Transforming America

Transforming America

Perspectives on U.S. Immigration

Volume 1
The Making of a Nation of Nations: The Founding to 1865

Michael C. LeMay, Editor

AN IMPRINT OF ABC-CLIO, LLC
Santa Barbara, California • Denver, Colorado • Oxford, England

Library of Congress Cataloging-in-Publication Data

Transforming America : perspectives on U.S. immigration / Michael C. LeMay, editor.
v. cm.
Includes bibliographical references and index.
Contents: v. 1. The Making of a Nation of Nations: The Founding to 1865—v. 2. The Transformation of a Nation of Nations: 1865 to 1945—v. 3. Immigration and Superpower Status: 1945 to the Present.
ISBN 978-0-313-39643-4 (hardcopy : alk. paper) — ISBN 978-0-313-39644-1 (ebook)
1. United States—Emigration and immigration—Government policy—History.
2. Emigration and immigration law—United States—History. I. LeMay, Michael C., 1941–
JV6483.T73 2013
325.73—dc23 2012018788

ISBN: 978-0-313-39643-4
EISBN: 978-0-313-39644-1

17 16 15 14 13 1 2 3 4 5

This book is also available on the World Wide Web as an eBook.
Visit www.abc-clio.com for details.

Praeger
An Imprint of ABC-CLIO, LLC

ABC-CLIO, LLC
130 Cremona Drive, P.O. Box 1911
Santa Barbara, California 93116-1911

This book is printed on acid-free paper ∞

Manufactured in the United States of America

Contents

Introduction

Immigration on the massive scale that the United States experienced from 1820 until today—totaling more than 70 million legal immigrants for permanent resident status, and probably more than 100 million if one includes those who came or stayed in an unauthorized status—inevitably produces substantial effects on all aspects of society. Immigration policy is inexorably intertwined with many other policy areas shaping American culture, economics, government, politics, and social life—as will be seen in this volume in greater detail. This volume is the first in a set of three that will examine the impact of immigration on America from a variety of perspectives and in terms of a multitude of related issues.

Each volume in this set brings together a collection of original chapters written by scholars with expertise from various disciplinary perspectives: cultural anthropology, economics, education, geography, history, law, political science, public policy, and sociology. Its contributors come from a considerable variety of institutional affiliations and include both well-established scholars and others at the beginning of their academic careers and doing cutting-edge scholarship.

This three-volume set is designed to give readers a broad, introductory review of the history of immigration and immigration policy in the United States and how that history has impacted a variety of related issues and concerns inexorably linked to the immigration flow. It seeks to encourage critical thinking by providing various sides to issues and allowing readers to trace the various arguments and concerns through time. These volumes are aimed at engaging readers and encouraging them to become involved in further study of the history of the issues surrounding immigration to the United States. The references provided at the end of each chapter provide a useful base for that further reading and study. Each volume in this set includes original chapters that trace the history of immigration during a particular time frame, the evolution of the different ethnic groups seeking citizenship status, ongoing debates about immigration and immigrants, unauthorized immigrant status, and what to do about those issues and possible solutions to the problems they raise. The volumes in this set note similarities and differences through time, as well as looking toward the future and the impact of immigration moving forward.

Volume 1, *The Making of a Nation of Nations: The Founding to 1865,* is comprised of 10 original chapters that discuss immigration history and that link immigration history and policy to related policy issues and concerns. It begins with an overview chapter that briefly identifies and discusses the major trends of immigration to the United States from 1790 until 1865. It focuses on what Professor LeMay, among others, labels the Open Door Era of immigration policy, and on what historians have termed the "old" wave of immigrants. It draws the relationship that the great migration, the first massive flow of immigration from Europe, had upon the development of passenger vessels to carry the millions of immigrants on their transatlantic or transpacific journey. This was migration on a size and scope unprecedented in human history.

The second chapter details the relationship between the perceived needs for national defense, at the time called domestic tranquility, and policy designed to determine the flow of immigration. In it, Professor LeMay describes the political forces who favored an open immigration policy and who controlled policy in a virtually unabated manner from the founding era through the Civil War period. It reviews the role that the German and the Irish immigrants played by their voluntary service in the War of 1812 and especially in the Civil War. It notes the important precedent set by that voluntary military service in defense of the nation for speeding up the naturalization of immigrants who thus served. The chapter briefly touches on the nativist political reaction to mass migration into the United States, a potent historical force, but one that ultimately was the less persuasive force in determining immigration policy prior to the Civil War. Simply put, the perceived needs for national security concerns trumped xenophobic reactions to the first massive wave of immigration.

In Chapter 3, "Mushrooming Cities," Professor LeMay traces the development of urbanization in the United States as the result of the immigration flow. Immigrants not only filled the first major cities of the nation, but also provided the labor force to build the cities and contributed substantially to the agricultural production that made big cities possible. It discusses, briefly, the "top 20 cities" in the United States that developed prior to the Civil War, indicating which immigrant groups played significant roles in each.

In Chapter 4, "Toward a More Perfect Union," LeMay shows the critical linkage between immigration and the developing nature of the federal system in the United States. It exemplifies the nearly coequal status of several state governments with the national government in determining immigration policy and in developing immigrant-receiving stations and the procedures used therein to administratively cope with the first massive wave of immigration.

In Chapter 5, "The Common and Uncommon Schooling of Immigrants to the United States," education historian Professor James McLaughlin discusses the impact of immigrants and immigration on the early development of education in the United States prior to the Civil War. He details the major challenges of access, religion, and language that most of the immigrant groups faced with respect to education, both public and private. He discusses the cultural views of various immigrant groups, and how those views at times differed with those of the majority of the native stock with respect to education. He focuses on Horace Mann and the common school movement that developed prior to the Civil War. Using the experiences of five immigrant groups in five exemplary American cities, he elaborates on their varied experiences and on the role they played in developing public or private educational approaches in their respective cities. Their experiences in those cities serve as instructive examples of the varied experiences of the nation as a whole in terms of how immigrants and the massive immigration flow effected the early development of education in the United States.

Political scientist Professor Scot Zentner examines the relationship between immigration and the development of political parties in the early republic in Chapter 6, "Political Parties and Immigration in the Early Republic." He focuses on how different perceptions of citizenship impacted opposition parties. He then traces how attitudes of nativism, attitudes regarding the slavery issue, and attitudes toward immigration and immigrant groups like the Irish and the Chinese, influenced the development of mass parties, resulting, by the time of the Civil War, in the basic two majority party system that has characterized American politics ever since.

In Chapter 7, "Naturalization Law, Immigration Flow, and Policy," immigration lawyer Carla Reyes offers an overview of naturalization law from the founding to 1865. Discussing the approach adopted in a series of enactments spanning from the Articles of Confederation to the Treaty of Guadalupe Hidalgo in 1848, she links the impact of naturalization law to immigration policy, and she details the relationship between that policy and the immigration flow. She demonstrates how naturalization law was employed as an incentive to draw immigrants to the United States. She uses brief discussions of German, Irish, Scandinavian, Dutch, and Mexican immigrants to illustrate how naturalization law impacted each group and their experiences in overcoming opposition and prejudice.

In Chapter 8, "Colonial Borders, New World Orders: Servants, Slaves, and the Founding Divisions of Labor in a Nation of Immigrants," political scientist Mark Hoffman argues the elaborate and at times intricate relationships between indentured and bonded servants, slaves, and immigrants interact with each other from colonial times and so shaped the development of racial slavery before the Civil War. He demonstrates how theories of colonialism modified over time and how variations in the approach of colonial elites shaped the ordering of immigrant workers, exploiting slaves, indentured servants, and immigrant labor alike to provide a consistent, compliant, and cheap labor pool for the colonial economies to the early republic's economy. He concludes with a discussion of post-abolition internal colonialism and contemporary continuities of the exploitation of immigrant labor.

In Chapter 9, "A Holy Experiment: Religion and Immigration to the New World," cultural anthropologist Sharon Kornelly discusses the intriguing relationship between immigration and entire religious-group resettlements. She examines the European origins of religious-group resettlement and the early, colonial foundations of such movements that essentially established a religious geography in the New World. She focuses on the Roman Catholic missions in the New World, on the Mayflower Compact and the Quakers, on religious-based settlements in the colonies of Rhode Island; Jamestown and Virginia in Maryland; the Carolinas, Georgia, and the Dutch colonies in New York; Pennsylvania; and Delaware. She elaborates on the transition from colonies to a nation and how established centralized churches continued post-Revolution. Kornelly shows the impact of the Great Awakening—the evangelism movement during the early years of the republic. She presents Thomas Jefferson's articulation, in Virginia's state constitution, of the doctrine of the separation of church and state, so critically important to religious freedom and to the various experiments in founding religious communities in the United States. She shows how migrations to the new nation from Scandinavia, Ireland, Germany, Eastern Europe, and Asia were influenced by religious freedom. She closes with a discussion of the long-term effects of religious community-driven resettlements.

Closing out this volume, in Chapter 10, "The Anti-Immigrant Social Movement: Racial and Religious Undercurrents and Their Political Effects," Professor LeMay develops further the topic touched on in prior chapters. He focuses on the *social movement* of anti-immigrant sentiment and nativist fervor, and draws parallels to the current movement commonly referred to as the Tea Party. He notes how the Order of the Star Spangled Banner began solely as a xenophobic social movement that quickly morphed into political action, finding temporary homes in existing political parties, and then developing into its own political party, the American Political Party, better known as the Know Nothing Party. He argues that today's Tea Party movement, partially directed by political party operatives, developed into a grassroots social movement that has deeply penetrated the Republican Party, but shows signs of perhaps spinning off into an independent, third-party organization just as the Know Nothing Party did in the 1850s. He notes the parallels, as well, in the attitudes and political thought expressed by the Know Nothing Party leaders to today's Tea Party advocates.

The volume closes with an "About the Editor and Contributors" section and a general subject index.

CHAPTER ONE

An Overview of Immigration to the United States: Founding to 1865

Michael C. LeMay

Introduction

It is not hyperbole to characterize the United States as a nation of nations. From its founding until the present, more than 75½ million persons have legally immigrated. If one includes the estimated number of unauthorized immigrants that total approaches 100 million persons. No other country in the world has received so many immigrants. Nor does any other society in human history approach the complex diversity of the American population, with tens of thousands of persons born in more than 170 other nations, some from which millions came. Nearly six million immigrants arrived during the period that is the focus of this volume. The official count is undoubtedly low since it does not include, for various reasons, many thousands who went uncounted. From 1820 until the Civil War, for example, official figures represent simply alien passengers arriving at U.S. seaports. Significant numbers arrived by land, coming across the borders with Mexico and, in particular, Canada, who went uncounted until 1908.

Prior to the Civil War, official immigration policy was unrestricted, a period we have described elsewhere as the Open Door Policy (LeMay, 1987). From the founding to 1819, an estimated 125,000 people arrived to permanently settle here, the majority of which were Protestants from the British Isles and northern Europe (Violet, 1980: 9). They came to a new nation with a population, according to the first census taken in 1790, of 3,227,000, most of whom were descendants of 17th- and 18th-century arrivals, or recent immigrants themselves. More than 75 percent of the then native stock were of British origin. Roughly 8 percent were of German origin. The remainder were Dutch, French, or Spanish in origin, although about one-half million were black slaves and about the same number were Native Americans. They occupied a sparsely settled land rich in soil and natural resources, with only 4.5 persons per square mile (LeMay, 1987: 7).

In 1740, a British naturalization law was enacted that systematized procedures regarding emigration, which it encouraged especially to the then American colonies. This basic emigration law set the precedent and established the pattern followed by the colonies and later by the U.S. government after independence (LeMay, 2004: 93). Indeed, when the U.S. Constitution was formally adopted in 1789, its first article had a section, Section 8, that empowered the newly established Congress to establish a uniform rule of naturalization. In doing so, the Constitution set in law that immigration and naturalization policies were appropriate responsibilities of the national level of government. And the next year Congress did meet, and among its very first actions, passed a uniform rule of naturalization, imposing a two-year residency requirement for aliens who are free white persons of good moral character. This first enactment by the Congress reflected the racial perspective of the founding fathers with regard to immigration and naturalization, a perspective evident in U.S. immigration law and policy until the mid-20th century.

Congress revised the Naturalization Act of 1790 to require a five-year residency and the renunciation of allegiance and fidelity to foreign powers, and reaffirmed the five-year residency requirement in 1813 in what was known as the Five-Year Residence Act (LeMay, 2004: 93).

Congress passed an act, in 1819, requiring shipmasters to deliver a manifest enumerating all aliens transported for immigration and requiring the secretary of state to inform Congress annually of the number of immigrants admitted to the nation. This 1819 law was the nation's first immigration law. It imposed no restrictions on entry, but merely required the government to keep count or track of the number of immigrants arriving at ports of entry. The precedent for this policy of enumerating the arrival of immigrants went back to colonial days, during which time immigrants were cautiously allowed as settlers, but in which the colonies were wary of those with religious differences (e.g., Catholics) or those who might become public charges (i.e., the indigent). The arrival, in the early 1700s, of Quakers and of Germans led to specific provincial immigration laws, which will be described more fully in the following text. Colonial laws (or provincial acts, as they were then called) established what became central concepts in American immigration policy and law. These laws, for example, required shipmasters to provide lists of the settlers and to provide bond in case such a person became a public charge. Their economic concerns were reflected in the laws' prohibition of the immigration of persons who were lame, impotent, or infirm unless security had been provided that the town into which they settled would not be charged with their support (LeMay and Barkan, 1999: 2). The interplay between national and state (or local governments in the colonial era) policies was established during colonial times. Provincial laws specified the requirement of shipmasters to submit their list (manifest) to town selectmen or the town treasurer. Continuing concern over the religious affiliation of immigrants was evident in provincial laws that provided for incentives for Protestant settlers to enter the colony, and indeed, encouraged French-speaking Protestants to settle in the provinces, requiring of them only one year of residency before they could naturalize and become citizens (LeMay and Barkan, 1999: 4–5).

Why so many emigrants chose to leave their nations of origin and to immigrate to the United States is an important consideration in understanding immigration laws enacted by the United States. By the 19th century, the old world (Europe) was experiencing massive social and economic changes brought about by overpopulation. This created a large mass of landless peasants from the British Isles to Russia. Moreover, the Industrial Revolution added new strains to the social order as the old employment patterns disintegrated. Displaced artisans and farmworkers moved first from rural Europe and the British Isles to the urban and often port cities of England, Ireland, and Germany. They soon joined the waves of emigrants. Population pressures contributed to economic disruptions and to religious and political persecutions. Religious and political minorities became scapegoats on which the blame for these problems was laid. When, by the mid-1800s, famine was added as a factor pushing emigration, the various governments of Europe encouraged emigration. Suddenly, those leaving Europe numbered in the millions.

The United States offered religious freedom to immigrants fleeing religious persecution. Its relatively politically open society drew those fleeing political persecution. The image of America as a land of nearly boundless opportunity drew those compelled to flee the economic deprivation and sometimes near-starvation conditions in their homelands. Open lands attracted the Europeans suffering from acute overpopulation. And the American colonies, and then the United States upon independence, needed to augment its population to defend itself from hostile Indians and from the potential threat of recolonization by European colonial powers.

The nation's burgeoning cities needed unskilled laborers. The nation's frontier lands needed farmers. The beginnings of industrialization in the United States prior to the Civil War were made possible by the cheap labor force provided by the vast numbers of unskilled laborers who were immigrating annually by the tens of thousands. Rapid industrialization made possible by cheap labor kept wages down and enabled the accumulation of the large sums of capital required to invest in establishing the base for industrialization. Immigration provided a large pool of unskilled labor at the most opportune time for the new nation.

The national government first began counting immigrants in 1820. From that year to 1865, a total of 5,855,743 legal immigrants arrived seeking permanent residence (Statistical Yearbook, 2003). Among them, 95 percent came from the British Isles and Northwestern Europe, 3 percent from North America (mostly Canada), and 2 percent from Southern and Eastern European nations (LeMay, 1987: 5). Among those coming from Canada, some overland and some by schooner ships sailing down the Eastern Coast, an estimated 10 percent were pass-through immigrants from the British Isles and Ireland, and many others from Germany, who entered Canada first, but had the intention from the start to remigrate to the United States. Immigrants arriving to the United States in the period 1820–1880 are often called the "old" immigrants. Their numbers swelled with each successive decade: from 1821 to 1830, 143,500 came; from 1831 to 1840 that number rose to just under 600,000; from 1841 to 1850 more than 1,700,000 arrived; from 1851 to 1860, they totaled more than 2½ million; and even during the Civil War years, from 1861 to 1865, more than 800,000 came, despite the war. Appendix I to this chapter details the annual totals of legal immigrants from 1820 to 1865.

Their impact can hardly be exaggerated. They had profound cultural, demographic, economic, and social effects. Their coming resulted from a correspondence between the needs of the overcrowded nations of Europe, and later Asia, and the needs of a vastly underpopulated America. How these millions mixed and mingled to become the American people is a dramatic and compelling story—one relevant today, another period of massive immigration.

Policy to regulate immigration blends domestic and international considerations in a gatekeeping function determining, at any given time, whether one will or will not be allowed entry for permanent residence. Immigration policy weighs four elements: (1) their impact on the economy, (2) their effect on the racial and ethnic mix of the American people,

(3) how they affect national identity—the composite sense of peoplehood, and (4) priorities of foreign policy and national defense (today termed "homeland security"—but during the period covered by this volume, referred to as "domestic tranquility") (LeMay, 2006: 5–6).

Sometimes these components harmonize, reinforcing each other. At others, they work at cross-purposes, as opposing groups seek to influence immigration policy by emphasizing different elements. But at all times, these four elements are a key to understanding U.S. immigration policy. They significantly influence the size and nature of the flow.

Historians distinguish two main factors influencing the decision to migrate: *Push factors* propel millions of persons to emigrate from their nation of origin—events such as wars, widespread epidemic disease (pandemics), famine, extreme social and political upheavals, and drastic economic disruptions. *Pull factors* draw those millions of migrating persons to a particular nation, like the United States. Examples of pull factors include subsidized travel, abundance of opportunity, a rich and rapidly developing economy, and the numerous freedoms afforded by the United States.

The 19th century was an age of mass migration; an age of pandemic diseases; an age of industrialization; an age of economic, political, and social revolutions. As we have seen, overpopulation in Europe caused extensive social and economic changes. Those changes necessitated societal reorganization to cope with these disruptions of the old order. The agricultural order changed from communal and subsistence farming to farms geared to cash crops for a market economy (enclosure). The Industrial Revolution began in England and gradually progressed across the European continent, adding new strains to the social order as feudalism and old employment patterns disintegrated. By the millions, displaced artisans and farmworkers comprised the waves of immigrants to the United States.

Overpopulation pressures and economic disruptions, religious and political persecutions, and then massive famine forced millions to leave the old world for the new, to stay and likely starve, or to take their chance on surviving the hazardous journey and try to improve their lot in America. Ireland, for example, saw its total population reduced by roughly one-half in the decade of the 1850s.

The United States pulled those millions by offering the reverse of conditions plaguing Europe. Religious freedom drew thousands fleeing persecution. A politically open society, with unprecedented access to politics and the vote, drew those fleeing political suppression. A land of nearly boundless opportunity drew those fleeing economic deprivation and near-starvation. The vast, open frontier attracted Europeans suffering from acute overpopulation. The United States sought and welcomed newcomers to fill and develop the land, and to defend against possible European efforts to recolonize or the perceived threat from tribes of hostile Indians.

By the mid-19th century, a nation of burgeoning cities drew unskilled laborers who made rapid industrialization possible, fueled by cheap labor and the accumulation of large sums of capital. The foreign-born population of a growing number of large cities commonly comprised from about a tenth to a fourth of their total populations. Many came, having heard that the streets of America were paved with gold, only to discover not only that the streets were unpaved, but also that they would be doing the paving. Immigrant labor did much of the building of the new cities.

Early Laws Establishing the Open Door Policy and Naturalization and Immigration Laws and Procedures

The history of immigration and naturalization laws in the United States harkens back to colonial days and reflects a continuing struggle for control of the process (LeMay and Barkan, 1999: 2–10). Competing forces strove to achieve a politically acceptable consensus about the matter. Their interplay is central to the periodic reviews and revisions in both policy and procedure designed for consensus on how open or closed would be the borders at any particular time.

Among the first actions taken by the colonies was to require shipmasters to provide provincial authorities with a list of the settlers (known as a manifest) transported aboard ship and to provide bond in case such persons became public charges. A good example was the Massachusetts Province Law of March 12, 1700. The Massachusetts colony passed another act, in June 1722, that imposed a fine of 200 pounds on any shipmaster who landed a settler who became a public charge. On April 2, 1731, the Massachusetts colony enacted a province law that extended naturalization to all the foreign born who were Protestants and who took an oath of allegiance after residing in the province for a period of one year.

Another colonial-era precedent was the Plantation Act: The British Naturalization Act of 1740. It was aimed at attracting population to the colonies to increase the colonies' wealth and security. It induced settlers by making them British subjects with the rights and privileges of natural-born subjects after the person resided in the colony for seven years, and upon swearing an oath of allegiance to the Crown and the abjuration of allegiance to any other sovereign—which was exceptionally liberal for its time. It ensured a degree of religious freedom, specifically for Jews and Papists (their name for Catholics). It instructed Colonial authorities to send annually to the Commissioners for Trade and Plantations in London a list of names of persons so naturalized.

Among the earliest provincial immigration laws was that of Massachusetts enacted on June 8, 1756. It prohibited ship captains from landing passengers who were sick, lame, or otherwise infirm by imposing a fine of 100 pounds to be paid to the town at which they were landed.

What became the prevailing attitude of open policy was articulated, in a letter dated December 2, 1783, by the then commander in chief of the Continental Army, General George Washington, to the Volunteer Association of the Kingdom of Ireland in the City of New York, thanking them for their hospitality to American prisoners of war and proclaiming the idea of America as a nation of asylum: "The bosom of America is open to receive not only the Opulent and respected Stranger, but the oppressed and persecuted of all Nations and Religions, whom we shall welcome to a participation of all our rights and privileges, if by decency and propriety of conduct they appear to merit the enjoyment" (LeMay and Barkan, 1999: 10).

Despite philosophical differences among the founding fathers, notably factions led by Alexander Hamilton with those of Thomas Jefferson, they agreed on the need for the United States to isolate itself from Europe's political rivalries. Open immigration was viewed as a safeguard against England or France attempting to reassert colonialism (LeMay, 2006: 17).

In 1794, Indians in Ohio joined Canadian militia attacking General Wayne's forces at the Battle of Fallen Timbers. Wayne's forces won resulting in the Treaty of Greenville, by which the United States bought from 12 tribes the rights to the southeastern quarter of the Northwest Territory (what is now Ohio and Indiana and parts of Michigan and Illinois). Spain incited the Creeks, Chickasaws, and Cherokees in Ohio and renewed fears about Indian tribal coalitions with European colonial powers.

Likewise, the War of 1812 and Tecumseh's tribal coalition, and the Battle of Tippecanoe confirmed the idea that the British were inciting the Indians. After the War of 1812, a period of economic nationalism affected economic policy and cultural life (Tindall, 1984: 374–380).

After the Constitution was adopted, the new Congress passed a uniform rule of naturalization. Its wording, "being a free white person," reflected the racial bias in much of immigration and naturalization law. For the times, however, it was very generous or open in extending citizenship after residence of two years, and upon satisfaction of being a person of good character and taking the oath of affirmation, and that children of such persons were also thereby naturalized (Act of March 26, 1790).

The requirement of only two years of residency was amended in 1795—which extended the time to five years and required renunciation of hereditary titles of nobility (Act of January 29, 1795). Amended again, in 1798, Congress passed a more restrictive naturalization law—changing the 5-year residency requirement to 14 years, assessing fees, and stipulating in greater detail the process for naturalization and requiring a declaration of intention to become a citizen (Act of June 18, 1798—cited in LeMay and Barkan, 1999: 13–15). Another 1798 law reflected the xenophobic fears aroused by the French revolution. The Alien and Sedition Act required oaths of allegiance from aliens residing in the country and granted the president extraordinary power to remove aliens deemed to be seditious. The law expired after two years and was not reenacted when the Jeffersonian Democratic Republicans replaced the Federalists in power. It became the precedent whereby Congress would later enact laws controlling immigration and granting rather sweeping power to the executive branch concerning immigration matters (Act of June 25, 1798) (Tindall, 1984: 331). It served as precedent for granting sweeping enforcement powers seen today in the USA Patriot Act of 2001 and the Homeland Security Act of 2002.

Congress passed naturalization acts in April of 1802, 1804, and 1813 that dealt with the length of residency (reestablishing the five-year period) and covered widows and children of resident aliens. Then, in 1819, Congress passed, consistent with the precedent of provincial laws mentioned previously, the first purposive act concerning immigration. It called for captains or shipmasters to provide a list of the names and particulars concerning all passengers delivered to the United States, and established for the first time the collection of data on immigration and immigrants to the United States. It marked the beginning of formal immigration law (Manifest of Immigrants Act of March 2, 1819), and 1820 became the first year for which annual immigration totals were recorded at the national level of government (LeMay and Barkan, 1999: 20–21).

Congress further amended the naturalization process in 1824 (Act of May 26, 1824) with provisions dealing with alien minors—persons immigrating before the age of 21—who came to the United States unaccompanied by a parent (a somewhat frequent occurrence given that as many as 10% of persons making the voyage died in passage). It allowed for their naturalization to proceed when the person attained 21 years of age if he or she had resided within the United States for 5 years or more, and counted the years since the time of their arrival rather than making them wait and reside for 5 years after attaining the age of 21 (LeMay and Barkan, 1999: 22).

State governments (importantly, Massachusetts and New York, with their ports of Boston and New York City, respectively) passed laws (Massachusetts in April 1837, New York in May 1847) that dealt with the process by which the state handled immigrants that required the enumeration of immigrants, established boarding officers, and imposed landing fees, except for vessels coming ashore in distress, or where alien passengers were taken from any wreck where life was in danger (a fairly common event). These laws required sureties in bond to satisfy the landing officers that residents of the state would not have to bear the costs of immigrants becoming public charges. They established a system in which the federal and state governments were jointly and equally involved in the administration of immigration procedures, with most of such procedures being conducted by the state of the port of debarkation. Ports and cities with reception stations established by 1865 included the following: Baltimore, Boston, Detroit, Cape Charles, Charlestown, Galveston, Key West, New Orleans, Pensacola, Philadelphia, Portland, Maine, Port Townsend, San Diego, and San Francisco. It was not until the Act of March 3, 1891, that the U.S. government undertook sole responsibility for immigration matters (LeMay and Barkan, 1999: 66–70).

To secure domestic tranquility, the United States needed to increase its population to settle the land, defend against hostile Indians, and develop the abundant natural resources that would assure national power. After the depression of 1837, a period of dynamic growth ensued with an increase in population density and the rapid development of cities; a virtual revolution in transportation, with the development of steam-driven river traffic, canals, and especially railroads; and with the expansion of ocean transport. These pull factors coincided with the beginnings of the Industrial Revolution, with its development of New England's mills and factories. National commerce assured world-power status and likewise required sustained population growth through immigration.

In 1845, John Louis O'Sullivan coined a name for the spirit of expansionism: "Our Manifest Destiny is to overspread the continent allotted by Providence for the free development of our yearly multiplying millions" (Tindall, 1984: 535). Elected in 1844, President Polk urged Congress to annex Texas, which joined the Union in 1845.

Finally, in 1848, Congress ended the war with Mexico with the signing of the Treaty of Guadalupe Hidalgo wherein Mexico ceded to the United States most of its northern territory that today comprises all or parts of the states of California, New Mexico, Arizona, Nevada, Utah, and Colorado. Importantly, the treaty's Article 8 provided for the admission to U.S. citizenship of Mexicans remaining in those territories ceded to the United

States and not declaring their wish to remain citizens of Mexico. It exemplified the first of several treaty agreements entered into by the United States that contained provisions that impacted both naturalization and immigration laws and policies (LeMay and Barkan, 1999: 25–26).

State governments in the Midwest sent agents to European countries to recruit immigrants and assisted farmers and artisans to settle in those states and territories. In 1862, Congress enacted the Homestead Act, which provided free land of 160 acres by staking a claim and then living on the land for five years, or by paying 1.25 dollar an acre after six months (Document 24 in LeMay and Barkan, 1999: 29–30).

Throughout the period from the founding to the Civil War, the overarching aim of immigration policy was to attract immigrants to serve as a buffer against Native American Indian resistance to the Euro-American expansion across the land in their ever-expanding western push. This policy prevailed over calls for restricting immigration.

The Development of an Anti-Immigrant Political Movement

A precursor to today's Tea Party social movement, increasingly after 1830, an ever-growing number of Catholic immigrants began arriving and set off a dramatic xenophobic reaction. Immigrants became easy scapegoats on which to lay the blame for problems of a rapidly changing society as the United States began to urbanize and industrialize. Immigrants were hailed as importing crime, disease, drunkenness, and poverty. Social reforms bent on preserving the nation's institutions and Protestant evangelicals seeking to save the nation's purity joined forces to establish anti-immigration associations like the secret Order of the Star Spangled Banner. The social movement quickly morphed into what came to be called the Know Nothing political party.

The party advocated restrictive immigration policy and stringent naturalization laws. Xenophobic fever led to violent outbreaks of anti-Catholicism. Inflamed by virulent anti-Catholic literature, pamphlets, and cartoons, violent attacks took place on churches and convents during riots in such places as Baltimore, Boston, Cincinnati, Hartford, Louisville, Philadelphia, Providence, New Orleans, New York, San Francisco, and St. Louis (LeMay, 1987: 10).

In addition to these fears of cultural, economic, and social disruptions resulting from unrestricted immigration, there was a well-founded fear concerning epidemic diseases. In the early to mid-19th century, a number of deadly epidemic diseases became pandemic in nature. Europe was scourged with small pox epidemics in 1824, 1851, and 1854; with scarlet fever in 1822, 1847, and 1857; with Asiatic cholera in 1832, 1834, 1849, and 1854; with yellow fever in 1805 and 1822; with cholera in 1817, 1823, 1830–1833, 1846, and 1849–1850; and tuberculosis raged throughout the 1800–1850 period with mortality rates of 300–500 per 100,000 population, making it the greatest epidemic killer of the 19th century. That fear was borne out when epidemics struck the United States: yellow fever in 1820–1823; Asiatic cholera in 1831–1832; cholera in 1832–1834; typhus in 1837; yellow fever again in 1841, 1847, 1852, and 1855; a deadly bout of influenza in 1850–1851; and cholera again in 1851; and small pox struck Philadelphia again in 1860–1861 (LeMay, 2006: 41). These epidemics led to specific immigration legislation intended to protect the nation from such outbreaks.

Smith describes these epidemics:

> Epidemics are like waves; they rise and fall. Sometimes they seem to be spaced at fairly regular intervals of time. Measles may rise to a peak every second or third year. . . . Topography and climate seem to have something to do with both epidemics and endemics. . . . Ophthalmia is traditionally associated with Egypt, malaria with the Mediterranean shores, plagues with the East, yellow fever with the tropics of America. Moreover, some diseases spread and become threatening at one season of the year, some at another. Pneumonia is a winter disease, measles seem to reach its peak in the spring, babies die from diarrhea in the hot summer months, and one fears poliomyelitis most in the late summer. Some diseases, again, fall upon people of all ages, some upon children, some most severely on the old. (Smith, 1964: 122)

Typhoid fever was a deadly killer in Philadelphia, in1837, and in many sections of the United States in 1865. Yellow fever, often called the American Plague, is a viral hemorrhagic illness now known to be spread by the type of mosquito adapted to living in cities, towns, and villages. A severe infection often leads to shock, bleeding, and kidney and liver failure, which causes jaundice that gave rise to its common name. The disease crossed the Atlantic aboard ships, riding in water casks, and established itself in places where temperatures stay at about 72 degrees Fahrenheit. Yellow fever spread from sailor to sailor and remained aboard ships for weeks and even months, reinfecting sailors so the ships seemed to suffer unending chains of attack that no one understood. "Yellow jack" was particular dreaded in the Caribbean and other tropical seas (McNeill, 1989: 222). Philadelphia suffered an epidemic in 1793. In Haiti, in 1802, Napoleon's troops suffered an epidemic that wiped out more than half his army. New Orleans suffered a nasty outbreak in 1847, and again in 1852, when more than 8,000 died in one summer.

Smallpox was especially deadly—with mortality rates of 20 to 40 percent. An outbreak in Boston in 1721 had a mortality rate of 15 percent, and in 1792 another Boston outbreak claimed 30 percent. Epidemics brought by European settlers decimated Native American Indians who had no immunity. One scholar counted 33 smallpox epidemics that decimated many tribes. Boston endured 6 epidemics, and the virus spread among the 13 colonies. During the Revolutionary War, smallpox killed an estimated 125,000 people (Fenn, 2001: 28–29).

Cholera was another feared disease of the 19th century. It was a local disease in India in 1817 that became pandemic, crossing the frontier in 1818 and marching eastward to Japan in 1823, and into Europe by 1826. It struck Russia in 1830, migrated to Germany and England by 1831, and Ireland by 1832, where immigrant ships took it to Canada and the United States and where epidemics struck the Eastern seaboard in 1833. The disease marched westward to 1836, subsided until 1846, when it again spread intermittently in Europe and North America, reaching its height in the United States in 1849 and 1850, when it killed 3,000 in New York in 1849 (Fenn, 2001: 16; Smith, 1964: 17).

In 1848, the discovery of gold in California drew a vast population to the West Coast and created the demand for the construction of the transcontinental railroad, inspiring a building boom that opened up vast lands to settlement. Massive numbers of unskilled laborers were needed to construct canals and railroads, mine coal and ore, and work in the mills spurred to new levels by Civil War–generated production. The gold rush and the railroad developments drew thousands of Chinese immigrant laborers to the West Coast, and on the East Coast, the composition of immigrants started to change, with those coming from Northern and Western Europe declining, and those from Southern, Central, and Eastern Europe rising. These changes in the flow, coupled with post–Civil War recessions, created new pressures for restriction. Labor began to organize and its adherents feared the competition of cheap labor from ever-growing numbers of immigrants coming from ever-more diverse nations of origin.

An article written by a leader of the Know Nothing movement vividly describes the anti-Catholic, anti-immigrant bias of the new political party. In it, J. R. Graves says:

> Nothing is more evident than that our political parties have become sadly, deplorably corrupt. . . . Congress has become a most shameful and disgraceful scene of drunkenness, riot, and caucusing for the Presidency, and the minor offices of the government. The foreign element is increasing

> in fearful ratio. Nearly one million per annum of foreign Catholics and German infidels—who, though opposed in all else, are agreed in the subversion of our free institutions—are pouring in upon us, and the tide is increasing. These foreigners have already commenced their warfare upon the use of the Bible in our public schools—against our free school system—against our Sabbath—against our laws. They boldly threaten to overthrow our constitution, through profligacy of our politicians; and we see our candidates for political preferment pandering more and more to the Catholic and foreign influence. We see from the last census that the majority of the civil and municipal offices of this government are today in the hands of Catholics and foreigners: an overwhelming majority of our army and navy are foreign Catholics . . . so we believe. (Overdyke, 1969: 67)

In stark contrast, Abraham Lincoln wrote in a letter dated in 1855 his take on the Know Nothing movement:

> I am not a Know Nothing. That is certain. How could I be? How can anyone who abhors the oppression of negroes, be in favor of degrading a class of white people? Our progress in degeneracy appears to me to be pretty rapid. As a nation, we began by declaring that "all men are created equal." We now practically read it "all men are created equal, except negroes." When the Know-Nothings get control, it will read "all men are created equal, except negroes, and foreigners, and Catholics." When it comes to this I should prefer emigrating to some country where they make no pretense of loving liberty—to Russia, for instance, where despotism can be taken pure, and without the base alloy of hypocrisy. (LeMay and Barkan, 1999: 27)

President Lincoln's view prevailed. Congress and Lincoln enacted the Act of May 20, 1862, to secure homesteads. It was an enormous draw of immigrants. Anti-immigrant sentiment failed to become public policy, as the more politically and economically potent barons of industry, and the leadership of both major political parties, continued support for open and unlimited immigration. The need for cheap labor to supply the explosively expanding cities and factories simply trumped the social fears as the determining factor in public policy. Economic needs combined with a philosophical idealism that regarded America as the land of opportunity and freedom. This position prevailed over the narrow views of the anti-Catholic and anti-immigrant movements.

A Brief Review of the Old Immigrant Wave

During the founding to 1865 period, immigrants from Germany outpaced all other countries. German immigrants were often distinguished by the movement of entire communities bound by religious creeds unaccepted in their homelands: Mennonites, Dunkers, Lutherans, Calvinists, and some Jews. They cultivated some of the richest farmlands in colonial America. Scattered thinly, they were united only by language. They had little political clout and interest beyond their local and private affairs.

The Revolutionary War changed all that. By then they were the largest group after the English. Easy converts to the cause for independence, several German regiments fought prominently and well in the war, accelerating their assimilation. As their general social and economic conditions improved, they took a more active role in public affairs.

During the 1830s and 1840s, they emigrated in large numbers as the agricultural revolution hit central Europe forcing many to leave. When the potato famine struck what is today the nation of Germany, but was then a loose collection of fiefdoms, they chose to emigrate. This coincided with the opening of the American Midwest, and German immigrants were enticed to immigrate. Texas, the Great Lakes region, and the Ohio River Valley became home to large German settlements. Midwestern cities attracted large numbers of Germans. Chicago, Detroit, Milwaukee, Cincinnati, and St. Louis became part of what came to be known as the *German belt* (LeMay, 1987: 24).

Political turmoil in Germany culminated in the failed Revolution of 1848. German intellectuals fled. They became known as the "Forty-Eighters," and they contributed significantly to the liberal movement in states where they settled in large numbers. They wielded economic, political, and social influences far beyond their numerical strength.

In addition to the cheap land offered by the Homestead Act, those willing to serve in the Civil War were rewarded, by a law enacted in 1862, which granted naturalization to honorably discharged soldiers. It was an important inducement to serve in the Union Army, and large numbers of German immigrants did so. A famous example was the noted American statesman/reformer, Carl Schurz. He was born in Liblar, Germany (near Cologne) in 1829. In 1848, he founded the newspaper, *Bonner Zeifing*, noted for promoting democratic reform, and was a key leader among the Forty-Eighters. He came to the United States in 1852, settling in Wisconsin, and was instrumental in the beginning of the Republican Party. He was a Union Army general during the Civil War and was the first German-born American elected to the U.S. Senate. He and his sister were instrumental in founding the kindergarten school movement, and he was famous for his statement: "My country, right or wrong." He served as the first secretary of the interior from 1876 to 1881, and instituted civil service reform (the merit system) for the Bureau of Indian Affairs and in the Department of the Interior.

Another example was Major General Franz Sigel, 1824–1902. He was born in Baden, Germany, and served in the Baden Army. He, too, was a leader in the 1848 Revolution, where he served as a colonel in the revolutionary army. Like Schurz, he came to the United States in 1852 and he settled in New York City, where he taught school. In the Civil War, he rose to the rank of Major General. He was a leader in the Battle of Wilson's Creek and in the 1862 Battle of Pea Ridge. He was a commander in the Shenandoah Valley Division that fought against Stonewall Jackson. After the Civil War, he was a journalist in Baltimore and later an editor in New York City.

Irish immigrants can also be traced to the colonial period, when they settled mostly in Pennsylvania and Maryland. Their numbers and Catholicism generated strong and overt discrimination. Irish immigrants figured prominently in the cholera outbreak that hit Canada in 1832 and the United States in 1831–1833 in New York and other seaports. British political suppression swelled Irish immigration to a flood by the 1840s. The potato famine precipitated massive migration, when their choice became emigrate or starve. Between 1847—a year in which 100,000 Irish arrived in the United States—and 1854, approximately 1.2 million arrived. That surge peaked in 1851, when nearly a quarter million arrived (221,000). Famine-induced immigration became a deluge of poor Irish immigrants settling on the East Coast, activating existing prejudice. Their sheer numbers, their Catholicism, and open anti-British sentiment contributed to the antipathy toward them evident among the native stock. Their poverty trapped them in the nation's explosively expanding Eastern seaboard cities, in tenement slums in Baltimore, Boston, and New York. By 1860, 1 person in 8 residing in the United States was foreign-born, with the Irish then the largest group, at 1.6 million, followed by the Germans at 1.3 million, dwarfing those who were British-born, at 338,000.

The Irish came jammed into overcrowded emigrant vessels where disease often spread like wildfire. The famine in 1846–1847, their poverty, and weakened condition at departure, combined with an inadequate diet during the long voyage, which could take as long as one to two months, and the grossly unsanitary conditions aboard ship, all contributed to disease outbreaks. And British emigration authorities, wanting as many as possible to leave to relieve conditions in Ireland, eased almost all restrictions on ships bound for Canadian and American ports (O'Gallagher, 1984: 47–51). A typhus epidemic took thousands of lives. In 1847, of the more than 100,000 persons who left the British Isles for America, a total of 17,443, or more than 16 percent, died during the voyage, in quarantine or in hospitals upon landing (Guillet, 1937: 91, 145–54). Since the cause of diseases and how they spread was unknown, the quarantine measures sometimes spread the outbreak to the healthy, quarantined along with, or nearby the sick. And the passage was dangerous as ships were often lost at sea. During this period, an estimated 9 percent of emigrants leaving did not survive the journey.

Their high rates of illiteracy and inappropriate job skills forced them into the unskilled labor pool. Their lower-class status hampered their acceptance precisely when the United States developed class consciousness (Handlin, 1979). The Irish were the first ethnic group to experience overt job discrimination—where in Eastern seaboard cities job advertisements often included the line, "No Irish Need Apply." They crammed into tenement slums—Irish shanty towns—and took whatever jobs they could—stevedores, teamsters, ditchdiggers, dockworkers, and terriers. They comprised construction gangs who razed or erected buildings. They were the unskilled laborers who built the canals, roads, subways, and railroads connecting the East with the Midwest and beyond.

Their arrival sparked a nativist movement. In 1828, the Workingmen's Party began in Philadelphia. It spread west, becoming especially powerful on the West Coast. In 1837, the Native American Association of the Star Spangled Banner was founded in New York City. By 1854, it had become the Know Nothing Party (Tindall, 1984: 478).

Extensive urbanization between 1840 and 1860 required larger local government workforces, especially in sanitation, streets and roads, and police and fire departments. Immigrants—particularly the Irish—supplied much of that workforce. Gradually, they took over some of those agencies—for example, the Irish cop (Levine, 2006: 123).

Scandinavians is a term used to refer to immigrants from Denmark, Norway, and Sweden. They were among the earliest European explorers of America. By mid-1600, they had a settlement in what is now Delaware. By 1860, the average Scandinavian immigrant arrived with sufficient capital to leave the Eastern seaboard for the Midwestern states, where they concentrated in frontier settlements. They succeeded in setting up their own shops, stores, factories, and banks. They were excellent farmers, attracted to such states as Minnesota, Wisconsin, Iowa, and Illinois. Protestant and Caucasian, they escaped ethnic and racial prejudice and incorporated comparatively easily. Coming in smaller numbers at any time, and with enough capital to reach the Midwest, they were not viewed as threats to the labor force. The Homestead Act of 1862 was especially important to them, providing cheap land, which enabled them to become established without incurring heavy debt. Their middle-class standard of living soon enabled them to become politically involved as well. They organized political groups, and learned American-style politics while organizing new townships, levying and collecting taxes, and laying out new roads in their frontier settlements. By the 1860s, more than a fifth of the male Scandinavian immigrants participated in town affairs. Many local townships allowed noncitizens to vote in local elections. Many served in the state legislatures of Wisconsin, Minnesota, and the Dakotas after the Civil War, tending to be Republicans.

Several other groups arrived in considerable numbers during the period 1820 to 1865: Dutch, French, Scots, Scotch-Irish, and Welsh. Dutch influence was strongest in the colonial and early independence period in New Jersey and New York. Religious dissenters from the Netherlands founded colonies in Michigan and Iowa in 1846 and drew a wave of immigrants who also settled in Wisconsin and Illinois.

France was a source of a large and continuous flow of immigrants totaling about 850,000. French Huguenots, Protestants fleeing religious persecution, dominated the colonial-era flow from France, and they readily converted to the Anglican Church here and that, coupled with their rapid adoption of English, eased their incorporation. When, during the Revolutionary War, France became an ally against Great Britain, their assimilation was greatly facilitated (LeMay, 2006: 53).

The Louisiana French became part of the country by absorption in the Louisiana Purchase in 1803. They maintained a strong and persistent subculture that absorbed other groups in the area, which slowed their incorporation. French Canadians also exhibited a persistent subculture. They started arriving in considerable numbers during the 1830s, settling in towns in New England.

The Scots, Scotch-Irish, and Welsh started immigrating during the colonial era and came in a steady stream thereafter. Their religious preference for Presbyterianism and Anglicanism helped them to incorporate. Their strong work ethic and job skills made them widely accepted, and they were often desired as skilled workers who served as superintendents and foremen.

The Chinese were the only old immigrant group to face overt racial discrimination. They came in large numbers drawn by the gold rush of 1848. They fled economic depression and local rebellions, as well as floods and disease outbreaks (especially cholera epidemics). They were pulled here by the gold rush, and then recruited as laborers building the transcontinental railroad from the West Coast to the Midwest. They were willing to perform work unattractive to the domestic labor force, often organized into work gangs arranged with a single contractor. The lack of women on the Western frontier left women's work—domestic service—open to them. But they worked in mines, helped build the railroads, and served as ranch hands and farmworkers. The Central Pacific Railroad, for example, employed 9,000 Chinese immigrants a year. By 1860, they made up about 10 percent of California's population and roughly 25 percent of its labor force. As early as 1849, a Know Nothing–affiliated judge serving on the California Supreme Court had ruled that the Chinese could not testify in court against white men. Violence against them went unpunished (LeMay, 1987: 30).

Miscegenation laws were but one of the legal constraints aimed against them. By the 1850s, they were expelled from California schools, denied the right to testify against whites, and legally banned from obtaining citizenship.

Job discrimination was prevalent. Violence and legislation kept them out of the mines. The 1855 Foreign Miner's Tax in California required foreign-born miners to pay a tax of four dollars a month, an exceedingly heavy rate in 1855. Since they were banned from naturalization, they were forced to pay ever-higher rates.

They tended to cluster together in urban Chinatowns. But even there they failed to escape legal harassment. San Francisco, for instance, passed ordinances aimed solely at the Chinese after the Civil War (the Cubic Air Ordinance, the Queue Ordinance, and restrictions related to the shipping of human remains sent home for burial). Eventually these ordinances were ruled to be unconstitutional, but such ordinances formed a legal basis for an atmosphere of racism and a rigid social and geographic segregation of Chinese (LeMay, 2006: 57).

Immigration and the Development of Passenger Transportation

The immigrant effected the development of passenger ships. Wooden sailing vessels were the only form of travel from Europe to North America from the 1600s to the 1800s. Sailing ships of that period were not designed for passenger service. They were either merchant ships or warships. They began transporting people, quite specifically, as human cargo. The more important styles of sailing ships were the sloop, the schooner, packet ships, and brigantines. Ships developed to suit specific needs: speed, cost, safety, and the adaptation of new technology (steam-driven screws rather than sail). It wasn't until about 1850 that ships were designed to carry people rather than cargo.

The name schooner was derived from the Scottish word "scoon"—to skip or skim over the water. They were small ships used mainly for sailing fairly close to shore rather than transatlantic traffic. They were used for trade up and down the Eastern Coast from the maritime provinces of Canada to Boston, New York, and Baltimore, for example. They began to carry passengers for immigration purposes in the early 1800s.

The *Baltimore Schooner,* or *Clipper,* for example, was a three-mast wood ship launched in 1825. It was sleek and fast and plied trade between Baltimore and Canada. The 1840s and 1850s were the era of clipper ships, used more often by smugglers than for immigration transport.

Packet ships were somewhat larger wooden sailing vessels that sailed the oceans in the 1700s and 1800s. They were the first mail carriers of the British Empire—for example, the ships of the British and North American Royal Mail Steam Packet Company. The packet ships typically took weeks to even a month or two to cross the Atlantic, and began taking some passengers by the early 1800s to supplement their cargo and mail business. The British packets sailed out of Falmouth in Cornwell, England, and the packet service ran from 1689 to 1850, sailing the Empire for 150 years as the only mail carriers to and from the country. They were small, two-mast brigs. Service to New York began in 1755 and by 1784 they sailed to several American colonies. An example of this type of ship was the HMS *Princess Royal,* which sailed between 1750 and 1800 and was a brig-style ship of the British East Indian Company. At 142 feet long and 38 feet wide, it went 878 gross tons (GT), and was part of the British merchant fleet that dominated trade in 1700–1800. It was cheap rather than fast—an important feature in a merchant ship. Ships of this type were converted to carry immigrant passengers in the early 19th century. By the 1800s, the company ran a fleet of 40 ships. They were undone by the development of steamships.

Steven Fox describes the era of the packet ships that brought tens of thousands of immigrants to America, despite horrendous and dangerous conditions:

> At their worst, the emigrant ships ran aground, or sank in storms, or caught fire, or just vanished. In 1847, the *Exmouth,* a tiny vessel of only 320 tons, was blown by a storm onto a rocky Scottish coast, killing 240 emigrants; the *Carrick,* after six weeks at sea, hit a shoal and broke up off Newfoundland, with about 180 deaths; the *Canton* ran onto rocks near Durness, Scotland, leaving no survivors among the three hundred on board. On the *Ocean Monarch* in August, 1848, only a few hours from Liverpool, someone lit an illegal fire below deck. The ship burned to the water line, killing over four hundred emigrants bound for Boston. In 1849, the *Maria,* heading from Limerick to Quebec, ran into an ice field in a storm, could not get free, collided with an iceberg, and went down with 109 people. Together these five shipwrecks caused well over 1,200 deaths, and during the first six years of the famine, in all about fifty ships foundered on their way to North America. So it went, year after year, a steady drumbeat of disasters, with no evident remedy. (Fox, 2001: 170–71)

Fox goes on to describe the chain migration among the Irish:

> Yet despite all these dangers and difficulties, the annual totals of Irish emigration to the United States kept rising: 68,000 in 1846, then 118,000 and 180,000, and over 184,000 by 1850. From America, newly prospering recent Irish arrivals—who had made the ocean trip and so well knew its hardships—still sent home to relatives in Ireland more than a million pounds a year, "passage money," to bring them over as well. This swelling traffic, against the many known perils and burdens of crossing the North Atlantic, by itself suggests how truly desperate these emigrants were to escape the famine, and to try out what they had heard about the distant dream and reality of America. (Fox, 2001: 171)

The first ship to use steam power for ocean crossing was a wooden-hulled, British-built, Dutch-owned ship, *Curacao,* a steam and sail ship. It crossed from Rotterdam in April 1827 to Paramaribo, Surinam, on May 28, and spent 11 days under steam. The first to cross the Pacific was the *Beaver,* in 1836, which served the Hudson Bay's trading post in Puget Sound and Alaska. Among the earliest of steamships that used both sail and a steam engine was the SS *Savannah,* which crossed the Atlantic in 1810 from Savannah to Liverpool, England. Commodore Perry used the USS *Mississippi* to open Japan to Western trade in 1853, but it was a naval ship, not a transport vessel.

As immigration increased, shipbuilders began to design ships especially for transporting them, rather than roughly adapting cargo ships to carry people. This trend was begun in the 1840s and increased in the 1850s and 1860s with the introduction of steam- and sail-driven ships. The first steamboat of note, the SS *Robert Fulton,* launched in 1819, was a river-cruising steamship only 158 feet long and 33 feet wide. The first notable steamships for the transatlantic traffic were Brunel's ships, built for the Great Western Steamship Line. They provided regular service between England and the United States starting in 1838. Brunel's SS *Great Western* was launched that year. It was 236 feet long and 35 feet wide, had four boilers, two mighty cylinders 6 feet in diameter, and was a side-wheeler that carried 8,000 tons of coal, used 30 tons a day, and had a top speed on 9 knots. It sailed from London to New York in two weeks and held the Blue Riband award (for the fastest transatlantic crossing) from 1838 until 1843. It was sold to the Royal Mail Steam Packet Company and was scrapped in 1856. His SS *Great Britain* was launched in 1843 and started regular service in 1844. It was an iron-hulled ship, 322 feet long, 32 feet wide, and was a screw and paddle-wheel ocean-going ship with auxiliary sail. It carried immigrants to Australia. Brunel's SS *Great Eastern* had four masts and two side-wheel paddles. It was 700 feet long and could carry 4,000 passengers. It sailed from 1852 to 1888.

It carried 12,000 tons of coal, used 330 tons per day, and was capable of 14 knots. Brunel called her the "Great Babe." In its maiden voyage, it carried 36 passengers out and 212 back. It later helped lay the transatlantic cable (Fox, 2001: 140).

A competitor to Brunel, William Inman, 1825–1880, was born in Liverpool and founded the Inman Line with five fast ships that were cheaper to run, and thereby charged less for the transatlantic service. His line included such ships as the *City of Glasgow, City of Philadelphia, City of Brussels,* and *City of Richmond.* They were large variations of the clipper design capable of transatlantic crossing. His *City of Glasgow* was lost with 480 dead. In 1852, he began offering limited number (300) of third-class accommodations. His SS *City of Baltimore* was built in 1856 for the transatlantic service. It went 22,368 GT and was 330 feet long, 79 feet wide and was in service from 1855 to 1885. It carried 106 passengers in steerage and had 24 cabins.

The most important transatlantic ship magnate was Samuel Cunard, 1787–1865. The British shipping magnate was born in Halifax, Nova Scotia, and was a master carpenter, a timber merchant, and ultimately, the founder of the Cunard Line, which became *the* dominant transatlantic passenger ship company. Cunard began shipping timber from Nova Scotia to England to be used in ship building. He launched his line in 1840 as the transatlantic mail service, and he then started a passenger line. His first ship was the RMS *Britannia,* launched in 1840. It was a side paddle–wheeled ship. The Cunard Line was a joint British–American owned line that operated out of England, averaged 8.5 knots, and sailed from Liverpool to Halifax in 12 days, 10 hours, then on to Boston. His ships were of the North American Royal Mail Steam Packet Company. In 1879, it was reorganized as the Cunard Steamship Line. His company absorbed the Canadian Northern Steamship Line and the White Star Line.

The Hamburg-American Packet Company began in 1847. It sailed a regular route from Hamburg to Southampton then on to New York City. It went on to become known as HAPAG, for its German name, and became a principal carrier of immigrants from Germany to North America (Canada and the United States). The North American Lloyd Company, founded in 1857, ran its service from Bremen to London with six 500 GT steamers. It added transatlantic service, in 1858, and the Baltimore route in 1869. The line formed a partnership with John W. Garrett, founder of the Baltimore and Ohio Railroad (B&O RR) in 1838, and a close friend of Albert Schumacher and C. A. Heinecke, who were major proponents of the Bremen to Baltimore route of steamship passenger service. The initial route of the B&O RR was from Baltimore to Harpers Ferry, West Virginia, at the time one of the main gateways to the Ohio Valley and the U.S. Midwest.

Appendix 1.1 Annual Legal Immigration to the United States, 1820–1865

Year	Number	Year	Number
1820	8,385	1843	52,496
1821	9,127	1844	78,615
1822	6,911	1845	114,371
1823	6,354	1846	154,416
1824	7,912	1847	234.968
1825	10,199	1848	226,527
1826	10,837	1849	297,024
1827	18,875	1850	369,980
1828	27,382	1851	379,466
1829	22,520	1852	371,603
1830	23,322	1853	368,645
1831	22,633	1854	427,833
1832	60,482	1855	200,877
1833	56,640	1856	200,436
1834	65,365	1857	251,306
1835	45,374	1858	123,126
1836	78,242	1859	121,282
1837	79,340	1860	153,640
1838	38,914	861	91,918
1839	68,069	1862	91,985
1840	84,066	1863	176,282
1841	80,289	1864	193,418
1842	104,565	1865	248,120

References

Braynard, Frank O., and William H. Miller Jr. 1991. *Pictorial History of the Cunard Line, 1840–1990.* Mineola, NY: Dover Books.

Browne, Gary L. 1980. *Baltimore and the Nation, 1780–1861.* Chapel Hill, NC: University of North Carolina Press.

Casson, Lionel. 1964. *Illustrated History of Ships and Boats.* New York: Doubleday.

Department of Homeland Security. *2009 Yearbook on Immigration Statistics.* Available at: http://www.immigration.gov.

Department of Justice. 2003. *2001 Statistical Yearbook of the INS.* INS, Washington, DC.

Fenn, Elizabeth. 2001. *Pox Americana: The Great Smallpox Epidemic of 1775–82.* New York: Hill and Wang.

Fox, Stephen. 2001. *Transatlantic: Samuel Cunard, Isambard Brunel and the Great Transatlantic Steamship.* New York: Harper and Collins.

Guillet, Edwin. 1937. *The Great Migration: The Atlantic Crossing by Sailing Ships, 1770–1860.* Toronto: Thomas Nelson and Sons.

Handlin, Oscar. 1979. *Boston's Immigrants.* Cambridge, MA: Harvard University Press.

LeMay, Michael C. 1987. *From Open Door to Dutch Door: An Analysis of U.S. Immigration Policy since 1820.* New York: Praeger.

LeMay, Michael C. 2004. *U.S. Immigration.* Santa Barbara, CA: ABC-CLIO.

LeMay, Michael C. 2006. *Guarding the Gates: Immigration and National Security.* Westport, CT: Praeger Security International.

LeMay, Michael C., and Elliott Barkan, eds. 1999. *U.S. Immigration and Naturalization Laws and Issues: A Documentary History.* Westport, CT: Greenwood Press.

Levine, Edward. 2006. *The Irish and the Irish Politician.* Notre Dame: University of Notre Dame Press.

McNeill, William. 1989. *Plagues and People.* New York: Anchor Books.

Miller, William H., Jr. 1995. *Pictorial Encyclopedia of Ocean Liners, 1860–1994.* Mineola, NY: Dover Books.

National History Day. 2006. *Triumph and Tragedy: Immigration Resource Book.* Santa Barbara, CA: ABC-CLIO.

O'Gallagher, Marianna. 1984. *Grosse Ile: Gateway to Canada, 1832–1937.* Sainte-Foy: Livries Carraig Books.

Overdyke, S. Darrell. 1969. *The Know-Nothing Party in the South.* Gloucester, MA: Peter Smith Publishing.

Smith, Geddes. 1964. *Plagues on US.* New York: Oxford University Press.

Tindall, George B. 1984. *America: A Narrative History.* 2nd ed. New York: Norton.

Violet, Joyce. 1980. "A Brief History of U.S. Immigration Policy." Report 80-223 EPW (Education and Public Welfare Division) INS, Washington, DC.

CHAPTER TWO

To Ensure Domestic Tranquility: Immigration and National Defense, 1820–1865

Michael C. LeMay

Introduction

Between 1820, when the government first began keeping count of immigrants, and 1865, approximately six million immigrants entered the United States (see Table 2.1). Immigration scholars have called this first significant influx of immigrants the old immigrant wave. About 80 percent of them came from Europe, predominately Northwestern Europe; 6 percent came from the Americas, mostly Canada; and the other 14 percent from all other sources, including several hundred thousand from China. The old immigrant wave marked a dramatic increase in total immigration. From the end of the Revolutionary War to 1819, an estimated 123,000 persons entered, averaging about 3,000 a year, most of whom were Protestants from the British Isles and Northern Europe (Vialet, 1980: 9). By contrast, the old immigrant wave averaged more than 130,000 per year. It was dominated by German and Irish immigrants, the majority of which were Catholic. From 1840 on, most were peasants fleeing abject poverty, and in the case of the Irish, the potato famine and the economic depressions of the 1840s. This sudden shift in the character of the immigrants aroused an anti-Catholic reaction and calls to restrict immigration.

Immigration policy reflects the perceived needs of the nation as those needs shift over time and in response to changing economic and demographic conditions. It also responds to the changing nature and composition of the immigrant flow. Various national defense, economic, ethnic, and foreign policy issues have played and continue to play key roles in the debates over immigration policy, which reflect conflicting value perspectives that tug and pull at one another, causing policy to oscillate in varying degrees among them.

For example, among those value perspectives on the one hand was the view that valued the immigrant as a source of industry, of renewed vigor, of a desirable infusion of new blood into the American stock, enriching the heritage and spurring new economic growth, populating open lands, and developing and exploiting the country's rich natural resources. Many saw such development as essential to the national defense against foreign threat and intrusion, and against a threat from the Native American Indian tribes. This perspective formed the basis for the open immigration policy, espoused by almost every president from George Washington to Barack Obama. It affirmed the United States as a nation of nations, as a nation of asylum for which immigration expressed and reconfirmed the American spirit of liberty for all.

The other perspective called for restriction. Its proponents feared the stranger who could not or, in their view, should not assimilate. They feared the dilution of the U.S. culture that the millions of newcomers inevitably meant. They feared an influx they thought would destroy the economy, depressing wages and working conditions. They feared the very openness of society and its borders, which they held would invite attack from foreign enemies. Opponents of widespread immigration today, and especially those advocating strict policy against illegal immigrants and any sort of legalization policy (which they refer to as amnesty), do so on grounds of national security and obedience to law.

The Open Door Cycle of Immigration Policy

Immigration policy performs a gatekeeping function. Changes in it result from dramatic changes in the size and the composition of the immigrant flow. Who, and how many, are allowed to enter intent on permanent resettlement influences a collective sense of national security. This gatekeeping function suggests the door image to characterize cycles of immigration policy (LeMay, 1987). The cycle determining immigration during the founding to 1865 era can be thought of as the open door cycle during which few or no restrictions were placed on immigrants seeking entrance. Indeed, immigration policy sought out immigrants, particularly from Northwestern European countries like Germany, Ireland, and Scandinavia (LeMay, 1987: 20–37). Table 2.1 summarizes those numbers.

The asylum view determined the policy during the first cycle. With the successful establishment of an independent nation and soon its revised constitution, official policy was to keep the gates open to all. At first, little opposition was voiced. In its first census, in 1790, the United States recorded a population of 3,227,000, most of whom were descendants of 17th- and 18th-century arrivals, or recent immigrants themselves. Among them, 61 percent were of English origin, about 8.3 percent Scotch, 6 percent Ulster Irish, 4 percent Irish Free State; 8.7 percent German, 3.4 percent Dutch, 1.7 percent French, 0.70 percent Swedish, and 6.6 percent were unassigned a particular nation of origin (Statistical Yearbook of the United States, 1996, Table 3). Approximately one-half million were black slaves and about the same number were Native American Indians. They occupied a land that was vast, sparsely settled, and obviously rich in soil and other natural resources awaiting development and exploitation. The population density was then only 4.5 persons per square mile (LeMay, 2006: 17).

Table 2.1 Immigration to the United States, 1820–1865, by Selected Years

Dates	Number of Immigrants
1820	8,385
1821–1830	143,439
1831–1840	599,125
1841–1850	1,777,251
1851–1860	2,598,214
1861	91,918
1862	91,985
1863	176,282
1864	193,418
1865	248,120
Total	5,924,128
Av./Year	131,600

Source: U.S. Department of Justice. 2003. *2001 Statistical Yearbook*. Table 1, Immigration to the U.S.: Fiscal Years 1820–2001. Washington, DC: U.S. Department of Justice, Immigration, and Naturalization Service. Available at: http://www.immigration.gov/graphics/shared/aboutus/statisics/Yearbook2001.pdf.

Table 2.2 lists the population of the United States by decade, 1790–1860, showing the steady increase in the total population, the general increase in density (persons per square mile), and the number of net immigration for the decade.

Obviously, the country needed laborers to build the cities, clear the farmlands on the frontier, push back the Indians, and strengthen defenses to avert coming under control of European colonial powers. The Constitution enshrined the prevailing sentiment among most citizens of the time—that this was a nation of a bold and noble experiment in freedom. A majority of citizens felt that freedom should be broadly shared by any and all who desired it, regardless of their former nationality.

In 1819, Congress passed the first official immigration act—the Manifest of Immigrants Act of March 2, 1819 (3 Stat. 489). The law simply charged the captain or master of any ship or vessel arriving in the United States to deliver a manifest of all passengers taken on board to designate the age, sex, and occupation of said passengers, and to set forth whether any had died on the voyage.

The wave of Catholic immigrants coming during the 1830s and 1840s set off a dramatic antiforeign reaction as they became scapegoats for all the problems arising from growing urbanization and industrialization. Immigrants were allegedly importing crime, disease, poverty, and drunkenness. Social reformers and Protestant evangelicals sought to preserve the nation's purity, and joined with the anti-immigrant and the often violent movement of the secret Order of the Star Spangled Banner, later and better known as the Know Nothing Party (Jones, 1960: 147–276; Beals, 1960; Billington, 1938 [1974]).

Table 2.2 Population of the United States, 1790–1860, by Census Year

Year	Total U.S. Population	Persons PSM	Net Immigration (Thousands)
1790	3,929,625	4.5	4
1800	5,308,483	6.1	12
1810	7,239,881	4.3	13
1820	9,638,453	5.5	21
1830	12,866,020	7.4	54
1840	17,069,453	9.8	91
1850	23,191,876	7.9	330
1860	31,443,321	10.6	123

Source: U.S. Bureau of the Census. *Statistical Abstract of the U.S., 2002*, Table 1, p. 8.

The antiforeign social movement, however, did not control public policy. The more economically and politically powerful forces in the native stock continued their potent support for open immigration as a source of cheap labor to supply the cities and factories mushrooming up across the nation. Then, in 1848, the discovery of gold in California drew a vast population to the West. A dramatic influx of Chinese to the West Coast, and increased immigrants from Southern, Central, and Eastern Europe to the East Coast, changed the complexion of immigrants after the Civil War, ushering in a new era of policy, the Door Ajar Era, during which time the first restrictions were enacted (LeMay, 1987: 38–72).

National Defense Considerations and Immigration

The founding fathers were in close agreement on foreign policy—that the most effective safeguard was isolation from Europe's geopolitical rivalries. In large measure as a reaction to the excesses of the French Revolution, the Federalists, who controlled Congress in the 1790s, enacted the Alien and Sedition Act of 1798 (1 Stat. 570). This law empowered the president, in the Alien Enemies Act, to expel dangerous aliens on pain of imprisonment (Tindall, 1984: 331; LeMay and Barkan, 1999: 15–16).

In his farewell address to the nation, President Washington articulated the strategy of isolation from Europe's wars and turmoil as "the Great Rule of conduct for us, in regards to foreign nations" (Kupchan, 2003: 165). He said, "our true policy is to steer clear of permanent alliances with any portion of the foreign world" (Tindall, 1984: 325). The nation's security depended on its geostrategic position, with vast oceans on both the East and the West, and with abundant land with rich natural resources in between, which meant that if the country refrained from meddling in the business of other nations, those powers would have no excuse to intervene in its affairs (Eland, 2001: 2).

Their fear of the colonial powers was well-founded—especially of Britain, France, and Spain. Americans feared those powers were attempting to recolonize the United States, with the aid and support of the tribes. In 1794, Indian tribes in Ohio reinforced with some Canadian militia, attacked General Wayne's force at the Battle of Fallen Timbers. General Wayne's troops won the skirmish, resulting in the Treaty of Greenville in which the United States bought from the 12 tribes the rights to the Southeastern quarter of the Northwest Territory (now Ohio and Indiana) and enclaves in Vincennes, Detroit, and Chicago. Similarly, Spanish intrigues among the Creeks, Chicksaws, and Cherokees kept up the same type of turmoil that the British stirred up along the Ohio. These raised national security fears about Indian tribal coalitions with European colonial powers (LeMay, 2006: 34).

When Jefferson became president, he initiated the Louisiana Purchase, which brought Jeffersonian Democrats support from the South, the West, and even some New Englanders. The War of 1812 and the rise of Tecumseh and his coalition of tribes renewed national defense fears. The Battle of Tippecanoe reinforced suspicions that the British were inciting the Indians. The Treaty of Ghent, negotiated by Secretary of State James Monroe, ended the war. The War of 1812 generated a new spirit of nationalism and came to be viewed as the Second War of Independence. It launched a period of economic nationalism that affected economic policy and cultural life (Tindall, 1984: 374–380). Throughout the early- to mid-19th century, U.S. military action abroad was sporadic, short-lived, and typically involved sending small raiding parties to protect U.S. traders and citizens abroad (Kupchan, 2003: 170; LeMay, 2006: 34–35).

The Tariff of 1816 raised federal finances to a level where the national government could support internal improvements, such as canals and the national road (1811–1838). When James Monroe became president in 1823, he issued the Monroe Doctrine. General Andrew Jackson took Florida in a military campaign against the Seminole Indians, and by 1819, Spain ceded all of Florida to the United States. The new nation was expanding geographically and in the powers exerted by the federal government.

Foreign policy focused on the Western hemisphere. National leaders saw the nation as expanding across the entire North American continent (Jordan et al., 1984: 47). When Andrew Jackson became president in 1828, he initiated the Indian Removal Act of 1830, and by 1840, the removal of virtually all tribes from the East to the West of the Mississippi River (Tindall, 1984: 423–27).

The U.S. military was kept small, typically averaging about 10,000 men in arms. The new nation depended on the vast oceans separating it from Europe and Asia. But isolation alone could not ensure national security, or as it was referred to then, "domestic tranquility." To secure domestic tranquility, the country would need to increase its population to settle land, defend against hostile Indians, and develop its natural resources to secure the United States' place among the nations of the world. After the Panic of 1837 (a national depression), the country experienced a period of dynamic growth. The agricultural industry, spurred with the invention of the cotton gin and the steel plow, tamed the prairie sod and increased population density with the rapid development of cities whose populations could be fed by the increased agricultural production. It greatly increased foreign trade as well, as cotton, wheat, and corn was exported to Europe. In transportation, the development of river traffic, the building of canals, and especially the expansion of railroads opened up the frontier land to development. The expansion of ocean transport brought ever-increasing numbers of immigrants, who provided cheap labor for the beginnings of the Industrial Revolution and the expansion of factories. So too, the development of the national commerce depended on a growing population. The widely accepted answer to rapid population growth was to draw immigrants to the "grand experiment in liberty" that would be the beacon to the world for a democratic republic (Tindall, 1984: 447–85).

The Industrial Revolution in America

The Industrial Revolution, which took place roughly from 1750 to 1850, was of great importance to the economic development of the United States, and certainly to its military power and status. The term refers to the change from hand and home production to machine and factory production, resulting in profound changes in agriculture, mining, transportation, and technology. The First Industrial Revolution saw the inventions of the spinning and weaving machines, operated largely by water power. These were later replaced by steam-driven machinery. The Industrial Revolution spurred America's economic and population growth, eventually transforming the United States to its modern urban-industrial state (Kornblith, 1998).

The first impetus to the American Industrial Revolution was the Embargo Act of 1807, and then the War of 1812. The Embargo Act stopped the export of American goods and effectively ended the import of manufactured goods from Europe. This led to the war with Great Britain in 1812. The war made evident the need for a better transportation system and greater economic independence. During the First Industrial Revolution (1750–1850), transportation was expanded as the nation built its first canals, established its first national road, and began its first railroad systems. It was during this era that electricity was harnessed. Improvements to industrial processes accelerated the refining process and production. Early manufacturing was enhanced by the use of the protective tariff (Olson, 2002).

Mass production became possible with technological innovations, in part encouraged by a patent system that favored innovation, and in part by new forms of factory organization. The nation was blessed with abundant natural resources just begging to be developed and exploited. These resources drew foreign investment to capitalize industrialization. Millions of immigrants from around the world, as we have seen, came to the United States seeking a better life and greater economic opportunity. They, in turn, provided both a massively increased demand for mass-produced consumer goods and as well the cheap labor force necessary to supply such goods. Industrialization and immigration led to the emergence of the labor movement and to women's organizations advocating industrial reform (Hoke, 1990).

James Watt's invention of the steam engine in 1775 literally moved production from the home to the factory, and from the basement to the first floor of factories. The mechanization of many complicated crafts soon reached deep into American society and life. By the 1850s, the nation established what became known as the "American system of manufacturing" (Hounshell, 1984). This system, by the time of the Civil War, propelled the United States to become a major world power. These changes, especially as seen in the metal industries, came with the replacement of organic fuel (wood) with fossil fuel (coal and later oil). North America was blessed with an abundance of both natural resources of fossil fuel.

The first factory systems in the United States developed in the 1810 to 1830 decades in the textile industry located along the East Coast (mostly in New England). It was followed by the chemical and metallurgical industries in the 1840s, and to all market-oriented industries by the 1860s. Textile and iron-making became the leading sectors spurring the key innovations and the nation's average income and population growth. Average per capita income increased tenfold. Average population growth increased sixfold. The living standards of ordinary Americans enjoyed sustained growth as never before witnessed. The textile industry was centered in New England. Boston merchants developed large-scale textile manufacturing and expansive markets that grew as the cost of production was lowered by manufacturing processes and the cost of transporting those goods to markets declined with the opening of canals and with steamboat transportation by river. In the 1830s and 1840s, government and private investors poured huge capital sums into canal construction, and after 1835, into railroad construction. Most notable were the Erie and Champlain canals in New York, and the coal canals in Eastern Pennsylvania and New Jersey. Early railroads carried passengers and cargo, typically over routes of 50 to 100 miles.

The Second Industrial Revolution began in the 1850s, when technology progress led to the development of steam-powered ships, railways, internal combustion engines, and electrical power generation of a mass-scale. The great advancements of the Industrial Revolution were made possible by the development of machine tools, spurred significantly by military production (especially the Armies of the North during the Civil War).

Industrialization led to factories that in turn spurred urbanization. As the Industrial Revolution concentrated labor into mills, factories, and mines, abuses evident during its early stages facilitated the organization of trade unions to protect workers' rights, working conditions, and wages.

As a growing number of successful farmers, professionals, and skilled craftsmen in the agricultural areas of the country accumulated capital, they invested in the economic sector, and manufacturing was the most important recipient of this capital. Entrepreneurs who owned small workshops and factories received that capital to expand and turn out a wide range of goods like boards, boxes, utensils, building hardware, furniture, and—especially for the topic of this chapter—weapons. These manufacturers expanded their market areas as they gained production efficiencies. Select manufactures such as shoes, tinware, buttons, and cotton textiles were especially in demand by urban residents and by prosperous farmers in agricultural areas. Such products were of high value relative to their weight; thus shipping costs were low (Weiss, 1992: 51).

Cotton textiles developed as an industry built on low-wage, especially female, labor. The burgeoning industry required capital, technical skills, and growing markets. Starting in the 1790s, New England, and particularly Rhode Island, became the site of the early cotton textile manufacturing. British immigrant machinist, Samuel Slater, trained many of the first important textile machinists. Investors in Rhode Island, Connecticut, Massachusetts, New Hampshire, and New York employed such machinists to build mills. Between 1815 and 1820, power-loom weaving became commercially feasible. Boston merchants began marketing cotton textile manufactured products on a large-scale basis.

Continued National Defense Policy Initiatives to the Civil War

President Polk, in 1840, cautioned European countries from standing in the way of America's westward expansion. As he put it: "We must ever maintain that the people of this continent have a right to decide their own destiny" (LeMay, 2006: 35).

In 1845, John O'Sullivan, editor of the *United States Magazine and Democratic Review,* coined a term to give name to the spirit of expansionism—manifest destiny—by which he meant "to overspread the continent allotted by Providence for the free development of our yearly multiplying millions" (Tindall, 1984: 535).

President Polk encouraged expansion and urged Congress to annex Texas, which joined the Union in 1845. Northern borders with Canada were settled with the Oregon Treaty in 1846. War with Mexico, in 1847–1848, ended with the Treaty of Guadalupe Hidalgo, which resulted in the annexation of California (LeMay and Barkan, 1999: 25–26).

Since the 1840s, the United States became foremost among the nations of the world in the degree to which it absorbed immigrants from other nations. No other country has experienced so many and varied an immigration of various ethnic groups. The open door policy welcomed all who would come. Midwestern and Western state governments particularly actively sought immigrants by sending agents to European countries to recruit and assist farmers and artisans to settle those states and territories. In 1862, Congress enacted the Homestead Act offering free land—an incredible pull factor to an overpopulated Europe (LeMay and Barkan, 1999: 29–30). It provided 160 acres of free land by staking a claim and then living on the land for five years; or by paying 1.25 dollar an acre after six months. When John Deere invented the steel plow and moldboard, in 1838, the Great Prairie sod was conquered with impressive results. By 1880, one single farm in South Dakota cultivated more than 13,000 acres of wheat (Tindall, 1984: 773). By the mid-1860s, the pacification of Indian tribes in the West and their removal to reservation lands sped up the settlement of the Western plains by Euro-Americans.

Throughout the Open Door Era, the overarching aim of immigration policy was to attract immigrants. This provided support to national security. European immigrants were seen as necessary to protect the nation from European ambitions and to serve as a buffer against Native American Indian resistance to the Euro-American expansion across the land in their ever-expanding Western push.

Germany became the source of the single largest contingent of immigrants. In the colonial to founding era, they came mostly for religious and economic opportunity reasons. From 1848 to 1865, they came largely for political and economic reasons. Religious factions came in groups: Mennonites, Dunkers, Lutherans, Calvinists, and Jews. Geographically, they were Palatines, Salzburgers, Wurttenburgers, and Hanoverians. They cultivated some of the richest farmlands in colonial America and served as the breadbasket of the revolution. They brought with them industrial skills important in later decades to establishing a domestic steel industry and the building of the railroad from the East to the Midwest.

Their Revolutionary War service, in which several German regiments fought prominently and well, accelerated their acceptance and assimilation. As their social and economic conditions improved, they took a more active role in public affairs, affiliating with the Democrats, reflecting their small farmer backgrounds.

During the 1830s and 1840s, Germans immigrated for different reasons. The agricultural revolution hit Central Europe forcing many off the land. They turned to manufacturing, but even this development left them overly vulnerable to economic change. When the potato famine struck, they were forced to emigrate. Fortunately for them, and for the United States, that coincided with the opening of the American Midwest. State governments, railroads, shipping lines, and manufacturers enticed immigrants. The development of ocean-going steamship lines by 1850 made the journey cheaper and less arduous. Texas, the Great Lakes region, and the Ohio River Valley attracted the newcomers. Midwestern cities exploded in population, attracting large numbers of German immigrants to cities like Chicago, Detroit, Milwaukee, Cincinnati, and St. Louis. A swath of land 200 miles wide, stretching from New York down to Maryland and across to the Mississippi River, became known as the German belt. By the 1860 census, German immigrants made up 36.63 percent of the total immigrants coming during the 1851–1860 decade (U.S. Bureau of the Census, 1909–1990).

Political turmoil in Germany, culminating in the failed, liberal 1848 Revolution, caused many German intellectuals to flee to America. The Forty-Eighters, as they came to be known, numbered some 10,000, but they wielded influence far beyond their numbers as they started newspapers, reading societies, theatres, and other cultural activities. They provided important leadership in the American labor movement, were prominent in the antislavery movement, and instrumental in the founding of the Republican Party. The Act of July 17, 1862 (40 Stat. S46), granted naturalization to honorably discharged soldiers and became an important inducement to recruit aliens to serve in the Union Army during the Civil War, in which large numbers of German immigrants fought. A German American brigade was led by Major Generals Franz Sigel and Carl Schurz, both German-born Forty-Eighters who had served in the revolutionary forces in Germany and came with military experience and skills. Their ability to speak with the German-speaking volunteers who served in the Civil War was especially important to their fighting effectiveness in a number of key battles of the war.

An estimated 516,000 German Americans served in the Civil War, more than 23 percent of all Union soldiers. Prominent units were the 6th Kentucky Infantry Regiment and the 4th Kentucky Cavalry, and the 2nd Volunteers Regiment. From Kentucky alone 1,940 German-born served. The most notable battles in which they fought include Chancellorsville, Gettysburg, Chattanooga and Nashville (with Sherman's 11th Corp), Shiloh, Missionary Ridge, Chickamauga Creek, and Vicksburg. Eleven German

Americans were recipients of the Congress Medal of Honor for Valor, begun in 1861.

After the Civil War, when settlers flocked to the West drawn by free land grants through the Homestead Act, by land grants given to Civil War veterans, and by the easing of the migration to West enabled by the expansion of the railroads during the war, the interior was opened to settlement and the successive and successful prosecution of the Plains Indian wars lasting from the late 1860s to the late 1870s. The pacification of the Indian tribes and their forced resettlement on reservations promoted the settlement of the Western Plains by Euro-American settlers (LeMay, 2006: 37).

Prior to the Civil War, Irish immigrants were second only to the Germans. In 1790, they comprised about 2 percent of the population of just over three million. After 1830, emigrants began fleeing political and religious persecution under British rule, and Irish immigration swelled to a flood. By the 1851–1860 decade, immigrants from Ireland rose to more than 914,000 and comprised more than 35 percent of the total immigrants who came to the United States during that decade, mostly forced by the potato famine to emigrate. Between 1847 and 1854, about 1.2 million Irish arrived in the United States in a surge that peaked in 1851, when nearly a quarter million arrived (Tindall, 1984: 447). Their sheer numbers and their Catholicism activated existing prejudice. They arrived dirt-poor, essentially trapping them in the nation's rapidly expanding Eastern seaboard cities where they concentrated in tenement slums in cities like Boston, New York, and Philadelphia. Their illiteracy and lack of job skills forced them into unskilled labor, and they comprised a lower-class just when the United States developed class consciousness. They were the first ethnic group to face overt job discrimination in New York, Boston, and other Eastern cities. They took whatever jobs were open to them—unskilled work as stevedores, teamsters, ditchdiggers, dockworkers, and terriers. They comprised the construction gangs who razed or erected building in the ever-expanding cities. They built the canals, roads, and railroads connecting the East with the Midwest and beyond.

This flood of immigrants sparked a nativist reaction. In 1828, the Workingmen's Party began in Philadelphia. It spread west, becoming especially powerful on the West Coast. In 1837, the Native American Association began. It was soon surpassed in importance, however, when, in 1849, the Order of the Star Spangled Banner was founded in New York. By 1854, it had evolved into the American Party, more commonly known as the Know Nothing Party (Tindall, 1984: 478; LeMay, 2006: 47).

A steadily growing urbanization between 1840 and 1860 required an increasing local government workforce, especially police departments. The Irish were quick to join, and rose rapidly to levels of responsibility. Where, in Ireland, they had been oppressed by the police—evicted, taxed, seized for questioning, imprisoned or forced to emigrate, and even killed—in America, they exercised such power. They soon realized that job security lay in the success of the growing number of urban political machines, and Irish-dominated police departments became the mainstays of ward and district organizations of the Democratic Party. They paved the streets of Eastern seaboard cities, dug out by hand the canals and later the subways, razed and erected the buildings of rapidly expanding cities.

Like the Germans, Irish immigrants served in the Union Army during the Civil War, speeding their naturalization and assimilation. Their military service in the Civil War, and especially their work in building the railroads, particularly the first transcontinental railroad from the East westward, enabled them to spread from Eastern seaboard cities to the Midwest. Many Civil War veterans were given grants of land in the Midwest for their service in the Union military. More than 144,000 Irish Americans served in the Civil War. A number of states sent thousands each of Irish volunteers: New York State sent more than 51,000, Pennsylvania more than 17,000, Illinois more than 12,000, Massachusetts more than 8,000, Missouri more than 4,000, and Wisconsin more than 3,000.

The famed Irish Brigade, of which the "Fighting Irish" was coined, was led by several Irish-born immigrants who achieved brigadier general rank: Thomas Meagher, Thomas Cobb, Thomas Smyth, and Robert Nugent. Among those in the Irish brigade alone, more than 4,000 were killed or wounded. Five Irish-born volunteers were recipients of the Congressional Medal of Honor for their valor in the Civil War. They fought in the Pennsylvania Campaign; at Bull Run; at the First and Second Battles of Manassas; at bloody Antietam (the costliest battle taking American lives in a single day in all of U.S. history); at Fredericksburg, Chancellorsville, Gettysburg, and the Siege of Petersburg, and at Appomatox Court House. Tens of thousands of Irish foreign-born immigrants sped up their naturalization process as a result of their service and honorable discharge.

Scandinavians were likely the first Europeans to explore America, with Viking exploration and minute settlements dating back to 800–1050. In the mid-1600s, they settled in what is now Delaware. They came from Norway, Sweden, and Denmark prior to the Civil War, although their peak period was later. They were a successful group of immigrants, typically arriving in better economic condition than most other immigrant groups, enabling them to escape the poverty, slums, and resulting social stigma of the Eastern seaboard cities with their teeming immigrant masses. The Homestead Act, particularly, enabled them to settle in the Midwestern states whose soil and climate so reminded them of their homeland. Minnesota, Wisconsin, Iowa, Illinois, and the Dakotas all saw dramatic increases in their population due to the Scandinavian influx. The 1850 census found more than 18,000 Scandinavians, and by the 1860 census they exceeded 72,500. They set up their own shops, stores, factories, and banks. Their assimilation was eased by their being Caucasian, escaping racial prejudice. They were strongly Protestant, avoiding the anti-Catholic sentiment. They came in smaller numbers over more decades, compared to the huge wave of Irish who came by over a million in a decade. Scandinavians were not viewed as threats to the dominant society's labor force. Many were anti-Catholic, and thus more accepted by the native stock with whom they shared a common enemy. Their rapid financial success in the Midwest led to their early political involvement. Forming cities in the then frontier settlements provided them with an understanding of American-style politics. They organized political groups to get information on laws and elections, organized new townships, worked in town governments, levied and collected taxes, and developed new roads. The first Scandinavian-born politician to enter statewide politics was a Norwegian, James Reymert, who represented Racine County in Wisconsin in 1847.

Other immigrant groups among the old immigrants that arrived in significant numbers between 1820 and 1865 included the Dutch, French, Scots, Scotch-Irish, and Welsh. Total immigration from the Netherlands numbered about a quarter million prior to the Civil War and they had a significant impact on U.S. society during the colonial and early independence periods. Dutch influence was strongest in New Jersey and New York. Brooklyn, the Bowery, and the Bronx, for instance, all take their names as derivates of Dutch words. In the 1850 census, nearly 10,000 were born in the Netherlands, and more than 28,000 claimed that origin in the 1860 census. Dutch religious dissenters founded settlements in Michigan and Iowa in 1846. Their departure from their homeland coincided with the potato blight and the accompanying economic depression that hit much of Europe in the mid- to late 1840s. Their religious separatists established a settlement in what became Holland, Michigan. It served as a prototype for a new wave of immigrants who settled in Wisconsin and Illinois, as well as Michigan and Iowa, where the soil was so favorable and the climate so familiar.

The unifying force among Dutch settlements was religion rather than national identity. Schisms eventually resulted in the formation of the Dutch Reformed Church, the Christian Reformed Church, and the Netherlands Reformed Church. The Holland, Michigan settlement established Hope College; and the Christian Reformed Church, a more conservative group, emulated their example in founding Calvin College in Grand Rapids, Michigan.

France was the source of a large and rather steady flow of immigrants, from France proper, from the French Louisianans, or Cajuns, who were expelled from Acadia French Canada by the British in 1755; and other French Canadians who settled in New England. Colonial-era French immigrants were dominated by the Huguenots. Protestants fleeing religious persecution most readily became Anglican in the United States, which coupled with their rapid adoption of English eased their assimilation. Frequent hostilities between France and England spilled over to some animosity in the colonies and such friction, though short-lived, encouraged them to anglicize their names and customs. When, during the Revolutionary War, France became an ally against Great Britain, their assimilation was greatly facilitated. It was the French diplomat, De Crevecouer, who first used the concept of the United States as the asylum for the poor of Europe, and who first popularized the concept of America as being "the melting pot" (Rischin, 1976: 24).

The French Revolution led to thousands leaving for the United States. Unlike their earlier counterparts, this group of largely former French aristocrats kept separate and avoided the native stock, who they felt to be socially inferior. They were slow to assimilate and naturalize, and many returned to France after the fall of Napoleon. The French Revolution briefly aroused anti-French sentiment as Americans began to fear and detest the excesses of that revolution. As we have seen, this contributed to the Federalist Party pushing through the Alien and Sedition Acts.

The Louisiana French became part of the country by absorption in the Louisiana Purchase in 1803. They exhibited a strong and persistent subculture that has absorbed other ethnic groups in the area, largely through intermarriage and their socialization process (LeMay, 2006: 53). The French Canadians also exhibited a persistent subculture. Overpopulation at home and the diminishing size of agricultural land led many to immigrate to the United States in the 1830s, where they settled in large numbers in the mill and factory towns of New England. Other substantial settlements were in New York, Michigan, Illinois, and Wisconsin, where their family and church structures accounted for their persistent subculture and slower rate of assimilation.

In the 1850 census, more than 58,000 claimed French birth, and by the 1860 census, that number was slightly less than 110,000. Between 1851 and 1860, more than 76,000 arrived from France, comprising nearly 3 percent of all the immigrants coming in that decade.

The Scots, Scotch-Irish, and Welsh showed similar patterns of immigration and assimilation. They began arriving during colonial times and incorporated rather easily. Their religious preference for Presbyterianism,

Episcopalianism, and Anglicanism—all of which espoused the Protestant work ethic—earned them a widespread reputation for frugality and honesty, and made them readily accepted by the Calvinist New Englanders. They settled in considerable numbers in Pennsylvania, the Carolinas, and New England where they worked as farmers or miners, and in the latter occupation, they were often desired as skilled workers who served as superintendents and foremen.

While they did experience some anti-immigrant feeling, they often settled in large numbers in what were then frontier regions where they might become the dominant group. The native workforce perceived them as an economic threat due to their job skills, which made them highly desired as workers by the native elite who controlled business enterprises (LeMay, 2006: 53).

Another major group arrived after 1848 on the West Coast—the Chinese. They are unique among the old immigrant groups in that they faced a racial stigma and became the first target of specific restrictive laws. Between 1850 and 1860, more than 35,500 immigrants arrived in the United States.

After discovery of gold in California in 1848, Chinese laborers surged into the state. They were fleeing political upheavals in Kwantung and Fukien provinces in Southern China resulting from economic depressions and labor rebellions, but also floods, famine, and general social discontent. They were pulled by the demand for labor caused by the California gold rush and by heavy labor recruitment by the railroad and steamship lines. The Central Pacific Railroad, for example, employed some 9,000 Chinese and by 1860 they made up about 10 percent of California's population and roughly 25 percent of its workforce (Thompson, 1979). By 1850, they experienced growing hostility. In mining regions, they were often beaten, and occasionally murdered. In 1849, a Know Nothing judge on the California Supreme Court had ruled that they could not testify in courts against white men. As a result, crimes against them—even violent ones—went unpunished.

Miscegenation laws forbade them marrying white women. By the 1850s, California had expelled them from the mining camps, segregated them in schools, denied them the right to testify in courts, and barred them from obtaining citizenship. By 1865, calls for their outright restriction in immigration were heard nationally, and especially on the West Coast, where anti-Asian sentiment was strongest. Although not successful in passing federal legislation until 1882, the Chinese Exclusion League formed in California, then spread to neighboring states, and eventually morphed into the Asian Exclusion League (Schumsky, 1991: 178; LeMay, 2006: 54–57).

Nativist Political Reaction

Many White Anglo-Saxon Protestants among the native stock welcomed the immigrants. As we have mentioned, several state governments and businesses, particularly the railroads and various manufacturing concerns, and the transatlantic shipping lines being organized in the 1840s and 1850s, actively recruited immigrants.

But not all of the native stock reacted so favorably. The American Party, founded on July 4, 1845, was a specific anti-immigrant party whose main platform was the total rejection of the foreigner. Their party platform stated:

> The danger of foreign influence . . . threatens the gradual destruction of our national institutions . . . rendering the American system liable to the poisonous influence of European policy—a policy at war with the fundamental principles of the American Constitution, but also its still more fatal operation in aggravating the virulence of partisan warfare—has awakened deep concern in the minds of every intelligent man from the days of Washington to now. (O'Connor, 1968: 122)

Prior to the Civil War, by far the most prominent nativist movement was the Know Nothing Party, originally called the Order of the Star Spangled Banner. It began as a secret patriotic society founded in New York in 1849. The party achieved early success in Massachusetts, Pennsylvania, and Maryland. In the 1854 elections, it added striking successes in Rhode Island, New Hampshire, Connecticut, Delaware, Kentucky, and Texas. The movement wielded a strong influence in Virginia, Georgia, Alabama, Mississippi, and Louisiana (Smith, 1969: 141; Nevins, 2001: 329).

Historian John Highman captured the essential philosophy of Americanism as espoused by the nativist themselves:

> Here is the ideological core of nativism in every form. Whether the nativist is a workingman or a Protestant evangelist, a southern conservative or a northern reformer, he stood for a certain kind of nationalism. He believed—whether he was trembling at a Catholic menace to American liberty, fearing an invasion of pauper labor, or simply rioting against the great English actor William Macready—that some influence originating abroad threatened the very life of the nation from within. Nativism, therefore, should be defined as intense opposition to an internal minority on the ground of its foreign (i.e., "un-American") connections. (Higham, 1955: 4)

In 1856, Millard Fillmore was the party's nominee for president. Its platform was narrowly based on an anti-immigrant, anti-Catholic stance and it did not appeal nationally. It was silent on the number-one issue of the day—slavery. It carried only one state (LeMay and Barkan, 1999, Document 23: 28–29).

In order to join the party, a person had to be native-born and a Protestant, to swear an oath to vote for whomever or whatever the party told him to vote. If asked about their goals or stands on an issue, they were told to reply, "I know nothing," which gave rise to the party's popular name. On occasion, some party members would close one eye and place a thumb and forefinger over the nose, signifying "eyes nose nothing" (Bailey, 1976: 135).

Deep-rooted feelings caused many among the native stock to oppose immigrants by joining the new militant nativist party. Massive immigration following the potato famine aroused fears and hostility, which fed the movement and contributed to the party's rapid rise and temporary successes.

The slavery issue, which led to the party's demise, loosened ties so that many voters who were unwilling yet to cast their vote with either the proslavery Democratic Party or the antislavery forces coalescing in the formation of the Republican Party, found a temporary home in the Know Nothing Party. It attracted many from the working class, who feared their jobs would be taken and the institutions and order of society as they knew it would be undermined by so vast an influx of foreigners. They feared the increasing electoral clout of the immigrant bloc vote becoming evident in the emergence of the political party machine. Large-scale immigration, they feared, led to the overall low-pay rates and deplorable working conditions that characterized the early years of the industrialization period.

Others were attracted out of a deep-seated fear of Catholicism, which was increasingly evident among the immigrants flooding in during the 1840s. In New York, mobs of Irish and Know Nothing adherents clashed, leaving two dead (the situation depicted in the film *Gangs of New York*). In Newark, an estimated 2,000 Protestants and Catholics squared off, which left 20 dead, and hundreds of others wounded. In Baltimore, where the party was especially strong, numerous clashes took place and a riot in 1854 left eight dead. The Plug Uglies, a spin-off group of the party, were often behind the physical violence.

Not all citizens reacted so negatively. The famous writer, Ralph Waldo Emerson, attacked the xenophobic hysteria and the nativist movement by stressing what he considered to be the advantage of open immigration—what he termed "the smelting-pot theory":

> I hate the narrowness of the Native American Party. It is the dog in the manger. It is precisely opposite to true wisdom. . . . Well, as in the old burning of the Temple of Corinth, by the melting and intermixture of silver and

> gold and other metals, a new compound more precious than any, called Corinthian brass, was formed; so in this continent—asylum to all nations—the energy of the Irish, Swedes, Poles, and Cossacks, and all the European tribes—of the Africans, and the Polynesians, will construct a new race, a new religion, a new state, a new literature, which will be vigorous as the new Europe which came out of the smelting pot of the Dark Ages, or that which earlier emerged from the Palasogic and Etruscan barbarianism. (Orth and Ferguson, 1971: 299–300)

But those attracted to the nativist movement and party feared the smelting-pot theory. They did not want a new race, nor a new religion, nor a new language, state, or literature. They supported a change in immigration policy to restrict immigration. Many called for the outright banning of all further immigration to the country.

In 1854, the Know Nothing Party articulated well their antiforeign sentiment:

> Nothing is more evident than that our political parties have become sadly, deplorably corrupt . . . Congress has become a most shameful and disgraceful scene of drunkenness, riot, and caucusing for the Presidency, and the minor offices of government. The foreign element is increasing in fearful ratio. Nearly one million per annum of foreign Catholics and German infidels—who, though opposed in all else, are agreed in the subversion of our free institutions—are pouring in upon us, and the tide is increasing. These foreigners have already commenced their warfare upon the use of the Bible in our schools—against our free school system—against our Sabbath—against our laws. They boldly threaten to overthrow our constitution, through profligacy of our politicians; and we see our candidates for political preferment pandering more and more to the Catholic and foreign influence. We see from the last census that the majority of the civil and municipal offices of this government are today in the hands of Catholics and foreigners; an overwhelming majority of our army and navy are foreign Catholics. They hear the editors of Catholic papers, who are endorsed by their Archbishops, threatening in these words: "If Catholics ever gain an immense numerical majority, religious freedom in this country is at an end." So say our enemies. So we believe. (Overdyke, 1968: 67)

Then Republican activist and leader, Abraham Lincoln, in 1855, decried the Know Nothing Party and movement, stating his position on nativism as follows:

> I am not a Know Nothing. That is certain. How could I be? How can anyone who abhors the oppression of negroes, be in favor of degrading a class

> of white people? Our progress in degeneracy appears to me to be pretty rapid. As a nation, we began by declaring that "all men are created equal." We now practically read it "all men are created equal, except negroes, and foreigners, and Catholics." When it comes to this I would prefer emigrating to some country where they make no pretense of loving liberty—to Russia, for instance, where despotism can be taken pure, and without the base alloy of hypocracy. (LeMay and Barkan, 1999, Document 21: 27)

Rapid in its rise, the party experienced an equally rapid decline. Its 1855 convention split wide open over the slavery issue. Its northern members were antislavery; its southern wing would not budge from their proslavery position. After the 1856 election, the party essentially disintegrated, with its southern wing going Democratic (and later, secessionist), and the northern wing joining the Republicans (LeMay and Barkan, 1999: 28–29; see also Severance, 1970: 16–17).

Conclusion

A coalition of groups favoring restrictionist immigration policy developed but did not prevail during the closing decades of the Open Door Era. The coalition of groups favoring immigration was financially and politically more powerful. Their view that the nation needed open immigration to support the expansion of the nation and its increasing industrialization (spurred on by the Civil War) was seen as essential to national security. The United States had to have a large pool of cheap labor to enable industrialization. Industrialization was necessary to support a world-class navy and military force. The prevailing perception that was increasingly accepted as valid was the concept of Manifest Destiny—that it was the destiny of the nation to fill the land from coast-to-coast, and the destiny of the nation to become the beacon of democracy from the new world to the old world. Only open immigration would enable the United States to achieve its manifest destiny. And as a result, despite some tinkering with policy at the edges, the major thrust of immigration policy remained supportive of massive, large-scale immigration. The triumph of that perspective, and an illustration of the link between national security and immigration policy, was perhaps best exemplified by the opening, in 1855, of the Castle Garden immigration station in New York City by the New York State Emigration Commission (LeMay and Barkan, 1999, Document 27: 32–33).

During the Civil War, recruiting officers of the Union Army erected two huge tents adjacent to the Castle Garden immigration station. They sought to enlist the newly arrived immigrants into the army by offering bounties if they could not persuade them to sign up with arguments in their own language. The recruiters were quite successful in their endeavors as eventually more than 400,000 foreign-born from 20 different countries fought on the Northern side (LeMay, 2006: 64).

References

Bailey, Thomas H. 1976. *Voices of America.* New York: The Free Press.

Beals, Carleton. 1960. *Brace Knuckle Crusade.* New York: Hasting House.

Billington, Ray. 1938 [1974]. *The Origins of Nativism in the United States, 1800–1844.* New York: Arno Press.

Eland, Ivan. 2001. *Putting Defense Back into U.S. Defense Policy.* Westport, CT: Praeger Press.

Higham, John. 1955. *Strangers in the Land: Patterns of American Nativism.* New Brunswick, NJ: Rutgers University Press.

Hoke, Donald. 1990. *Ingenious Yankees: The Rise of the American System of Manufacturers in the Private Sector.* New York: Columbia University Press.

Hounshell, David. 1984. *From the American System to Mass Production, 1800–1932: The Development of Manufacturing Technology in the United States.* Baltimore, MD: Johns Hopkins University Press.

Immigration and Naturalization Service. 1997. *Statistical Yearbook of the United States, 1996.* Washington, D.C.: U.S. Government Printing Office.

Jones, Maldwyn Allen. 1960. *American Immigration.* Chicago, IL: University of Chicago.

Jordan, Amos A., et al. 1984. *American National Security.* Baltimore, MD: Johns Hopkins University Press.

Kornblith, Gary, ed. 1998. *The Industrial Revolution in America.* Boston, MA: Houghton-Mifflin.

Kupchan, Charles A. 2003. *The End of the American Era.* New York: Alfred A. Knopf.

LeMay, Michael. 1987. *From Open Door to Dutch Door: An Analysis of U.S. Immigration Policy since 1820.* New York: Praeger Press.

LeMay, Michael. 2006. *Guarding the Gates: Immigration and National Security.* Westport, CT: Praeger Security International.

LeMay, Michael, and Elliott Barkan, eds. 1999. *U.S. Immigration and Naturalization Laws and Issues: A Documentary History.* Westport, CT: Greenwood Press.

Nevins, Allan. 2001. *Ordeal in Union: A House Dividing.* New York: Routledge.

O'Connor, Thomas. 1968. *The German Americans.* Boston, MA: Little, Brown.

Olson, James Stuart. 2002. *Encyclopedia of the Industrial Revolution in America.* Westport, CT: Greenwood Publishing.

Orth, Ralph, and Alfred Ferguson, eds. 1971. *The Journals and Miscellaneous Papers of Ralph Waldo Emerson.* Cambridge, MA: Harvard University Press.

Overdyke, S. Darrell. 1968. *The Know-Nothing Party in the South.* Gloucester, MA: Peter Smith Publisher.

Rischin, Moses, ed. 1976. *Immigration and the American Tradition.* Indianapolis, IN: Bobbs-Merrill.

Schumsky, Neil. 1991. *The Evolution of Political Protest and the Workingmen's Party of California.* Columbia, OH: Ohio State University Press.

Severance, Frank H. ed. 1970. *Millard Fillmore Papers.* Vol. II. New York: Krause Reprint.

Smith, Theodore. 1969. *Politics and Slavery.* New York: Negro University Press.

Thompson, James J., Jr. 1979. "Southern Baptists and Anti-Catholicism in the 1920s." *Mississippi Quarterly* 32(4): 611–625.

Tindall, George Brown. 1984. *America: A Narrative History.* 2nd ed., New York: W.W. Norton.

U.S. Bureau of the Census. 1990. *A Century of Population Growth from the First Census to the Twelfth, 1790–1900.* Washington, DC: U.S. Bureau of the Census.

U.S. Bureau of the Census. 2002. *Statistical Abstract of the U.S., 2002,* Table 1, p. 8. Washington, DC: U.S. Department of Commerce, Economics and Statistical Administration, Bureau of the Census.

U.S. Department of Commerce, Bureau of the Census. 1997. *Statistical Yearbook of the United States, 1996.* Washington, D.C.: U.S. Government Printing Office.

U.S. Department of Justice. 2003. *2001 Statistical Yearbook.* Washington, DC: U.S. Department of Justice, Immigration and Naturalization Service.

Vialet, Joyce. 1980. *A Brief History of U.S. Immigration Policy.* Report 80-223 EPW. Washington, DC: Education and Public Welfare Division.

Weiss, Thomas. 1992. "U.S. Labor Force Estimates and Economic Growth, 1800–1860." In *American Economic Growth and Standards of Living Before the Civil War,* ed. Robert Gailman and John Waltis. Chicago, IL: University of Chicago Press.

CHAPTER THREE

Mushrooming Cities: Immigration and the Beginnings of Urbanization, 1790–1865

Michael C. LeMay

Introduction

Today, the United States is an overwhelmingly urban nation. More than two-thirds of the population lives in metropolitan areas, of which there are more than 300. In 2005, of the 296,410,404 residents of the United States, more than 62 percent live in cities, and 16 percent live in the 50 largest cities. As of 2005, there are 32 cities of 500,000 or more population in which 13 percent live, and 222 cities that each exceed 200,000 in population (Gaquin and DeBrandt, 2006: ix). By 2010, 83.7 percent of the population of the United States lived in the nation's 366 metropolitan areas (www.census.gov/prod/cen2010/briefs/c2010br-o1.pdf). Immigration was a defining factor of urbanization of the United States. The urbanization of America began before the Civil War. Cities grew in number and size in direct parallel to increased immigration. Like mushrooms popping up overnight, cities sprouted as immigration increased markedly.

In the 1790 census, the United States was a nation of farmers and frontiersmen. Its population was more than 99 percent rural. There were only two cities that were above 25,000 in population in 1790: New York at 49,401 and Philadelphia at 28,522 (U.S. Bureau of the Census, 1996). Among the nearly 4 million people, there were just over 200,000 urban dwellers, or roughly one-half of 1 percent. The Mid-Atlantic region led the country with just over 83,000 urban dwellers, followed by New England with just over 76,000, and then the South Atlantic with just over 42,000 urban residents. Throughout the entire nation of then 13 states, there were only 24 cities (defined as a place of more than 2,500 residents).

Largely due to immigration, the total population of the United States grew steadily between 1790 and 1860, as detailed in Table 3.1, which lists the total population by census year, the persons per square mile, and the number of immigrants entering (in thousands).

Mostly because of immigration, by the 1860 census the number of chartered cities in the United States had grown from 24 to 392, 58 of which were in the 10,000 to 25,000 size range. Among the just over 31 million in total population, 6,216,518 were urban dwellers, or nearly 20 percent of the total population, up from 1 percent in 7 decades. Among the nearly 400 cities, a number were sizable for the times: 6 cities were in the 100,000–249,999 size range, and 7 ranged in 50,000 to 99,999. Another 19 cities were between 25,000 and 49,999 in population. In 1860, New York City became the first city in the United States to exceed 1 million in population, Philadelphia was more than 500,000, New Orleans was more than 168,000, Cincinnati exceeded 161,000, St. Louis was more than 160,000, Chicago was more than 144,000, Buffalo was more than 81,000, Louisville was more than 68,000, Albany was more than 62,000, Washington, DC was more than 61,000, and San Francisco nearly 57,000. Table 3.2 lists the number of urban places in the United States by census year from 1790 to 1860, by size of urban place, detailing the steady rise in both the number and size of cities.

Table 3.1 Total Population of the United States, by Census Year, 1790–1860

Census Year	Total Population	Density	Net Immigration (Thousands)
1790	3,929,625	4.5	4
1800	5,308,483	6.1	12
1810	7,239,881	4.3	13
1820	9,638,453	5.5	21
1830	12,866,020	7.4	54
1840	17,069,453	9.8	91
1850	23,191,876	7.9	330
1860	31,443,321	10.6	123

Source: U.S. Bureau of the Census. 2003. *Statistical Abstract of the United States, 2002.* Table 1, p. 8. Washington, DC: U.S. Bureau of the Census, Department of the Interior.

Table 3.2 Urban Places in the United States, by Size of City, 1790–1860

Year	Number	100,000+	50,000+	25,000–50,000	10,000–24,999	5,000–9,999	2,500–4,999
1790	24	—	—	2	3	7	12
1800	33	—	1	2	3	15	12
1810	46	—	2	2	7	17	18
1820	61	1	2	2	8	22	26
1830	90	1	3	3	16	33	34
1840	131	3	2	7	25	48	46
1850	237	6	4	17	36	85	89
1860	392	9	7	19	58	136	163

Source: Table by author. Data from U.S. Bureau of the Census. 1909. *A Century of Population Growth from the First Census of the United States to the Twelfth, 1790–1900*. Washington, DC: U.S. Bureau of the Census, Department of the Interior.

Table 3.3 Immigration to the United States, 1820–1860

Year	Total U.S. Population	Total Immigrants Arriving	Foreign-Born (Percent)
1820	9,638,453	8,385	0.09
1821–1830	12,866,020	143,439	1.11
1831–1840	17,069,453	599,125	3.51
1841–1850	23,191,876	1,713,251	7.39
1851–1860	31,443,321	2,598,214	8.26

Percent of the foreign born in total population as of census year:
1850 Census 9.7%
1860 Census 13.2%

Source: Table by author. Data from U.S. Bureau of the Census. 1996. *Population of States and Counties of the United States: 1790–1990*. Washington, DC: U.S. Bureau of the Census, Department of Commerce.

Not surprising, the urban population was spreading regionally as well. By the 1860 census, there were more than 1,100, 000 city dwellers in the New England region, more than 2,600,000 in the Mid-Atlantic region, nearly 1 million in the East North-Central region, almost 300,000 in the West North-Central area, more than 600,000 in the South Atlantic region, more than 200,000 in the East South-Central region, more than 200,000 in the West South-Central region, just over 17,000 in the Mountain region, and just over 80,000 in the Pacific region (about 70 percent of whom resided in San Francisco, which topped 56,000 in 1860 due largely to the California Gold Rush). Of the 31 million residents in the United States in 1860, just over 4,100,000 were foreign born (just over 7.6%), so immigrants played a key role in that urban growth. Table 3.3 lists the number of immigrants to the United States during 1820–1860, the total population of the nation, and shows the steady growth in the percent of foreign-born among the total population.

Cities and Disease Epidemics

A significant problem facing the United States as a direct result of the rapid growth in the size and number of cities prior to the Civil War was that of coping with pandemic diseases that often broke out in cities and spread from them to the rural populations of the surrounding regions. Prior to the late 1880s, medical science did not know the cause of disease, nor how to effectively cope with epidemic outbreaks of contagious diseases other than quarantine of afflicted persons and waiting for the epidemic to burn itself out. Pandemics refer to when an epidemic disease spreads to entire countries, or regions of countries, and becomes multinational or even global in scope. The 19th century might justifiably be called the Age of Pandemics. A number of old-world epidemic diseases spread to the new world, often coming with immigrants. These diseases found virgin populations with little or no natural immunity to the disease, and epidemic outbreaks took hundreds to even thousands at a time. After contact with European settlers, the population of Native American Indian tribes was literally decimated through deaths by epidemic diseases, which killed many times more than those who were killed in battles with whites.

The more prominent epidemics that came to the United States with immigrants from Europe and Asia were such diseases as typhoid, tuberculosis, cholera, diphtheria, measles, bubonic plague, and the deadliest of all, smallpox. Southern cities suffered especially from malaria and yellow fever. To illustrate the point, New Orleans suffered from yellow fever epidemics in 1847 and again in 1852. In that later outbreak, more than 8,000 inhabitants of New Orleans died from yellow fever in the summer of 1852 alone.

Much more will be said about the battle against pandemic diseases by the immigration service in chapter 3 in Volume 2 of this set, but it will be useful here to illustrate the problem faced by the rapidly growing number of cities in the pre–Civil War years. Most often, epidemics of these maladies broke out in city populations and spread from the point of origin to outlying areas, to Indian tribes, and to other cities as persons infected with the disease travelled to them, often along river routes and canals. This chapter will briefly discuss two such epidemic diseases—cholera and smallpox—as these two were the deadliest and exemplary of many of them.

Cholera, we now know, is spread by contaminated water. It was a classic epidemic disease of the 19th century. Port cities, as the receiving stations for the mass waves of immigrants arriving in the mid-1800s, were particularly susceptible to epidemic outbreaks of cholera. Boston, New York City, Philadelphia, Baltimore, and New Orleans, for example, all suffered cholera outbreaks, a couple of which were especially deadly, as did hub cities in the interior to which immigrants traveled by river boats: like St. Louis and Louisville. A notably severe outbreak occurred in 1832. New York City was among the hardest hit, with more than 5,000 deaths in the summer of 1832. It established a cholera hospital to quarantine and care for the infected. That model was followed in other cities that same summer as outbreaks spread to Philadelphia, Baltimore, Louisville, St. Louis, and Cincinnati (LeMay, 2006: 41).

By far the most deadly of epidemics that were the scourge among cities of the United States prior to the Civil War, however, was that of smallpox. In *Pox Americana,* author and scholar Elizabeth Fenn (2001) has documented the great epidemic outbreaks of smallpox in the United States that ravaged the country between 1775 and 1882. She estimates the minimal mortality rate from smallpox between 1775 and 1782 in the United States at 130,658 persons (Fenn, 2001: 274). A few of the then major cities of the time that suffered smallpox episodes are highlighted here.

During the Revolutionary War, the two largest cities of the time, New York City and Philadelphia, were the hardest hit. As Fenn (2001) puts it: "Nowhere in North America was smallpox more persistent than in the city of Philadelphia" (41–42). The epidemic first broke out in those cities in 1774, and 300 died from it in Philadelphia that year. It festered in the city in 1775, and again in 1779–1780 (39–40).

One medical practice to cope with smallpox that was used at the time was inoculation. Slivers of wood, or needles and thread, were inserted into the pox of infected persons and then into healthy persons. Although medical practitioners of the time knew nothing of germ theory, they had learned that suffering a mild case of the disease made the survivors immune from further or more deadly outbreaks. The practice of inoculation against smallpox, however, was more restricted and unpopular in New England (Fenn, 2001: 39). As Fenn (2001) notes:

> Inoculation offered the risky alternative to a life of fear. Utilized for hundreds of years in parts of Asia and Africa, the procedure was nevertheless unknown among Europeans until the early eighteenth century. Shortly after 1700, word of the practice reached Europe from a number of sources. One was the Puritan minister Cotton Mather. (31–32)

In 1764 an epidemic of smallpox struck Boston, and more than 500 died. But Cotton Mather convinced many to receive free inoculations and many were saved and he was hailed as a hero in the city (Fenn, 2001: 42). Boston suffered three more episodes of smallpox outbreaks in 1775–1776. During the Revolutionary War, the disease so threatened the Army that General George Washington ordered mandatory inoculation of all soldiers. When Baltimore was struck by an epidemic of smallpox in 1769, the practice was prohibited by the city leaders, but many persons owning slaves disobeyed the law to have their slave laborers inoculated to prevent their deaths (Fenn, 2001: 40).

St. Louis was the site of several deadly outbreaks, in 1764 and 1767–1768, and from that river-port city that was a hub of transit to the frontier, the epidemics spread from the city to the Missouri River tribes of the Sioux Indians with devastating effects (Fenn, 2001: 201). In similar manner, San Francisco, in 1776 a small Mexican outpost, suffered an outbreak when it was spread to that city from an epidemic begun in Mexico City. And in that year, Detroit suffered an epidemic when Indians returning from Quebec carried the pox to Detroit, from which it spread all the way to Mickilimakinac (Fenn, 2001: 74).

Exemplary City Growth: The Top 15 Cities of the United States, 1820–1865

The following section details the growth of some of the key cities. It discusses exemplary cities characterized by particular national-origin groups among the old immigrant wave who arrived in substantial numbers prior to 1865.

The top 15 cities in the United States, as of the 1860 census, were as follows, rank-ordered by their size of population: (1) New York, 1,174,779; (2) Philadelphia, 565,529; (3) Baltimore, 212,418; (4) Boston, 177,840; (5) New Orleans, 168,675; (6) Cincinnati, 161,044; (7) St. Louis, 160,773; (8) Chicago, 144,900; (9) Buffalo, 81,129; (10) Louisville, 68,033; (11) Albany, 62,367; (12) Washington, DC, 61,122; (13) San Francisco, 56,766; (14) Pittsburgh, 49,221; and (15) Detroit, 45,619. In 1860, the total population in the United States was 31 million. Among them, more than 6,200,000, or essentially 20 percent, lived in cities. This section draws on the official websites of these cities, each of which are discussed in the following text.

New York City

By 1790, New York City was the largest urban center in the United States. It was the leading port of entrance for immigrants from Northwestern Europe and from the British Isles. European settlement of the area began with the founding of a Dutch fur-trading site in what is now lower Manhattan, in 1613, called New Amsterdam by 1625. By 1647, it was a colony governed by Director General Peter Stuyvessant, who ruled as a member of the Dutch Reformed Church. It was self-governed in 1652, and New Amsterdam was formally incorporated as a city in February 1653 (Kurlansky, 2006; Burrows and Wallace, 1999).

In 1664, the English conquered New Amsterdam and renamed it New York after the Duke of York. By 1754, what is now Columbia University was founded as a charter college by George II, King's College in lower Manhattan. The Stamp Act and similar British laws fermented dissent, for example, by the Sons of Liberty between 1766 and 1776. The Stamp Act Congress met in New York City in 1765, the first organized resistance to British rule among the colonies.

In 1785, the Congress met in New York City, the first capital under the Articles of Confederation. The new United States Constitution created the current Congress, which first met at Federal Hall on Wall Street, as did the first Supreme Court. New York City was the site at which the Bill of Rights was drafted and ratified. The Northwest Ordinances were also enacted there. New York City became the first capital of the newly formed United States in 1788, under the new Constitution, and in April 1789, George Washington was inaugurated president at Federal Hall on Wall Street. It remained so until 1790, when Philadelphia became the capital city.

New York grew as the new nation's economic center with the opening of the Erie Canal in 1825, which connected the Atlantic port to the vast agricultural markets of the interior. Immigration resumed after the War of 1812, and immigrants probably brought cholera with them in epidemics that broke out in 1832 and 1834 (LeMay, 2006: 41). The Great Irish Famine brought such a massive wave of Irish immigrants that by 1850 they comprised one quarter of the city's population. Epidemics of cholera, typhoid fever, and influenza, coming with immigrants, struck the city again in 1850–1851. Government bureaucracies, like the New York City Police Department and the public schools, were established in the 1840s and 1850s to respond to growing demands, and the Irish became increasingly important in city government.

In 1855, Fernando Wood became the first mayor from Tammany Hall, the Irish immigrant-dominated Democratic political machine. New York City was transformed by immigration, and development followed a proposal that expanded the city street grid to encompass all of Manhattan spurred by the opening of the Erie Canal. By 1835, the city surpassed Philadelphia as the largest city in the country. The city's old merchant aristocracy successfully advocated the establishment of Central Park, which began in 1857, and became the first landscaped park in any American city.

Table 3.4 details the population growth of the city, by census year, from 1790 to 1860. During the Civil War, the city's strong commercial ties to the South and its ever-growing immigrant population fed anger about conscription and resulted in the Draft Riots of 1863. After the war, immigration rose exponentially and New York (via the Castle Garden station)

Table 3.4 City of New York Population, by Census Year, 1790–1860

Year	TotalPopulation
1790	49,401
1800	79,216
1810	119,734
1820	152,056
1830	242,278
1840	391,114
1850	696,115
1860	1,174,779

Source: U.S. Bureau of the Census. 2003. *Statistical Abstract of the United States, 2002.* Washington, DC: U.S. Bureau of the Census, Department of the Interior.

became the first stop for the millions seeking a new and better life in the New World (LeMay, 1987: 58).

Philadelphia

Another city that was among the earliest and most important immigration receiving port cities was that of Philadelphia. European settlers arrived in the Delaware Valley in the early 17th century, and the first settlements were by the Dutch, English, and Swedish. Sweden's first expedition was in 1637, and they settled just below the Schuykill River in what is today Philadelphia, and named it Fort Nya Korsholm (New Korsholm), after a town that is now in Finland. The English took control of the colony in 1664, and in 1682, the area was included in William Penn's charter for Pennsylvania. As a Quaker, William Penn experienced religious persecution, and he established a colony where anyone could worship freely, encouraging rapid growth of the city to where it became America's most important city. He named it Philadelphia, Greek for brotherly love. It was planned as a rural town rather than a city. It was chartered as a city in 1701. Benjamin Franklin, a leading citizen in the 1750s, advocated for improved city services and the establishment of one of the first hospitals in the American colonies, as well as the Philadelphia Society for Promoting Agriculture (1785), the Society for the Encouragement of Manufactures and the Useful Arts (1787), the Academy of Natural Sciences (1812), and the Franklin Institute (1824). These attracted new industries and skilled craftsmen from Europe.

Table 3.5 City of Philadelphia Population, by Census Year, 1790–1860

Year	Total Population
1790	28,522
1800	41,220
1810	53,722
1820	63,802
1830	80,462
1840	93,665
1850	121,376
1860	565,529

Source: U.S. Bureau of the Census. 2003. *Statistical Abstract of the United States, 2002.* Washington, DC: U.S. Bureau of the Census, Department of the Interior.

Its central location among the 13 colonies made it a natural place for the revolutionaries to meet, and it hosted the First Continental Congress, the Second Continental Congress, which signed the Declaration of Independence, and the Constitutional Convention. It served as a temporary capital, 1790–1800, while the District of Columbia was under construction.

In 1793, an epidemic of yellow fever killed an estimated 5,000 people, about 10 percent of its population at the time, and one of the deadliest outbreaks in American history. Indeed, the city suffered periodic epidemics, including a notable typhus epidemic in 1837, that accompanied increased immigration (LeMay, 2006: 41).

Despite these setbacks, Philadelphia continued to grow steadily throughout the 19th century, a growth spurred by industry. Philadelphia became the nation's first industrial city, with textile manufacturing and other business, including the Baldwin Locomotive Works, the Pennsylvania Railroad, and ship-building leading the way, and fed by a steady stream of immigrant labor. Germans were the largest immigrant population until the 1850s, when the Irish exceeded them. Table 3.5 shows the steady growth of the city's population from 1790 to 1860.

Baltimore

The largest city and the economic and cultural center of Maryland, the city was founded in 1729 and quickly became a major seaport for the Mid-Atlantic region and among the most important immigration-receiving port cities prior to the Civil War. In 1625, the city was named after Lord

Baltimore of the Irish House of Lords, the first Lord Baltimore of County Cork, Ireland, and the founder of the Maryland colony. The Maryland colonial General Assembly established the Port of Baltimore at Locust Point in 1706, primarily as the port of export in the tobacco trade, and the city grew quickly in the 18th century as a granary for the sugar colonies of the Caribbean.

The city played a key role in the American Revolution, when city leaders such as Jonathan Plowman joined the resistance. Congress met there in December 1776, effectively making the city the first, unofficial, capital of the United States. The area around Fells Point incorporated as the City of Baltimore in 1797, but remained a part of Baltimore County until 1851, when it became an independent city.

The Battle of Baltimore was fought on September 13, 1814, during the War of 1812, after the British burned Washington, DC, and U.S. forces from Fort McHenry successfully defended the harbor. During the battle, Francis Scott Key penned "The Star Spangled Banner." His poem was set to music in 1780, ironically using a British tune, and it became the national anthem in 1931.

The city's population blossomed after the War of 1812 as construction of the National Road began, and as the private Baltimore and Ohio railroad made it a major shipping and manufacturing center linking the city to the Midwest. It was a major port city for German immigrants, and the city took on a distinctive German cultural flavor. For a time, it rivaled New York City as an immigrant reception station. Prior to the Civil War, immigration control was largely run by the state rather than the federal government.

Table 3.6 City of Baltimore Population, by Census Year, 1790–1860

Year	Total Population
1790	13,503
1800	26,514
1810	46,555
1820	62,738
1830	80,620
1840	102,313
1850	169,054
1860	212,418

Source: U.S. Bureau of the Census. 2003. *Statistical Abstract of the United States, 2002*. Washington, DC: U.S. Bureau of the Census, Department of the Interior.

Maryland remained in the Union during the Civil War, but Confederate sympathizers led the Baltimore Riot of 1861, causing 16 deaths. The city was occupied by federal troops and under federal administration until April 1865 (Krugler, 2004). That year also marked a nasty cholera epidemic outbreak (LeMay, 2006: 41).

Boston

In 1630, the British changed the name of a French settlement, Trimountaine, after the peninsula's three hills, to Boston. Colonial Governor Winthrop founded the City of Boston, named after the town of Boston in Lincolnshire, England, from which several of the prominent colonists had emigrated. Early on the city evidenced its Puritan heritage of legislated morality, hard work, moral uprightness, and education. The first school in America, Boston's Latin School, began in 1635. The first college, Harvard College, started a year later. In 1660, Mary Dyer was hanged in Boston Common for repeatedly defying a law-banning Quakers from the colony—the last religious martyr in North America. In 1689, when King James II was deposed, Bostonians revolted and seized his appointed governor, Sir Edmund Andros, and sent him back to England for trial. The colony, then known as the Dominion of New England, was dissolved and Massachusetts granted a new charter. It was an important colonial port, and the city was a colonial hub, connected by road to New York and the major settlements in Central and Western Massachusetts and Connecticut (Worcester, Springfield, and New Haven), and with Providence, Rhode Island.

The city played a major role in the American Revolution. It was the site of the Boston Massacre, the Boston Tea Party, the Battle of Bunker Hill, and the Siege of Boston; and was near several of the early battles of the War, like Lexington and Concord. It was home to noted patriots like Paul Revere, William Dawes, and Samuel Prescott—of midnight-ride fame. Its prominent role in the Revolutionary War earned it the nickname "Cradle of Liberty."

After the revolution, it became one of the world's wealthiest international trading ports, exporting rum, fish, salt, and tobacco. It was chartered in 1822, and by the mid-1800s was one of the largest manufacturing centers in the nation—particularly of clothing, leather goods, and machinery. Traffic along the Merrimack and the Nashua rivers connected Boston to the surrounding region, affording easy transport of goods and contributing to the proliferation of New England's mills and factories. By the 1850s, a network of railroads helped the region's industry and commerce grow to renewed heights.

The 1840s brought large waves of new immigrants from Europe, notably the Irish and then Italians, giving the city a large Roman Catholic population. The port and the city of Boston became one of the leading immigrant reception stations in the country. From the 1830s through the Civil War, Boston was also a leading center in the abolitionist movement.

Boston went on to become the haven city for Irish immigrants, especially those fleeing the potato famine, and to this day it has the largest percentage of Irish-descended people of any city in the United States. The Irish left their mark in heavily Irish neighborhoods like Charlestown and South Boston, in the name of local teams like the Celtics, in the dominant Irish American political families like the Kennedy's and the Curley's, in the establishment of Catholic Boston College—the rival to the WASP (White Anglo-Saxon Protestant) dominated Harvard University—and in crime bosses like James Whitey Bulger. Boston Female Medical School, opened in 1848, was the nation's first medical school for women that trained nurses. These developments were, in part, spurred by epidemics, like a cholera epidemic in 1832–1833 that broke out with increased immigration from both Germany and Ireland, areas which suffered cholera epidemics. The city established a cholera hospital to cope with the epidemic (LeMay, 2006: 41).

Table 3.7 City of Boston Population, by Census Year, 1790–1860

Year	Total Population
1790	18,320
1800	24,937
1810	33,787
1820	43,298
1830	61,392
1840	93,383
1850	136,881
1860	177,840

Source: U.S. Bureau of the Census. 2003. *Statistical Abstract of the United States, 2002*. Washington, DC: U.S. Bureau of the Census, Department of the Interior.

New Orleans

New Orleans began as a French settlement that was ceded to Spain in 1762 to compensate for the loss of Florida to the British, who also took Louisiana east of the Mississippi River. Spain did not send a governor to take control until 1766. French and German settlers, who wanted the city returned to French control, forced the governor to flee in 1768. Spain reasserted control in 1769, sending another governor, although the city was effectively under control of the Spanish garrison in Cuba.

During the final period as a Spanish colony, the city suffered two massive fires that destroyed most of the city's buildings—in 1788 and in 1794. After the fires, the city was rebuilt in the Spanish style, with brick buildings, firewalls, iron balconies, and open courtyards. Much of the 18th-century architecture, so distinctive of the French quarter, reflects the Spanish colonial period, exemplified by the St. Louis Cathedral, the Cabildo, and the Presbytere.

In the 1790s, the sugar industry flowered, and the growth of commerce along the Mississippi River led to the development of international interests of New Orleans, and the city became the South Atlantic region's commercial and political center, and a leading reception station for immigration, particularly from South and Central America and from the Caribbean. The construction of levees around Lake Pontchartrain via Bayou St. John, which opened in 1794, further boosted the city's commerce.

The population of the city suffered epidemics of yellow fever, malaria, and smallpox periodically throughout the 19th century, all influenced by primitive sanitation, and the lack of public water. An especially nasty epidemic of yellow fever struck in 1847, and another of typhoid fever during the Civil War, in 1863 (LeMay, 2006: 41).

In 1795, Spain granted the United States use of the city's port facilities. In 1800, Spain and France signed the Treaty of Ildefonso, which returned Louisiana to France. In 1803, Napoleon sold Louisiana to the United States—the Louisiana Purchase. By 1800, the city's population was 10,000 people.

In the first decade of 1800, immigration from Cuba and French planters expanded the population. Its cosmopolitan polyglot population reflected the American, African, French, and Creole-French cultural heritages, especially with an influx of immigrants fleeing the revolution in Haiti in 1804. Haitian refugees, both whites and free blacks, arrived in New Orleans. As more and more refugees fled to Louisiana, about 90 percent settled in New Orleans. For example, an 1809 migration brought 2,731 whites, 3,102 free blacks, and 3,226 black slaves to the city, doubling its French-speaking population; and in 1809–1810, thousands more French-speaking refugees came from St. Domingue, fleeing persecution by Cuban officials responding to Bonapartist schemes in Spain.

During the War of 1812, when the city was under martial law, the British tried to capture New Orleans but were defeated by Andrew Jackson's army. The city was attacked by a naval force sent down from Halifax, Nova Scotia. The battle took place after the Treaty of Ghent was signed in January 1815, but before word could reach the combatant forces that the war was over.

The city's population doubled during the 1830s (see Table 3.8), among whom were French settlers who were friends of the Marquis de Lafayette, and some who had newly founded the city of Tallahassee, including a nephew of Napoleon Bonaparte, and a large contingent of Creole. The large Gallic community had become a minority by 1820. In the 1830s and 1840s, however, a renewed influx of German and Irish immigrants arrived, and by 1840 New Orleans was the wealthiest and third most populated city in the United States, with a population more than 100,000. By 1850, it was the largest city in the South.

The use of natural gas in 1830 and the building of the Pontchartrain Railroad in 1830–1831, one of the earliest in the United States, plus the introduction of the steam cotton press in 1832, all contributed to the rise of New Orleans as the leading city in the South. The city began a public school system in 1840. Foreign exports in the 1830–1840 decade made it an important commercial port. Commerce was further enhanced by the opening of the New Basin Canal, constructed by immigrant labor, which enabled shipping from the lake to uptown New Orleans. Riverboats and steamers joined ocean-sailing vessels in plying a thriving commercial trade.

Table 3.8 City of New Orleans Population, by Census Year, 1810–1860

Year	Total Population
1810	17,242
1820	27,176
1830	46,082
1840	102,193
1850	116,375
1860	168,675

Source: U.S. Bureau of the Census. 2003. *Statistical Abstract of the United States, 2002*. Washington, DC: U.S. Bureau of the Census, Department of the Interior.

The city's cultural diversity was boosted by slavery, the quadroon balls, a medley of Latin languages, and a distinctive subculture of the river-men. Though still a frontier city of sorts, its seemingly boundless prosperity led to the city's advancement—despite a short setback during the Panic (Depression in today's terms) of 1837. In 1849, Baton Rouge replaced New Orleans as the capital of Louisiana. In 1850, the city was linked to St. Louis and New York City by telegraph. In 1851, the New Orleans and Jackson Railway opened, becoming the first rail outlet northward. It joined what became the Illinois Central Railroad. Then, in 1854, a Western outlet, now the Southern Pacific Railroad, began. Immigrant laborers were the majority who built these railroads (LeMay, 1987: 34).

During the 1830s, what was effectively three municipalities made up New Orleans—the French Quarter and Faubourg Treme, the Uptown (upriver from Canal Street), and the Downtown (the rest of the city from Esplanade Avenue down to the river). They were governed essentially as separate cities for 20 years, with the office of the Mayor of New Orleans being largely a ceremonial role.

The importance of New Orleans as a financial and commercial center was enhanced when, in 1838, the national government established the United States Mint there, largely due to then President Andrew Jackson. The New Orleans Mint produced both silver and gold coinages until 1861, when Confederate forces took over the building and began minting Confederate money until it was recaptured by Union forces in 1862. A massive flood occurred in 1849, leaving about 12,000 homeless; one of many floods that plagued the city as portions of its often poorly constructed levees failed. Again, immigrant labor was essential to the construction and maintenance of levees.

Cincinnati

Located just north of the Ohio River at the Ohio–Kentucky border, Cincinnati was the first American boomtown in the heart of the country, and for a while it rivaled the larger coastal cities in size and wealth. By the end of the 19th century, however, inland Midwest cities, notably Chicago, surpassed Cincinnati in size, as European immigrants bypassed the city for greater opportunity further inland. The University of Cincinnati was founded as the Medical College of Ohio, in 1819.

Cincinnati was noted for its large number of 19th-century Italianate architecture buildings, concentrated in a downtown area known as Over-the-Rhine, a distinctive neighborhood of German immigrants, and one of the largest historic districts listed on the National Register of Historic Places. Skilled Italian artisans were prominent in their construction.

The city was founded in 1788. In 1790, the governor of the Northwest Territory changed the name of the settlement to Cincinnati, in honor of the Society of Cincinnati, of which he was a member. The society honored General George Washington who was considered a latter day Cincinnatus, the Roman farmer who became Rome's dictator, an office he resigned after he saved the city by defeating the Aequians. The city was home to many descendants of the Revolutionary War, including German and Irish former soldiers, who were granted land there as payment for their Revolutionary War service.

In 1802, it was chartered as a town when David Ziegler, a war veteran from Heidelberg, Germany, became its first mayor. It was incorporated as a city in 1819. The introduction of steam navigation on the Ohio River in 1811 and the completion of the Miami and Erie Canals, constructed mostly by immigrant labor, helped the city to grow to more than 115,000 by 1850 (see Table 3.9). It began as the Miami Canal, in 1825, related to its origin on the Miami River. In 1827, it connected Cincinnati to Middletown; and by 1840, it reached Toledo, when its name was changed to the Miami and Erie Canal, as it connected the Miami River to Lake Erie. Cincinnati was dubbed the "Queen City" during its period of rapid expansion in the 1830 (Aaron, 1992). Immigrant labor also figured heavily in the construction of the Little Miami Railroad connecting Cincinnati with the Lake Erie Railroad and access to the ports of Sandusky Bay on Lake Erie in 1836. In 1859, the city laid out six streetcar lines (Stradling, 2003).

During the Civil War, the city was a major supplier of goods and troops for the Union Army and the headquarters for the Department of the Ohio, charged with the defense of the region and directing the Army's offensives into Kentucky and Tennessee. In 1863, the Union Army imposed martial law due to the imminent danger posed by Morgan's Raiders, who brought the war to the North.

Between 1810 and 1860, Cincinnati grew steadily in population, recorded in each census: 2,540 in 1810, 9,642 in 1820, 24,831 in 1830, 46,338 in 1840, 115,435 in 1850, and 161,044 in 1860. By 1860, Cincinnati was a major industrial hub city.

St. Louis

St. Louis was founded in 1764, near the confluence of the Missouri and Mississippi rivers, by colonial French traders who named the settlement after King Louis IX of France. Its early wealth was dependent on the fur trade. The settlement became part of the Spanish Empire when Spain defeated France in the Seven Years' War. It reverted back to France in 1800 and was part of the Louisiana Purchase sold by Napoleon to the United States in 1803. It was nicknamed the "Gateway to the West" as westward expansion funneled through it.

Immigrants flooded to St. Louis after 1840, especially from Germany, Bohemia, Italy, and Ireland. Many arrived by river steamboat from New Orleans. The city grew from 4,977 in 1830 to 16,469 in 1840 to more than 77,860 in 1850 and to 160,773 in 1860. Nativist sentiment increased when cholera broke out with the waves of immigrants from major ports to the South and East in the 1830s and 1840s (LeMay, 2006: 41). A cholera epidemic in 1849 took the lives of one-tenth of the population. A major fire that year destroyed many steamboats and a portion of the city and led to reforms: cemeteries were moved to the outskirts, sinkholes were filled and swamps drained, water and sewer utilities were begun, and a new building code required structures to be built of brick or stone. The city developed with a second channel of the Mississippi River and, as levees were built, again mostly with immigrant labor, on the Illinois side of the river.

The Civil War brought only a few skirmishes to the region in which Union forces prevailed, but the war cut off trade with the South, crippling the city's economy. The city was the site for the militantly antislavery association, the Knights of Liberty, which began there in 1846. The arsenal at St. Louis was used during the Civil War to construct the North's ironclad ships.

Chicago

The name "Chicago" is the French version of the Miami-Illinois Indian word for "stinky onion," a plant common along the Chicago River. Its location at a short portage connecting the Great Lakes and the Mississippi River attracted French explorers, like Louis Jolliet. French use of the Chicago portage was abandoned in the 1720s due to North American raids during the Fox Wars. The first permanent settlement was founded by Jean Baptiste du Sable at the mouth of the Chicago River in the 1780s, though he left the area in 1800.

After the Northwest Indian War, in the Treaty of Greenville signed in 1795, tribes ceded the area of what became Chicago to the United States for a military post. Fort Dearborn was constructed in 1803, although it was destroyed during the War of 1812. It was again ceded to the United States by the Treaty of St. Louis, in 1816, and Fort Dearborn was rebuilt in 1818 and continued in use until 1837. In 1832, troops involved in the

Black Hawk War brought cholera with them from the East Coast (LeMay, 2006: 41).

In 1829, the State of Illinois located a canal and layout for the surrounding town, and the town of Chicago began with a population of less than 100. Entrepreneurs saw the potential of the site for a transportation hub, and in 1833 the Town of Chicago was incorporated. Great Lakes schooner shipping came to the area in 1834 and trade began that benefited both the cities of New York and Chicago. The city charter was granted by the state in 1837 and the boomtown had a population of 4,000, which grew to 4,500 in 1850 and exploded to 144,900 by 1860.

The rich farmland of the area attracted settlers, and Cook County commissioners built roads to the South and the West. These enabled hundreds of wagons a day to pass through the area. Soon, grain elevators were built and docks constructed to load ships bound for the East Coast through the Great Lakes. As produce was increasingly shipped through the Erie Canal to the Hudson River and thence to New York City, Midwest farms expanded, as did the New York City port. These began a dramatic influx to Chicago.

It was during the 1850s, however, when the construction of railroads made Chicago a major transportation hub. By then, more than 30 railroad lines converged on the city from the East, ending in Chicago, and those oriented to the West began in Chicago. By 1860, Chicago was the nation's transshipment and warehousing center. Factories followed, most notably, the harvester factory that opened in 1847. It soon processed produce for natural resource commodities extracted in the mines of the West. The forests of Wisconsin fed a lumber industry. Illinois farmland fed the wheat industry. Hundreds of thousands of hogs and cattle were shipped to Chicago for slaughter, preserving in salt, and transport to Eastern city markets, and Chicago became the nation's slaughterhouse capital.

In 1848, the opening of the Illinois and Michigan Canal allowed shipping from the Great Lakes through Chicago to the Mississippi River and on to the Gulf of Mexico. That year saw the Galena and Chicago Union Railroad completed and the city went on to become the major transportation hub of the budding nation—with its roads, rail, and water connections. Its population literally exploded. In 1840, it was the 90-second most populous city in the United States. Twenty years later, it ranked ninth. Its pivotal year was 1848, which saw the completion of the Illinois and Michigan Canal, the first steam locomotives, the introduction of steam-powered grain elevators, the arrival of the telegraph, and the founding of the Chicago Board of Trade. By the end of the Civil War, it grew to the nation's second largest city. In 1857, it was the largest city in the Northwest. From 1848 to 1900, it grew by an average of nearly 34,000 in population annually, becoming the most explosively growing city in the nation.

German immigrants were attracted to the area's rich farmland and many German immigrant skilled tradesmen settled in the city. Many of the Irish immigrants constructing the transcontinental railroad from the East westward ended up in Chicago, and the city's Irish population grew rapidly before the Civil War, giving the city an Irish flavor exceeded only by Boston's and New York's.

Buffalo

Buffalo began in 1789 as a settlement near Buffalo Creek. It grew to a city with the opening of the Erie Canal in 1825, as its Western terminus, and later as a railroad hub and a grain-milling center. The city design was established in 1804 by Joseph Ellicott, principal agent of the Holland Land Company, and is one of the few radial design and grid system cities in the country.

The opening of the canal brought a large population to the then town, and it was incorporated as a city in 1832. It long had a large African American population and was home to the abolitionist William Wells Brown, who made the city a terminus point of the Underground Railroad.

The port developed in the 1840s with both commercial and passenger services heading West, as grain and commercial goods were shipped via steam-powered vessels. In 1843, the city boasted the first steam-powered grain elevator, enabling fast uploading of lake freighters of bulk grain from lake boats to canal boats and, later on, railcars.

During the Civil War, the city grew markedly from 81,209 in 1860 to 94,210 by 1865. Its census year populations were as follows: 1,508 in 1810, 2,095 in 1820, 8,668 in 1830, 18,213 in 1840, 42,216 in 1850, and 81,209 in 1860.

Louisville

Louisville began as a Spanish settlement, although it had a sizable French-speaking population and they sided with the colonists in the Revolutionary War. In colonial times, it suffered from Indian attacks and the population had to live within forts up to the Revolutionary War, the last of which, Fort Nelson, was considered the strongest West of Fort Pitt. Then Virginia Governor Thomas Jefferson approved the town charter in 1780, and in 1803, President Jefferson sent Meriwether Lewis and William Clark on their expedition West, surveying the land of the Louisiana Purchase.

With the purchase, American ships could bring cargo upstream, especially after the arrival, in 1811, of the *New Orleans,* the first steamship plying trade between Pittsburgh and Louisville. In 1815, the *Enterprise*

Table 3.9 City of Louisville Population, by Census Year, 1790–1860

Year	Total Population
1790	200
1800	300
1810	1,357
1820	4,012
1830	10,341
1840	21,210
1850	43,194
1860	68,033

Source: U.S. Bureau of the Census. 1909. *A Century of Population Growth from the First Census of the United States to the Twelfth, 1790–1900*. Washington, DC: U.S. Bureau of the Census, Department of the Interior.

arrived, the first steamship from New Orleans. Industry and manufacturing thrived as steamships were built in Louisville, and soon mills and factories followed. In 1830, the Louisville and Portland Canal was completed, allowing still more commercial traffic. The Marine Hospital was built in 1825 to treat the ill or injured river workers. By 1828, the city became the largest in Kentucky. The first public school opened in 1829; and in 1831, a Catholic school for girls and the St. Vincent Orphanage were built. The Kentucky School for the Blind opened in 1839, the third oldest such school in the country. By 1850, the city was the fifth largest in the country. That year marked the opening of the Louisville and Nashville Railroad, completed in 1859, and it became a source of the city's development as a center for rail and water transportations.

In 1855, an election riot between supporters of the Democrats and the Know Nothing Party broke out and mobs rioted in the large neighborhoods of the city populated by German and Irish immigrants, destroying property and killing many. The city was a large slave-trading center from 1820 to 1860, but during the Civil War, Louisville was a Union stronghold, which kept Kentucky in the Union, and throughout the war it was a center of planning, supplies, recruiting, and transportation for numerous campaigns in the Western Theater.

Albany

One of the oldest surviving settlements from the original 13 colonies, Albany's first European settlement—a Dutch village and fur-trading post

Table 3.10 City of Albany Population, by Census Year, 1790–1860

Year	Total Population
1790	3,498
1800	5,349
1810	10,762
1820	12,630
1830	24,209
1840	33,721
1850	50,763
1860	62,367

Source: U.S. Bureau of the Census. 1909. *A Century of Population Growth from the First Census of the United States to the Twelfth, 1790–1900*. Washington, DC: U.S. Bureau of the Census, Department of the Interior.

called Fort Nassau—began in 1614, and the city of Albany was chartered in 1686. It became the first capital of New York State in 1797. English and Scottish people were in the majority when the city was officially chartered in 1686, named after the then duke of Albany who became James II of England and James VII of Scotland.

Albany was a center of transportation along the Hudson River and was the original Eastern terminus of the Erie Canal. The city became home of the first railroad system in the country. It was the first American city to develop electricity, natural gas lines, public water system, and a sewer system. Home to a large German and Dutch immigrant population, for a time beer was among its main exports, along with lumber, published works, and ironworks. By 1810, it was the 10th most populated city in the nation. Albany was the turnpike center of the state by 1815, and the turnpike and railroad conjunction with the canal made the city a transportation hub for settlers heading West through Buffalo and to the Michigan Territory. It was the location of two major regional railroad lines: the Delaware and Hudson Railway and the New York Central Railway.

And in 1807, Robert Fulton began a steamship line between New York and Albany. With the completion of the Erie Canal in 1825, the city grew continuously, based on its central role as a transportation hub for people and products linking the East with the Midwest.

Washington, DC

In early 1781, President Washington appointed Pierre L'Enfant to devise a plan for the new national capital city. His plan was revised by Andrew Ellicott,

Table 3.11 City of Washington, DC, Population, by Census Year, 1800–1860

Year	Total Population
1800	3,210
1810	8,208
1820	13,247
1830	18,526
1840	23,364
1850	40,001
1860	61,122

Source: U.S. Bureau of the Census. 1909. *A Century of Population Growth from the First Census of the United States to the Twelfth, 1790–1900.* Washington, DC: U.S. Bureau of the Census, Department of the Interior.

which became the basis for the capital city's future development. In 1800, the national government moved to the city, and in February 1801, the District of Columbia Organic Act established the District and the cities of Washington, Georgetown, and Alexandria under the jurisdiction of Congress.

Congress began funding construction of the Washington City Canal in 1809, which opened in 1816, connecting the Anacostia River with Tiber Creek. In 1828, construction commenced on the Chesapeake and Ohio Canal, which opened in 1831 with its first section going to Seneca, Maryland. It reached Cumberland, Maryland, in 1850, but was by then nearly obsolete as the Baltimore and Ohio Railroad, begun in 1835, arrived in Cumberland in 1842. It operated freight and passenger traffic, and by the Civil War connected Washington to the West. Table 3.11 presents its population, by census year, 1800–1860.

San Francisco

In 1776, the Spanish built a fort and mission named for Francis of Assisi. Upon independence from Spain, in 1821, the area became part of Mexico. In 1835, the first English settler erected the first independent homestead, and the area soon attracted American settlers. In 1846, during the Mexican–American War, Captain John Montgomery arrived and claimed the area for the United States. It was renamed San Francisco in 1847.

The California Gold Rush in 1848 propelled the city into a period of rapid growth. In one year it grew by 24,000 in population, transforming it into the largest city on the West Coast at the time. California was granted statehood in 1849, and the military built Fort Point at the Golden Gate, and a fort on Alcatraz Island to secure San Francisco Bay.

Capitalizing on the wealth generated by the Gold Rush, a group of businessmen founded Wells Fargo, in 1852, and the Bank of California, in 1864, establishing the city as the center of the banking industry on the West Coast. It had a large Chinatown by 1850, housing the city's significant pre–Civil War Chinese population. The Port of San Francisco boomed with the establishment of the Pacific Railroad. By 1860, the city population was 56,766.

Pittsburgh

In 1768, William Penn purchased from the Six Nations the Western land that included the present site of Pittsburgh. Following the Revolution, the village of Pittsburgh grew steadily as the site of the industry building boats for settlers headed for the Ohio Territory. In 1784, the Town of Pittsburgh was laid out, and in 1785 it became a possession of the state of Pennsylvania. Glass manufacturing began in the city in 1797.

The War of 1812 cut off British manufacturing and spurred domestic manufacturing, and by 1815 Pittsburgh began producing significant quantities of iron, brass, tin, and glass products. The city was incorporated in 1816. In the 1830s, large numbers of Welsh immigrants arrived, drawn to its factories. By the 1840s, it was one of the largest cities west of the Allegheny Mountains. A great fire burned more than 1,000 structures in 1845, but the city rebuilt and by 1857 it boasted 1,000 factories. The Civil War spurred its economy with a booming production of iron and armaments. Table 3.12 presents its steady growth from 1800 to 1860.

Table 3.12 City of Pittsburgh Population, by Census Year, 1800–1860

Year	Total Population
1800	1,565
1810	4,768
1820	7,348
1830	12,568
1840	21,115
1850	46,601
1860	49,221

Source: U.S. Bureau of the Census. 1909. *A Century of Population Growth from the First Census of the United States to the Twelfth, 1790–1900*. Washington, DC: U.S. Bureau of the Census, Department of the Interior.

Detroit

Detroit was incorporated as a town in 1802 and when Ohio became a state, the eastern part of Michigan was attached to the Indiana Territory. Nearly all of the settlement was destroyed by fire in 1805. The city of Detroit was rebuilt, incorporated in 1806. The British surrounded the area during the War of 1812. In 1824, the Territorial Legislature created the Common Council of the City of Detroit.

By the Civil War, 45,000 people were living in the city, which was by then a key railroad stop, especially for slaves, along the Underground Railroad. Industry and commerce was spurred by the War, and the city attracted a large black population, as well as Germans, added to the French descendants who populated the city from its original village and town days. The city population grew steadily from 1,422 in 1820 to 2,222 in 1830, to 9,102 in 1840, to 21,019 in 1850, and to 45,619 in the 1860 census. Detroit was a major immigrant receiving city of those coming overland down from Canada.

Conclusion

Immigration fed the industrialization and urbanization of the United States from its founding to the Civil War. By that time, 20 cities exceeded 45,000 in population, and the foreign-born population of those cities spanned from 10 to as much as 25 percent of their respective populations. Immigrant labor built the railroads and the canals that formed the transportation base of so many of the new cities; and they laid the streets, dug the sewers, and erected many of the buildings that made urban life possible in the United States. Immigrants were active—indeed leaders—of the budding labor movement. Unions first appeared in the 1820s, although they were small, local, and short-lived (Brooks, 1971). By the 1860 census, more than 4 million foreign-born were in the population of 31 million. Among those, more than 3,800,000 came from Europe and just over 2 million of them from the British Isles. Ireland was the place of birth to more than 1,600,000, Scandinavia sent more than 72,000, Germany more than 1,200,000, Canada more than 288,000, and China more than 35,500.

References

Aaron, Daniel. 1992. *Cincinnati: Queen City of the West, 1819–1838*. Columbus, OH: Ohio State University Press.

Andrews, Anthony. 1995. *First Cities*. Washington, DC: Smithsonian Books.

Archdeacon, Thomas. 1976. *New York City, 1664–1710: Conquest and Change.* Ithaca, NY: Cornell University Press.

Avery, Ron. 1999. *A Concise History of Philadelphia.* Philadelphia, PA: Otis Books.

Bookchin, Murray. 1995. *From Urbanization to Cities: Towards a New Politics of Citizenship.* New York: Cassell.

Boyer, Paul S., et al. 2010. *The Enduring Vision: A History of the American People.* 5th ed. Boston, MA: Wadsworth Publishing/Cengage Learning.

Brooks, Thomas R. 1971. *Toil and Trouble: A History of American Labor.* 2nd ed. New York: Delacorte Press.

Burrows, Edwin, and Mike Wallace. 1999. *Gotham: A History of New York City to 1898.* New York: Oxford University Press.

Fenn, Elizabeth. 2001. *Pox Americana: The Great Smallpox Epidemic of 1775–82.* New York: Hill and Wang.

Gaquin, Deidre, and Katherine DeBrandt, eds. 2006. *Places, Towns and Townships.* Lanham, MD: Bernan Press, 2006.

Hartnell, Edward, et al. 1916. *Boston and Its Story, 1630–1915.* Boston, MA: City of Boston. Available at: http://mapserver.lib.virginia.edu/ Historical Census Browser.

Krugler, John D. 2004. *English and Catholic: The Lords of Baltimore.* Baltimore, MD: The Johns Hopkins University Press.

Kurlansky, Mark. 2006. *The Big Oyster: History on the Half Shell.* New York: Ballantine.

Quincy, Josiah. 1952. *A Municipal History of the Town and City of Boston, 1630–1830.* Boston, MA: Little, Brown.

Sammarco, Anthony. 1995. *Boston: A Century of Progress.* Boston, MA: Arcadian, 1995.

Steen, Ivan. 2006. *Urbanizing America: The Development of Cities in the United States from the First European Settlements to 1920.* Malabar, FL: Krieger.

Stradling, David. 2003. *Cincinnati: From River City to Highway Metropolis.* Boston, MA: Arcadian Publishing.

U.S. Bureau of the Census. 1909. *A Century of Population Growth from the First Census of the United States to the Twelfth, 1790–1900.* Washington, DC: U.S. Bureau of the Census, Department of the Interior.

U.S. Bureau of the Census. 1996. *Population of States and Counties of the United States: 1790–1990.* Washington, DC: U.S. Bureau of the Census, Department of Commerce.

U.S. Bureau of the Census. 2003. *Statistical Abstract of the United States, 2002.* Washington, DC: U.S. Bureau of the Census, Department of the Interior.

Ward, David. 1971. *Cities and Immigrants: A Geography of Change in 19th Century America.* New York: Oxford University Press.

Wells, Jonathan D. 2005. *The Origins of the Southern Middle Class, 1800–1861.* Chapel Hill, NC: University of North Carolina Press.

CHAPTER FOUR

Toward a More Perfect Union: Immigration and Federalism

Michael C. LeMay

Introduction

The United States is a federal system of government that divides political power in a particular way. Immigration is a prime example of a public policy area that reflects the impact of federalism and illustrates how federal relations changed over time. Before the Civil War, immigration policy-making exemplified what political scientists have called dual federalism (e.g., Beer, 1978; Diamond, 1981; Lowi, 1995). It will be useful here to define some key terms or concepts that are used throughout this chapter to better understand types of government and the structuring of power between or among political subdivisions, like states, provinces, counties, parishes, cities, or towns. Political scientists typical distinguish three major types of governmental arrangements between or among levels of government: the unitary system, the federal system, and the confederal system, or confederation.

The unitary system is the most common form of country or nation-state. It is characterized by the centralization of political power at the national government, with little power held at the political subdivision level—such as provinces, counties, cities, and towns. Those subdivisions are creatures of the national-level government of the country and are organized by the national level for administrative purposes. They cannot enact policy-binding on the country as a whole, and are limited in local policy-making to those areas of public policy-making granted to them by the national government. China is an example of a large nation-state that has a unitary form of government. The unitary system is preferable to the political ideology of China's ruling elite.

Nowhere in the constitution are the words "federalism" or "federal system" used. The term "federal" denotes alliances between independent sovereigns, as the division of government powers between the national and state governments. But a federal system is inherent in the original federal design (Beer, 1978: 10; Adams, 1980; Lowi, 1995; Wood, 1991). The founding fathers conceived of the American federal system as a structural device, a design to better ensure the Republic as a democratic, representative polity (Diamond, 1981; LaCroix, 2010; Mullins, 1999; Nash, 2005; Patrick, 1995). Beer puts it as follows: "To the colonial dissidents, liberty meant certain personal rights, such as freedom of conscience, but above all, political liberty, and the right to govern by consent of the governed." The constitution they wrote declared that it was ordained by "We, the people" (Beer, 1978: 10–11).

In a federal system—such as that found in the United States, Canada, Australia, Brazil, and the former USSR—the national government holds significant political power, but the political subdivisions—the states in the case of the United States—hold significant political and legal powers of their own as well. This form of government seems especially suited to geographically large nations, and/or ones with complex and diverse demographic populations and regional differences, and nation-states with complex and dynamic economic systems (Reimer and Simon, 1994). Although small, the language diversity of Switzerland accounts for its choice of a federal system to better represent its diversity of population. The United States, with its enormously complex and diverse population from literally hundreds of nations of origin, and with its complex industrial and agricultural economy, is one for which federalism is especially well suited.

In a confederation, the subdivisions (states) hold equal power and they delegate some power and responsibility to the national level for common administrative purposes. Confederations, for example, the United States under the Articles of Confederation from 1776 to 1789, the Confederate States of America from 1861 to 1864, and the United Emirate Republics, tend to break down as their constituent units develop conflicting interests and can no longer agree on common policy direction for the national level. Those conflicting interests can be especially the result of divergent views and needs as immigration from diverse sources change the demographics of the states, and as immigration influences variation in their developing economies.

From 1787 until 1865 (and beyond), the federal system operated in practice in the United States as dual federalism. In the dual federalism form, the national and the state governments are considered as coequals, each sovereign, and each having their own major public policy areas of primary concern (Drake and Nelson, 1999). Daniel Elazar (1987) depicts this metaphorically as a layer-cake. Various parts of the Constitution were interpreted narrowly—for example, the Tenth Amendment, which set the guidelines for federalism in the United States, the Supremacy Clause, the Necessary and Proper Clause, and the Commerce Clause. Traditionally, the powers of government are categorized into three types: reserved, granted, and concurrent. The dual federalism perspective held that the federal government has jurisdiction only if the Constitution clearly grants it such. A very large group of powers belonged to the states (i.e., were *reserved* to them), and the federal government was limited to only those powers explicitly listed in the Constitution (its *enumerated* powers). Reserved powers are those reserved specifically for the states and concern policy areas that are traditionally state-run: police powers, such as providing fire and police protection, establishment of health regulations (which, as we shall see in the following text, were especially important for immigration regulation prior to the Civil War), licensing, education, and so on. *Granted* powers are also known as express, enumerated, implied, delegated, and inherent powers. For instance, Article 1, Section 8 grants the national government, specifically the Congress, power to coin money, to raise an army and navy, to provide for patent and copyright protections, to establish a post office, to regulate commerce, to establish rules of naturalization, to establish federal courts, and to make treaties with other nations. *Implied,* or inherent, powers are those that exist to carry out express or enumerated powers, as stated in Article 1, Section 8: "To make all Laws which shall be necessary and proper to carry into Execution the foregoing Powers, and all other Powers vested by this Constitution in the Government of the United States, or in any Department or Officer thereof." In essence, since the Congress can raise an army, the Necessary and Proper Clause means that it can specify regulations as to who may or may not join the army, whether military service shall be voluntary or compulsory, and can stipulate the size and composition of the army and naval forces. It can determine whether such military forces are standing or are more temporary. The Congress can delegate to the president, in his constitutional role as commander-in-chief, the authority to call into service or nationalize any or several state militia (the National Guard units among the various states during a time of war) (American Federalism, 1776–1977).

Finally, concurrent powers are those held by both federal and state governments. Under concurrent powers, both the national and state governments (and by delegation, local government units as well) may levy a tax, construct and maintain roads or build canals, or spend money for the general welfare of citizens. During the period of dual federalism, concurrent powers meant that both the national and the various state governments in which ports of entry of immigrants were located, shared the responsibility to regulate and control immigration and to process immigrants through reception stations jointly administered by them.

This design for this distribution of government power was unique—essentially invented in Philadelphia in 1787 for the American republic (Diamond, 1981; Beer, 1978; Lowi, 1995). *The Federalist Papers,* a compilation of 85 anonymous essays published in New York City, argued the case for ratification of the Constitution. In the *46th Federalist,* James Madison wrote, "we must consider both of them as substantially dependent on the great body of the citizens of the United States. . . . The federal and state governments are in fact but different agents and trustees of the people, constituted with different powers, and designed for different purposes" (Patrick, 1990). Among the founding fathers, Alexander Hamilton, James Madison, and John Jay especially discussed the concept of the sovereignty of the people as the way to protect the values, freedom, and identity of the new nation, and as a protection against the nations of Europe that might seek to take away those values and freedoms. They feared recolonization, especially by Great Britain. They favored a stronger national government and a mercantile rather than an agricultural economy.

Those who opposed the new Constitution became known as the Anti-Federalists. Their perspective favored the local rather than the country as a whole. They were oriented toward plantations and farms rather than commerce and finance. They preferred strong state governments and a weak national government (Reid, 1986).

The essence and the genius of the invention of 1787 was the use of the same electorate to choose two sets of government, each with constitutional protections and thus independent bases of political power (Beer, 1978: 14; see also Cooke, 1961; Reimer and Simon, 1994).

The American Revolution posited a new conception of popular sovereignty than from what was accepted in Europe as popular sovereignty. In late 18th-century Europe, sovereignty was viewed as residing in the person of the king or queen. The American founding fathers viewed it as residing in the people—although in their eyes and as written into the Constitution, "the people" meant free white male property-owners and therefore excluded women, blacks, Native Americans, those Euro-American whites who lacked property (e.g., indentured servants), and children. Popular sovereignty embodied the idea of consent of the governed, the principle over which they fought the Revolutionary War. This concept informed the 13 state constitutions as well as the national Constitution (Fritz, 2007). In the newly established republic, at both the national and the state levels, "the people" meant citizens who exercised plenary authority as the sovereign—a view that persisted from the revolution to the Civil War (Morgan, 1988).

As the dispute over slavery increased, by the mid-1840s and in the wake of the Mexican American War, the term "popular sovereignty" gained currency and a connotation as the method by which the slave question might be resolved. Through the war with Mexico, the United States acquired lands formerly held by Mexico, and whether these territories should enter as free states or slave states boiled over the long-simmering question of the extension of slavery or whether slavery should be permitted, protected, or abolished in the new states (Reimer and Simon, 1994). Congressional attempts to resolve the issue ended in deadlock and moderates, particularly as advocated by Senator Stephen Douglas of Illinois, held that the people in each territory, like the people in the then existing states of the union, were the sovereign thereof and should therefore decided for themselves whether to enter the union as free states or slave states. Douglas was convinced that this concept was the formula for bridging the differences between the North and the South, thus preserving the union. He anticipated that slavery as an economic system would gradually die out and need not be ended by force of arms.

The failure of the principle of popular sovereignty to avert the Civil War, however, meant that the idea as the people as sovereign both unified and divided American thought about government and as the basis of the union. As Fritz (2007) notes:

> The constitutional melt-down of the Civil War, while significantly altering the terms of constitutional debate, did not banish the idea that the people were sovereign. After the war, as before it, the argument that the national government now exercised the sovereignty the people once held was challenged as inconsistent with the constitutional legacy of the Revolution. (19)

The Evolution of Federalism, 1790–1865

The federal system established in the Constitution of 1787 embodies five basic characteristics:

1. A division of legal authority between the national and the respective state governments. Although some overlap occurs, there are two legally distinct spheres of government. To describe federalism for the period prior to the Civil War

(and beyond), some political scientists suggest the metaphor of a layer cake to depict federalism (Diamond, 1981: 47; Walker, 1995: 93; see also, Grodzins, 1961; Elazar, 1987, 1994).

2. The states are subordinate to the national government in such areas as the management of foreign affairs and the regulation of interstate commerce and in the establishment of a military force to secure the national defense.
3. Federalism enables the cooperation between state and national governments in policy areas pertaining to education, interstate highway construction, protection of natural resources, and the health of citizens. As we will see in the following text, the latter was especially relevant with regard to immigration and immigration policy prior to the Civil War.
4. The U.S. Supreme Court is the legal arbiter of the federal system, resolving any conflicts between the national government and the states with regard to their respective powers, and claims of primacy in certain policy area (Article III, especially as interpreted by the Supreme Court in decisions like *McCulloch v. Maryland* and *Gibbons v. Ogden*). The Supreme Court took to itself the role are the final arbiter of how the rights specified in the Bill of Rights shall apply to both the national and to the various state governments. As will be seen more fully in the following text, it stipulated by its decisions that the national level of government has the primary and almost exclusive role of stipulating immigration policy and of the process of naturalization of citizens.
5. The two levels (national and state) exercise their respective authority simultaneously over people within their territory. Dual citizenship exists and individuals have a wide range of rights and privileges from both the state and the national governments, as stipulated in Article IV, and especially in the Bill of Rights, the first 10 amendments to the Constitution.

There are still evolutionary changes in the politics and the understanding of the federal system as it operates in the United States. Proponents of states' rights and powers hold that the Constitution is a compact between the states and the federal government. Both states and the national government retain supremacy within their respective spheres of policy. Advocates of dual federalism argue that the national government cannot invade the power that is reserved for the states.

Proponents of the position that the people, not the states, established the national government favor a cooperative approach to state–national relations, metaphorically depicted as a "marble-cake rather than a layer-cake" (Walker, 1995: 132; see also Wildavsky, 1967). *Cooperative federalism* emphasizes the General Welfare clause and the Necessary and Proper Clause of the Constitution. This perspective regarding national power increasingly prevailed after the Civil War, and especially after the 1880s. It justified an expansion of the national-level government and the primacy of that level when the national government became involved in policy areas that were traditionally state functions (Gerston, 2007; Peterson, 1995; Riker, 1987; Shapiro, 1997). This view justified the national government taking over sole administration of immigration policy-making and enforcement after 1890, as we will see more fully subsequently.

Prior to the Civil War, the federal system operated with fairly clear distinctions between the policy-making and administrative operations of the national government and those of the various states, although even in the early period of federalism there were some relationships marked by partnership and cooperation (Elazar, 1987). Immigration was one such area. Government finances were largely separate—each level having its own emphasis on funding sources. There were few of the intergovernmental transfers of monies (grants) that characterize the system today. Both the state and the national governments cooperated in establishing new territories as the nation expanded westward. Both worked on development of the transportation needed to exploit those new lands (canals, roads, and railroads). There were only a few grants of land from the federal government to the state(s), although those few were quite important for drawing immigrants to the new territories or newly incorporated states, such as the Homestead Act of 1862.

Two political forces (not yet distinct political parties as we know them today) quickly emerged, divided in large measure over the question of how the federal system ought to operate in practical political terms. The Federalists—best exemplified by Alexander Hamilton, James Madison, and their allies—advocated a strong central government that could and would provide the country the economic, political, and military cohesiveness necessary to assure maintaining its independence. The Federalists, as argued in *The Federalist Papers,* 10th, 14th, 45th, and 51st, saw the lack of cohesiveness as the principal flaw under the Articles of Confederation. The Federalists argued that the national-level government under Confederation was, simply put, too weak, too dysfunctional (Cooke, 1961; Patrick, 1990).

By contrast, the Anti-Federalists—best exemplified by Thomas Jefferson and his supporters, and later by Andrew Jackson—believed that a strong central government constituted a threat to their newly won liberty. They feared a central government's propensity toward tyranny. They preferred that the governing of daily life be carried out by the states—closer to the people, the ordinary farmers, and frontiersmen who made up the vast majority of the population—rather than the economic—largely commercial—elite of cities like Boston, New York, and Philadelphia. This political conflict revolved largely around interpretations of the Tenth Amendment, which says simply: "The powers not delegated to the United States by the

Constitution, nor prohibited by it to the States (i.e., section 10), are reserved to the States respectively, or to the people" (Peterson, 1995).

By 1810–1820, the Supreme Court, under Chief Justice John Marshall, expanded the national government's powers by interpreting the role of the Supreme Court and its powers as being coequal with the executive and legislative branches and as the final arbiter in cases of conflict between the levels of government. It provided for a relatively expansive interpretation of the Supremacy, Commerce, and Contract Clauses of the Constitution, thereby increasing the national government's economic authority. In 1819, for example, the Court ruled, in *McCulloch v. Maryland,* that the national government had the authority, through the Necessary and Proper Clause, to establish a national bank. The Court took a broad construction of the meaning of the clause, viewing the constitution not as a compact among sovereign states but as a national constitution established *by the people,* and thus construed, the national government could take actions that were appropriate to implementation of its prescribed powers, and not only those that were indispensable (Beer, 1978: 6).

His successor as chief justice, Roger Taney (1835–1863), however, decided cases that tended to favor equally strong national and state governments, and that the national government should be limited to its enumerated powers and that all others belonged to the states. Political Scientist Theodore Lowi summarized the dual federalism system as operating at the time of the Taney Court as follows:

1. Domestic policies associated with the national government included internal improvements such as canals and a national road and a national railroad, subsidies (e.g. to shipping), tariffs, the disposal of public lands, immigration and naturalization law, centralized national defense, foreign policy, copyrights, patents, and currency.
2. State government policies included property law, estate and inheritance law, commerce laws and laws of ownership and exchange, banking and credit laws, labor and union laws, family laws, morals laws, public health and quarantine laws, public works laws, including eminent domain, and building codes, corporation laws, land-use laws, water and mineral resource laws, judiciary and criminal procedures laws, electoral laws, including political parties, local government laws, civil service laws, and occupations and professions laws.
3. Local government policies (granted by the state through state statutes or by recognizing city charters) included variances (adaptation of state law to local conditions), public works, contracts for public works, licensing of public accommodations, assessable improvements, and basic public services (police, fire, sewer, water supply, hospitals and so on).

> The clash between the Federalists and the Jeffersonian Democrats continued after the election, in 1828, in which Andrew Jackson became President of the United States. Jacksonian-Democrats challenged the emerging economic dominance of the central government and particularly its banking powers. They sought to strengthen the states and individual liberties. But a return to a simple agrarian society and economy was no longer possible by the 1830s. Commerce, especially inter-state commerce, and the growing industrial sector of the economy, more notably so in the north and in the Mid-Atlantic states, had progressed too far to return to an agrarian dominated economy. As a result of these economic developments, Northern and Southern states clashed over tariffs and slavery—both seen as primarily economic issues. The Jacksonians opposed the national governmental policies favoring banking and commercial interests as antidemocratic. They equated the states' economic control with personal liberty and favored economic decentralization. As president, however, Jackson asserted the primary importance of maintaining the union. He opposed Senator John C. Calhoun's doctrine of nullification. Sectional strife, however, continued and ultimately led to the Civil War (Peterson,1995; Beer, 1978).

In a decision that carried import for the administration of immigration procedures by state governments, the Court articulated a negative or dormant notion of the Commerce Clause in the 6–2 decision of *Cooley v. Board of Wardens* (S. Ct. 1851). Shipmaster Aaron Cooley had protested a port regulation making him pay half the normal fee for a pilot even though he did not use one. He claimed the regulation was an unconstitutional infringement of Congressional authority over foreign and interstate commerce as stipulated in Article 1, Section 8. The Court ruled that the states had limited authority over local aspects of interstate commerce, absent conflicting federal legislation, and provided it was otherwise within state authority. The Court maintained final judgment whether the matter was nationwide in scope, in which case state laws could not have jurisdiction. In the absence of the Congressional action regarding the Commerce Clause, the Supreme Court could and did define the boundaries of state and national actions.

In another action with particular importance for subsequent immigration regulation regarding paupers or persons who might become public charges, President James Pierce vetoed a Congressional land grant for the mentally handicapped. He argued that if Congress were to make provisions for paupers, bestowing the national government's means on the societal wants of their people, than the states and their localities would be strongly tempted to shift such burden from themselves to the federal government, reversing their true relation to the Union and imposing a financial burden beyond the capacity of the funding sources enjoyed by the national government at the time (May, 1854).

But by 1862, the land-grant authority of the federal government was advanced by the Morrill Act of 1862 (7 U.S.C. 301), providing for land grants to states to support public institutions of higher education (begun as state agricultural colleges), the first time the national government participated financially in a program of state welfare. The land-grant act was introduced by a congressman from Vermont, Justin Smith Morrill. He envisioned the financing of agriculture and mechanical education to assure that education would be available to those in all social classes. There were several of these grants, the first passed in 1862, signed into law by President Abraham Lincoln on July 2. The act gave each state 30,000 acres of public land for each senator and representative, based on the census of 1860. The land was to be sold (often to settlers and among whom were very often immigrants drawn to the United States by the prospects of such cheap land) and the money from the sale of the land was to be put into an endowment fund that would provide support for the colleges in each of the states. The land grants drew settlers, including immigrants, to the states, particularly the newer states in the Midwest.

And in a law having even greater impact as a pull factor of immigration, the Congress enacted the Homestead Act of 1862, and signed into law by Lincoln on May 20th (Session II, Ch.75, 1862: 392–93; see also LeMay and Barkan, 1999: 29–30). Although not its stated purpose, the law was a powerful inducement to immigration (LeMay, 1987: 24). A land claim was open to any citizen *or intended citizen*. In order to encourage the opening and settlement of the West, the Congress enacted the law that gave to a settler 160 acres of land if he worked it for five years. A land claim had to have a house with a window (hence the title of "Homestead Act"). The rule requiring a 12 by 12 house did not specify feet, however, and a 12 by 12 inch house sheltered many an owner only from the law. Ingenious devices like that, or the building of a cabin on wheels to roll from claim to claim, were used to stake claims under the law. It was an inducement particularly to immigrants coming from Germany and Scandinavia, and pushed the frontier westward (LeMay, 1987: 35).

The Homestead Act offered free or relatively cheap land and was an inducement drawing farmers from the overcrowded population of Germany. Western states advertised for German farmers, who had a reputation of being hardworking and highly productive. State governments joined with the railroad companies of the time in sending agents to induce German immigrants to settle and develop the abundant lands of the Midwest and prairie states. An additional draw was that America was viewed as a haven from the military conscription during the years of the German wars of unification. Scandinavian immigrants were likewise drawn to the frontier settlements of Minnesota, Wisconsin, Iowa, Illinois, and North and South Dakota, all of which saw dramatic increases in their population as a result of this immigration flow (LeMay, 2009: 97–98).

Also in 1862, the Congress passed the Act of July 17, 1862 (40 Stat. S46), the Honorably Discharged Soldiers Act, regarding their naturalization. It stipulated that any alien, age 21 or over, who enlisted in the armies of the United States, either regular or volunteer, and was thereafter honorably discharged, shall be admitted to become a citizen of the United States upon his petition and requiring no more than one year of residency. It became an important inducement to recruit aliens to serve in the Union Army during the Civil War and was particularly an inducement for German and Irish immigrants (see LeMay and Barkan, 1999: 30).

In 1864, Congress passed the Contract Labor Law. It was an attempt to revive an 18th century device designed to stimulate labor migration from Europe. This law authorized employers to pay the passage and bind the services of prospective immigrants. While the law did not outlive the war, it underscored the hunger for population. Congress repealed the law in 1868, responding to political pressure from organized labor, which feared the lowering of wages encouraged by the importation of contract labor (LeMay, 1987: 35).

The Doctrine of Nullification, articulated by Senator Calhoun, was laid to rest by the force of arms of the Civil War. It settled the most important national–state interaction issue in the nation to that time, the issue of slavery and its consequences. Slavery embodied a fundamental contradiction between economic and personal liberties. Slavery treated humans as property. The issue set the North and the South in repeated opposition: over how the slaves should be counted, whether new territories could chose to permit slavery, and how slaves were to be treated when passing through free states. The Civil War involved the national government as protector of civil liberty of citizens and of persons (i.e., the former slaves) against state incursions, and with the Fourteenth Amendment (adopted July 9, 1868), the federal government set the standards of personal rights that were then funneled to the various states. In essence, it applied the Bill of Rights, which had been understood as applying to the national government only, to state governments. For the South, these actions were seen as violation of personal and property rights by the national government.

National and State Relations Regarding Immigration Matters

The Constitution is fairly silent on the matter of immigration. Article 1, Section 8 grants to the Congress the power to establish a uniform rule of naturalization. The Congress, among its very first acts, was to adopt a rule of naturalization (1 Stat. 103) that stipulated:

> That any alien, being a free white person, who shall have resided within the limits and under the jurisdiction of the United States for the term of two years, may be admitted to become a citizen thereof, on application to any common court of record, in any one of the states wherein he shall have resided for the term of one year at least, and making proof to the satisfaction of such court, that he is a person of good character, and taking the oath of affirmation such court shall administer; and the clerk of such court shall record such application, and the proceedings thereon; and thereupon such person shall be considered as a citizen of the United States. (LeMay and Barkan, 1999, Document 7: 11)

The very generous condition, requiring only two years of residence, was amended in 1795, changing the minimum time to five years, and requiring the renunciation of hereditary titles of nobility (Act of January 29, 1795; 1 Stat. 414). In 1798, concern for immigration aroused by fears developing about the excesses of the French Revolution gave rise to xenophobia, a pervasive fear of the foreigner. Xenophobic reaction to the French Revolution led Congress to amend the uniform rule of naturalization again—changing the time to 14 years, assessing fees, and stipulating in greater detail the process for naturalization including a fee for surety of peace and penalties for various failures to comply with the law (Naturalization Act of June 18, 1798; 1 Stat. 566). Responding to those same fears, Congress enacted the Alien and Sedition Act (the Alien Act of June 25, 1798; 1 Stat. 570). The act manifests the considerable degree of xenophobia evident at the time. It granted the president extraordinary power to remove aliens deemed to be seditious. The act expired after the two-year limitation of the law and was not renewed, but it provided precedent whereby Congress would later enact laws controlling immigration, and granting sweeping enforcement powers to the executive branch concerning immigration matters that were later used during times of war—World War I and World War II, and post-9/11 (LeMay and Barkan, 1999, Document 10: 14–16).

In 1804, Congress passed a law allowing for the naturalization of the wife or children of an alien who died while in the process of naturalization but before the process was completed (Act of March 16, 1804; 34 Stat. 603). In 1813, it reaffirmed the five-year residency requirement for the naturalization process (Act of March 13, 1813; 45 Stat. 1514). Although these laws addressed the process of naturalization not immigration, the more generous or more stringent requirements may have influenced the flow of immigration. Equally important for federalism matters, they affirmed the primacy of Congress in stipulating such matters, giving the various state governments, and by delegation their local governments, no say in the issue.

In 1819, however, when Congress finally gave its attention directly to the matter of immigration, it was influenced by state precedents (i.e., colonial provincial laws) and was vague enough in procedural issues that it allowed the states a significant role in the procedures and processes of dealing with immigrants arriving at their ports. This law illustrates the two-way street nature of dual federalism at the time. State government policy could influence and pave the way for national-level action as well as national policy could impact state and local policy-makings. The first purposive law enacted by Congress concerning immigration to the United States simply called for captains or masters of ships to provide a list of names and the particulars concerning all passengers delivered to the United States, and for collectors of customs at the receiving ports to deliver a quarterly report containing copies of the manifests to the secretary of state of the United States, who in turn reported to Congress annually. It established for the first time the collection of data on immigration and immigrants, and marks the beginning of formal immigration law (Manifest of Immigrants Act of March 2, 1819; 3 Stat. 489). It was very similar to colonial provincial laws of Massachusetts and New York and demonstrates the state-to-federal influence of federalism wherein state governments act as sort of laboratories of policy ideas.

Before the United States became fully engaged in regulating immigration, in the 1880s, the government of several states (Massachusetts, Maryland, New York, Pennsylvania, Louisiana, and Virginia) having major receiving ports of entry (Boston, New York City, Baltimore, Philadelphia, New Orleans, and Richmond) passed laws designed to regulate the immigration flow in order to protect those states from financial responsibility for immigrants. The other most frequent provision related to health issues was protecting their population from contagious diseases accompanying immigrants, and establishing emigrant or marine hospitals to care for the ill among the immigrant arrivals. An important example of that is the Massachusetts law of 1820, "To Prevent the Introduction of Paupers, from Foreign Ports or Places, February 25, 1820." Similar to the national law on the Manifest of Immigrants, the Massachusetts act required the master of such vessels arriving at the port to leave a list of the names and places of residence of such passengers coming ashore with the selectmen or overseers of the poor of the town where such passengers were landed, and if, in the opinion of the selectmen, any such passenger may be liable to become chargeable for their support to the Commonwealth (of Massachusetts), within five days of his arrival, to enter into bonds with sufficient sureties to the satisfaction of the selectmen, in a sum not exceeding 500 dollars for each passenger, to indemnify and save harmless such town as well as the Commonwealth (Chap. CCXC: 428–29). Such laws reflected the practice of requiring shipmasters to declare immigrants, establish fees and persons for processing immigration (most of whom, until the late 1880s, were *state* officials), and place certain restrictions on individuals who might immigrate into the state (i.e., lunatics and paupers).

As the incidents of disease epidemics increased in the 1840s, state laws created their own commissioners of immigration, for example, the May 5, 1847 "Act Concerning Passengers in Vessels Coming to the City of New York" (Laws of the State of New York, 1847, Vol. 1, Chap. 195: 182–88). Like the Massachusetts law, it required the master of the vessel to supply a manifest to a city official, report any who are "lunatic, idiot, deaf and dumb, blind or infirm," and if so, whether they are accompanied by relatives who are likely to be able to support them, to specify the names, ages, last place of residence, and specify the names and ages of any passenger who may have died during the voyage, and levied a fine on the shipmaster or vessel owner for any false reporting. It charged the mayor, or his appointee charged with carrying out those duties, to require the master or commander of any ship to pay the City of New York a sum of one dollar per passenger within three days of arrival. It specified the position of commissioners of emigration at the port of New York charged with the duty to examine the ship and passengers, and authorized them to board the ships for the purpose of examining passengers as to any lunatic, idiot, deaf, dumb, blind, or infirm, or likely to become public charges, requiring the master of the ship to provide sureties and bond in a penalty of 300 dollars for every such passenger, conditioned to indemnify each and every city, town, or county within the state from any cost or charge to support such person or persons named within five years of the date of the bond.

In practice, then, state governments established commissioners of emigration to process immigrants at the major ports of entry. In the 1820s, 1830s, and 1840s, they were met on the wharf, asked a few rudimentary questions that were checked against the manifests, and the ships logs were examined for any incidents of illness or death during the voyage, usually by local doctors contracted by the state to provide the service of such medical inspection, cursory though they were at the time. Much of the immigrant processing, then, was under the policy, implementation, and control of *state* governments. The federal government focused on the census aspect of the millions of arrivals. State and federal inspectors typically did so on board the ship or on the docks or wharfs where they landed, usually in or near the customs office in some convenient warehouse building.

New York

From 1820 to 1860, 70 percent of the nearly 5½ million immigrants arrived through the port of New York City, at a rate of about 5,000 per year. By the mid- to late-1850s, those numbers increased to tens of thousands a year. As their numbers soared, political pressure to better screen and process them led to the establishment of a reception center specifically organized to do so. The first such station in the country was Castle Garden, in 1855 (National Park Service, 1987; Novotny, 1971; Svejda, 1968).

Castle Garden was established in part to protect New York City's population from epidemic diseases, and in part to protect immigrants from a host of swindlers who met them as they disembarked. Agents met them on the piers, enticing them with offers to find housing, food, and railway tickets to inland destinations. City political connections and cronyism led to a system in which immigrants were often victimized by a network of crooked shippers, innkeepers, railroad ticket agents, porters, and money changers.

German and Irish immigrants soon formed protective organizations that lobbied the New York State legislature to cope with the corruption and exploitation of immigrants. In response, New York established a Board of Commissioners of Emigration, in May 1847. It, in turn, created the Emigrant Refuge and Hospital on Wards Island to treat noncontagious illness among immigrants. The Marine Hospital was placed under the Board's control as numbers swelled and became too great for local inspectors and immigrant societies to handle. In 1850, for example, more than 2,000 ships delivered more than 200,000 immigrants. By then, 1,000 immigrants a day were arriving at the port. Castle Garden was meant to better deal with instances of corruption and exploitation, although soon it, too, had lesser but still significant levels of corruption, cronyism, inefficiency, and exploitation in coping with the sheer volume of immigrants.

The danger of epidemic outbreaks remained ever present. New York City suffered a cholera outbreak in 1832, and cholera and smallpox epidemics in 1834, which resulted in several thousand deaths. In 1849, another severe cholera epidemic occurred. The massive numbers arriving in 1847–1848 with a typhus epidemic (then referred to as "ships fever") among them led lawmakers to conclude the outbreak came with them. Until the 1880s and the development of germ theory, medical doctors and legislators had no idea what caused contagious diseases, but they concluded the diseases came with immigrants. Quarantine of any ship and its passengers was the only procedure they understood to act as a barrier against spreading the disease among their population. In 1851, another smallpox outbreak occurred, and in 1854 more than 2,500 perished in a cholera outbreak. In 1847 alone, more than 200,000 Irish fled the poverty and disease of their homeland for America. They boarded ships hungry, weakened, and many already ill. At that time, there was no inspection at the ports of embarkation. Most immigrant passengers set off with barely enough money to cover their passage and food for the journey. At that time, the transatlantic voyage typically took a month or more. An estimated nine percent of those who embarked in England, Ireland, and Germany died during the voyage—by shipwreck or of illness during the long and arduous passage. News of that staggering death toll shocked both state and federal immigration authorities, and laws were enacted requiring shipowners to provide food for the journey, increased ventilation for passengers during the voyage, and to be inspected on arrival, with increased fines imposed for those shipowners or shipmasters breaking the laws. Too often, however, fines were set too low to effectively deter greedy shipmasters, and the death rates on board remained quite high until steamship lines developed to provide the transatlantic migration.

The much smaller stations at Baltimore, Boston, New Orleans, and Philadelphia were able to better cope with fewer problems since their annual arrivals were more manageable. Each of those ports will be briefly discussed to illustrate their experiences and to discuss and exemplify their federal to state to local relationships.

Baltimore

During the War of 1812, Baltimore was the home port to about a third of the nation's privateers (essentially, legalized pirates who by a letter of marquee were granted authority to attack, capture, and seize the booty of ships of the enemy nation—in this case, Great Britain). After the war, the city leaders saw their city as being able to compete with cities like New York and Philadelphia for the Western trade when the Cumberland Road was completed, in 1818, linking the Chesapeake Bay to the Ohio River at Wheeling. After 1820, European immigration increased from a few hundred a year to nearly 2,000 by 1828, when the first commercial steam railroad, the Baltimore and Ohio, opened. Baltimore's location as the western-most seaport on the East Coast, along with highway, canal, and rail connections, attracted thousands of German, Irish, and English immigrants. Workers were needed to build the city, to supply traders and merchants. By the Civil War, 25 percent of the city's population was foreign born, including more than 15,000 Irish and more than 32,000 Germans. Baltimore's Hibernian Society aided Irish immigrants. Rapid population increase brought increased density in poor neighborhoods jammed with immigrants, and epidemics of dysentery, cholera, and respiratory illness in the immigrant neighborhoods were common throughout the 1830s. The Hibernian Society also acted as an employment agency. The German Society of Maryland, organized in 1783, helped new arrivals. In 1817, a ship trapped by ice had more than 300 German immigrants aboard and their conditions became horrendous until aided by the Society. The German Society lobbied the legislature to regulate labor contracts, new laws against keeping immigrants aboard ship for more than 30 days after arrival, and care for the sick. The society was quick to bring to trial any ship captain who violated the protective laws. It's Intelligence Bureau, formed in 1845, found jobs for 3,500 immigrants and secured Baltimore's reputation as a favorable port of entry when immigrants wrote home to their friends and relatives. The city's one-quarter German population made it an attractive alternative to New York's port (Stolarik, 1988: 62–68). The smaller size of arrivals at any one time, moreover, made the processing by state officials and U.S. customs agents on the wharf at Piers 8 and 9 on Locust Point more manageable. Only steerage passengers were required to pass through the medical examination procedures, and even they were looked at only casually (Stolarik, 1988: 70–71). In 1833, schooner and smaller packet ships typically arrived with fewer than 50 to at most less than 150 passengers. The *Phoenix,* sailing from Bremen to Baltimore, arrived on September 10, 1833 with 163 passengers on board, 152 in steerage. The *Galliot Hendzika,* sailing from Amsterdam to Baltimore, arrived on September 17, 1833 with 70 aboard ship. The *Bremen Packet* arrived on October 15, 1833, with 117 aboard, and the *Brunswick,* also sailing from Bremen to Baltimore, arrived on October 17, with 133 aboard (Immigrant Ship Transcriber's Guild, hereafter noted as ISTG). Baltimore, as well as Boston and Philadelphia, was also a port of entry for secondary immigration from Canada. Immigrants from Ireland, the British Isles, and Germany sometimes found it easier to migrate first to Canada, settle for a time and improve their conditions, and then sail by schooner ships down the East Coast from Canada to New England or the Mid-Atlantic states.

Boston

Boston was less attractive than New York, Philadelphia, Baltimore, or New Orleans, which were more active ports than Boston every year from

1818 to 1848, except in 1844. Farmers could find richer soil more quickly in cities to the south or west, and skilled craftsmen and unskilled workers were more likely to find work within them. In only 3 of the 20 years between 1820 and 1840 did Boston rank as high as third among ports of entry, and only once was it second—in 1822. The low rate of immigration to Boston would have continued except for the Great Irish potato famine of 1845. From 1847 to 1854, 20,000 or more Irish immigrants arrived in Boston annually. In 1840, Boston became the terminus city for the pioneering steamship service of Britain's Cunard Line in 1840, whose fares were subsidized by the British government so that even the poor could cross, although it cost them all of their money. With the potato blight, emigration became a necessity, not a choice. Many died in passage. Barely able to afford the 17 to 20 dollars fare (or 10 pounds in British sterling, including provision) from Liverpool to Boston, immigrants increasingly came from Cork, Kerry, Galway, Clare, and Donegal in 1850–1855, when more than 20,000 to 27,000 plus arrived annually.

Immigrants from Sweden and Germany also came to Boston, but by 1850 the Irish made up more than three-fourths of the foreign born in the city and a quarter of the city population as a whole. Swedes and Germans arrived with more money and were better able to move West, so the 1850 census year found only 2,000 Germans and fewer Swedes among the city's population. A few Scots, French, and Italians made up the other minority immigrant population who worked in the textile factories or as domestic servants, and most immigrants remained crowded in slums that horrified the native-born population.

By the 1850s, the Know Nothing Party gained power in Boston, and the party carried Massachusetts in 1854, electing the governor, all statewide offices, the senate, and all but two seats of the statehouse. The number of immigrants coming through Boston declined sharply in 1858. Only in 1865, after the war ended, did new arrivals number more than 10,000 (Fuchs, in Stolarik, 1988: 17–20).

As was the case in Baltimore, before the Civil War immigrants arriving at the port of Boston were processed on ships and on the docks. The Boston immigration station as a dedicated structure for that purpose did not open until the 1890s. The smaller numbers per year and per ship enabled the largely state and local appointed immigration officials and workers to manage the process. Even in 1847, the beginning year of the flood of Irish immigrants, ships arriving in Boston carried passengers as few as a dozen and only one landed with 359 aboard. Some typical examples of ship arrivals in that year include the following: the steamer *Hibernia* arrived from Liverpool on January 25, 1847 with 109 aboard; the schooner *Flora* sailed from Halifax to Boston with a mere 9 immigrant passengers; the royal cutter, *Darig,* arrived from Sable Island, Nova Scotia, with 45 passengers; the ship *Mary Ann* sailed from Liverpool to Boston, arriving on March 10, 1847, with 136 on board; the brig *Armagh* came from St. John, New Brunswick with only 4 Irish on board; and the ship *Anglo Saxon* came from Liverpool to Boston, arriving April 1st, 1847, with 359 English and Irish immigrants (ISTG).

New Orleans

Because of the city's location near the mouth of the Mississippi River, New Orleans held a commanding position over access to the western interior and was key to President Jefferson's program for economic growth and development. By 1817, steamboats plied the inland waterway to Louisville, and made New Orleans a major gateway to the western interior. The period of major immigration to New Orleans took place between 1820 and 1860, when more than 550,000 immigrants came through the port, and by 1837 it was the second leading port of entry. From 1847 to 1857, more than 350,000 immigrants jammed the docks to be processed.

From 1820 to 1860, New Orleans rivaled New York as a commercial port, shipping more than 1.5 billion dollars worth of exports, almost a quarter of the nation's total exports. By 1846, it was the fourth leading commercial center in the world. Captains of cotton ships sailed from New Orleans to Liverpool, Le Harve, Bremen, and Hamburg, and returned with increasing numbers of human cargo comprised of Irish, German, and French immigrants. Since they could disembark themselves from their vessels, they were an economically desirable cargo. And while the journey to New Orleans was a bit longer than to New York or Baltimore or Philadelphia, it was cheaper. Most of the more than one-half million immigrants who came through New Orleans before 1860 went on to the western interior. Among the bulk of the foreign immigrants arriving at its wharfs, most stayed only long enough to secure inland passage on a steamer going upriver beyond the deep South (Logsdon, in Stolarik, 1988: 105–9).

Because of local swamps and little or no sanitation, New Orleans suffered regularly from epidemics of yellow fever. Thousands of immigrants stranded in the city filled its hospitals—and ultimately, its cemeteries. Local leaders who controlled the immigration processing wanted a wide-open port. They turned over management of the port to private lessees by 1820, but New Orleans still attracted many immigrants as an alternative port to the more stringent processing in ports to the north thereby attracting passengers who feared rejection for personal handicaps that might have excluded them by the custom officials in New York, or Philadelphia, for instance.

A scourge of yellow fever outbreak in 1853–1854, which killed 8,000 people in New Orleans, finally convinced business and local government leaders to secure state legislation that set up quarantine stations outside the city and forced most ships, particularly those from tropical ports, to stop for health inspection. Onshore facilities were not constructed until 1859, ironically, just as the heyday of immigration to the city was coming to an end (Stolarik, 1988: 109). Prior to 1840, ships arriving at the New Orleans port typically carried less than 100 passengers and could be processed aboard ship or on the docks. A few examples from 1836 will illustrate the point: the ship *Lyons,* from Le Havre to New Orleans, arrived on June 7 with 62 French and German immigrants aboard; the ship *Hamilton,* sailing from Liverpool to New Orleans, arrived October 31 with 41 English, Scotch, and Irish immigrants; the barque *Jane,* out of Greenock, Scotland, arrived on November 5 with 79 immigrants, mostly Scots and a few Irish; the ship *Orion,* sailing from Hamburg, arrived in New Orleans on the December 12 with 125 German immigrants and had 2 children who died at sea; and the brig *Weser,* which came from Bremen, arrived on December 29 with 127 aboard.

By 1854, steamships were typically arriving with more than 300 aboard, such as the ship *Henry Pratt,* coming from Le Havre, had 339 mostly Swiss and some French on board; the barque *Edmund,* out of Bremen, arrived on November 3 with 345 German immigrants; the ship *Hermann,* also out of Bremen, reached New Orleans with 372 passengers, including 285 in steerage and among whom there were 12 infants; and the ship *O' Thyen,* from Bremen, arrived on November 8 with 346 passengers.

Philadelphia

The voyage from Europe to Philadelphia is 200 miles longer than that to New York, a serious impediment during the years of wooden sailing vessels. Despite this relative handicap, however, between 1815 and 1873, about a quarter of a million arrived at the port of Philadelphia. From 1847 to 1854, one of its most important periods of immigration, the city's share of total immigration to the United States was 4.4 percent. The city was the country's most important immigrant port in the 18th century, and as early as 1717 the Provincial Assembly had ordered ship captains to submit manifests. At that time, Germans and the Scotch-Irish from Ulster were the primary sources. Between 1717 and 1733, for example, 36 ships arrived from Germany alone, and by 1754 were averaging 11 ships a year, but such ships typically carried only a dozen or so immigrants. Large-scale European immigration began after 1815, with the end of the Napoleonic Wars, and by then New York had become the major port of entry to America. Nonetheless, many of the city's merchants were active in overseas trade, and their merchant ships brought immigrants to Philadelphia. Fearing yellow fever, the city had established a quarantine hospital as early as 1798. Between 1815 and 1819, more than 60 ships arrived from Ireland. Between 1820 and 1831, more than 20,000 immigrants arrived. They accounted for one-eighth of the nation's total, with two lines of Philadelphia-owned ships regularly making the run from Liverpool, the main port for Irish and English emigrations. Steerage cost between five and seven pounds, typically the total wages for a month to two (Stolarik, 1988: 37–40).

Between 1830 and the great famine migration of 1847, more than 60,000 arrived in Philadelphia, and its share of all immigrant arrival rose to just under 5 percent, where it remained until the Civil War. From 1847 to 1854, more than 120,000 immigrants entered through the port. After 1850, the British government began subsidizing passage of the poorest emigrants and this policy made the migration more accessible.

The first steamship line, the Liverpool and Philadelphia Steam Ship Company, was owned by Liverpool Quakers, but the real force was their partner William Inman. In 1850, he persuaded them to expand from sailing packet ships to new steamships, which made the crossing in only 10 days. The line's ships, like the *City of Glasgow, City of Manchester,* and *City of Philadelphia,* were faster and cheaper than those of other lines. In 1854, the *City of Manchester* made 5 round trips with as many as 532 passengers each. But they were also less safe: that year saw the *City of Glasgow* disappear in March on its way to Philadelphia with 450 passengers aboard, and in September, the *City of Philadelphia* went aground near Cape Race, Newfoundland. Passengers were saved, but the ship was not. In 1857, Inman dropped the Philadelphia route, sailing to New York instead.

Immigrants were processed on the wharfs lining the Delaware riverfront. In 1851, the effects of the famine were still evident and 13 ships sailed to Philadelphia with about 2,500 passengers. In 1855, British officials reported 7,206 immigrants arrived in Philadelphia from all ports, including 2,890 from England and Wales, 3,374 from Ireland, and 425 from Germany—more than half the ships arriving from Liverpool. Between 1855 and 1864, about 50,000 arrived, about 3 percent of the national total (Stolarik, 1988: 40–41).

Again, the typical ship carried less than 200 passengers. This made it easy for local government officials to process them on the docks. State policy and largely local officials administered immigration policy by contract with the federal government. For example, in 1850, 14 ships arrived: among them the *Adam Lodge,* from Londonderry, with 158 passengers; the *Edmund,* also from Londonderry, with 158; the barque *Filergill,* with 145; and the barque *Creole,* with 183 (ISTG).

Conclusion

From 1790 to 1865, and particularly between 1820 and 1865, when immigrants were officially counted, the laws and procedures regulating immigration to the United States were clearly shared by both the federal and state governments. The national government, after 1855 and until 1890, contracted with state government boards of emigration to administer immigration regulations in the major ports on the East Coast through which European immigrants were entering the country. Thus, the immigration policy area is a prime example of dual federalism. Changes in the flow of immigrants aroused anti-immigration sentiment that influenced political party developments and were registered in demands for restrictions on immigration. Such restriction, however, were not enacted at the national level until the 1892 Chinese Exclusion Act. Cooperative Federalism, in which the national government led policy-making and state and localities followed its policy lead, was exemplified almost first with the development of national immigration policy-making and administration, with the immigration service clearly and solely at the national level, and with numerous immigration reception stations being established and administered by the federal government.

References

Adams, William P. 1980. *The First American Constitutions: Republican Ideology and the Making of State Constitutions in the Revolutionary Era.* Chapel Hill, NC: University of North Carolina Press.

American Federalism. 1776–1977. Available at: http://www.usinfo.state.gov/usa/infousa/facts/crsreport/federal.htm.

Beer, Samuel. 1978. "Federalism, Nationalism, and Democracy in America." *The American Political Science Review* 72: 9–21.

Constitution of the United States of America, ACLU.

Cooke, Jacob E. ed. 1961. *The Federalist.* Cleveland, OH: The World Publishing Co.

Diamond, Martin. 1981. *The Founding of the Democratic Republic.* Florence, KY: Cengage Learning.

Drake, Frederick D., and Lynn R. Nelson. 1999. *States' Rights and American Federalism: A Documentary History.* Westport, CT: Greenwood.

Elazar, Daniel J. 1987. *Exploring Federalism.* Tuscaloosa, AL: University of Alabama.

Elazar, Daniel J. 1994. *The American Mosaic: The Impact of Space, Time, and Culture on American Politics.* Boulder, CO: Westview Press.

Fenn, Elizabeth. 2001. *Pox Americana: The Great Smallpox Epidemic of 1775–82.* New York: Hill and Wang.

Fritz, Christian G. 2007. *American Sovereigns: The People and America's Constitutional Tradition Before the Civil War.* New York: Cambridge University.

Gerston, Larry N. 2007. *American Federalism: A Concise Introduction.* New York: Sharp.

Grodzins, Morton. 1966. *The American System: A New View of Government in the United States.* Chicago, IL: Rand McNally.

Immigrant Ship Transcriber's Guild. Available at: www.immigrantships.net/index2.html.

LaCroix, Alison. 2010. *The Ideological Origins of American Federalism.* Cambridge, MA: Harvard University Press.

LeMay, Michael. 1987. *From Open Door to Dutch Door: An Analysis of U.S. Immigration Policy since 1820.* New York: Praeger.

LeMay, Michael. 2009. *The Perennial Struggle.* 3rd ed. Upper Saddle River, NJ: Prentice-Hall.

LeMay, Michael, and Elliott Barkan, eds. 1999. *U.S. Immigration and Naturalization Laws and Issues.* Westport, CT: Greenwood Press.

Lowi, Theodore. 1995. *The End of the Republican Era.* Norman, OK: University of Oklahoma Press.

Morgan, Edmund S. 1988. *Inventing the People: The Rise of Popular Sovereignty in England and America.* New York: W. W. Norton.

Mullins, J. Patric. 1999. *A Historiography of the Motivation of the Constitutional Framers.* Boca Raton, FL: Florida Atlantic University.

Nash, Gary B. 2005. *Unknown American Revolution: The Unruly Birth of Democracy and the Struggle to Create America.* New York: Viking Press.

National Park Service. 1987. *Castle Clinton.* Washington, DC: National Park Service, U.S. Department of the Interior.

Novotny, Ann. 1971. *Strangers at the Doors.* Riverside, CT: The Chatham Press.

Patrick, John J. 1990. *James Madison and the Federalist Papers.* Bloomington, IN: ERIC Clearinghouse for Social Studies/Social Science Education.

Patrick, John J. 1995. *Founding the Republic: A Documentary History.* Westport, CT: Greenwood Press.

Peterson, Paul E. 1995. *The Price of Federalism.* Washington, DC: Brookings.

Reid, John P. 1986. *Constitutional History of the American Revolution.* Madison, WI: University of Wisconsin Press.

Reimer, Neal, and Douglas Simon. 1994. *The New World of Politics.* San Diego, CA: Collegiate Press.

Riker, William. 1987. *The Development of American Federalism.* Boston, MA: Kluwer.

Shapiro, David. 1997. *Federalism: A Dialog.* Evanston, IL: Northwestern University Press.

Stolarik, M. Mark, ed. 1988. *Forgotten Doors: The Other Ports of Entry to the United States.* Philadelphia, PA: Balch Institute/Associated University Presses.

Svejda, Dr. George. 1968. *Castle Garden as an Immigrant Depot, 1855–1890.* Washington, DC: National Park Service, U.S. Department of the Interior.

Walker, David. 1995. *The Rebirth of Federalism.* Chatham, NJ: Chatham House.

Wildavsky, Aaron, ed. 1967. *American Federalism in Perspective.* Boston, MA: Little, Brown.

Wood, Gordon S. 1991. *The Radicalism of the American Revolution.* New York: Knopf.

CHAPTER FIVE

The Common and Uncommon Schooling of Immigrants to the United States, 1787–1865

H. James McLaughlin

Introduction

The period in U.S. history from 1787 to 1865 saw the rise of a common or public school system, at the same time that millions of immigrants entered the country, especially after 1845. This chapter addresses general educational issues related to immigrants over these eight decades, and then focuses on five ethnic groups: the Germans in Cincinnati, the Irish in New York City, the Norwegians in Koshkonong and Southern Wisconsin, the Mexicans in San Antonio and South Texas, and the Chinese in San Francisco. By 1860, Cincinnati, New York City, and San Francisco were three of the five cities with the highest foreign-born percentage of population, and events in those cities influenced education in their state and sometimes the nation (see Appendix 5.1). Norwegians had an important presence in upper Midwestern states such as Iowa, Wisconsin, and Minnesota. Mexicans were really the only immigrants in the Southwest, although it had been their land for some time. Every group had its own educational trajectory, which was influenced by language, religion, culture, and others' perspectives of them. In each place, the immigrants made a new American home and created an uncommon education for their children.

Education before 1787

Before the signing of the U.S. Constitution in 1787 and its passage in 1788, schools were often not free, not compulsory, not open to girls, and never open to slaves or Native Americans. Immigrants to the territory of the current United States had come primarily from England. An early act in Massachusetts, passed in 1647 and commonly known as the "Old Deluder Satan" Law, declared that towns with more than 50 families should provide a school for the children, primarily to instruct them in religious principles by using the Christian Bible as the main text. Until well into the 19th century, however, schooling for rural children was sometimes tenuous because it depended on the availability of a teacher and the resources offered by local citizens. Also, because the immigrant population was largely English, the class-based system of education was recapitulated. Children of the wealthy had tutors or went to boarding schools, and then attended the few private colleges in the Northeast, or were sent to colleges in England.

1787

The U.S. Constitution, written in 1787 and passed in 1788, did not mention education. This left education as a matter to be handled by the states and not by the federal government, and set the nation on a decentralized course that would lead to local school board control of public schools, funding through local property taxes, and widely disparate resources and access to schooling in different parts of the country.

At the same time, the passage of the Northwest Ordinance in 1787 set a tone for future educational initiatives in areas newly settled by whites. The Ordinance stated: "Religion, morality and knowledge, being necessary to good government and the happiness of mankind, schools and the means of education shall forever be encouraged." The term "encouraged" signified a call for moral education without a concomitant commitment to equitable school funding, a minimum level of resources, or even access for all children to an education. For example, land had to be rented by each community for educational purposes, which frequently did not occur or was subject to mismanagement. Thus, "schooling remained a local, voluntary, and largely entrepreneurial undertaking" in rural areas until the mid-19th century (Kaestle, 1983: 184). It took the common school movement, set in motion 50 years later, to propel the nation on a more direct path toward its educational commitments, which we are still trying in some ways to fulfill.

Major Challenges for Immigrant Groups from 1787 to 1865

After the British, who comprised the bulk of immigrants before the 1830s, every new immigrant group had to adapt to its new country and to secure a formal education for its children. The first challenge was always to gain access to schooling, especially outside of the Northeastern urban centers.

Access to Schooling

Established citizens and new immigrants alike tended to value formal education for their children. In the more urban and industrializing Northeast, school enrollment was a relatively high 70 percent for children aged 5–19, even before the common school movement of the 1840s (Meyer et al., 1979: 597). In the cities, most children from families with some means attended an independent pay school or dame school, while poor children became apprentices or attended a church-sponsored charity school (Kaestle, 1983: 30–32). Many of these institutions were borrowed from England; beginning in the 1830s, educators also looked to Prussia for ideas because of its compulsory public education laws and its perceived widespread literacy.

A key point is that America was largely rural before the Civil War. In 1830, 91 percent of Americans lived in places with fewer than 2,500 inhabitants (Kaestle, 1983: 13). Being a farmer did not correlate with a lack of education for children; while rural school enrollment in the Northeast was slightly lower than or equal to urban children from ages 5–14, it was actually higher from ages 15–19, probably because many urban children worked outside the home at those ages (Meyer et al., 1979: 598). But in rural areas, school terms were short and resources were minimal. Students attended spare one-room schools for perhaps 60 days a year, and some children in more isolated areas had little or no access to schools.

Throughout the period from 1787 to 1865, the South was mired in a bifurcated system of plantations supported by slave labor and small landholdings that were largely resource-poor. Few children attended school, except for the wealthy landowners. Children in the South had much lower rates of school enrollment, less funding, and shorter school terms than elsewhere in the country (Meyer et al., 1979: 600). There was little immigration aside from England, and the common school movement did not take hold there until well after the Civil War. European immigrants therefore tended to settle in the new Midwest states, such as Indiana (1816),

Illinois (1818), Missouri (1821), Michigan (1837), Iowa (1846), Wisconsin (1848), and Minnesota (1858).

Postrevolutionary education writers focused often on the purposes of schooling, and called for "a balance between freedom and order" that could occur by educating citizens to be patriotic and virtuous (Spring, 2008: 48). Economic and demographic changes would make this balance seem precarious. After 1830, cities grew at a faster rate, and beginning in the mid-1840s, the immigrant population exploded because of European economic conditions, the war with Mexico, and the California gold rush, among other social dynamics. Increased immigration brought with it struggles over religion, language, and culture.

Religion

The relationship between religion and education has long been debated in the United States. Thomas Jefferson wrote in "Notes on the State of Virginia" that the Bible should not be used to teach children how to read; moral instruction should first teach them "how to work out their own greatest happiness, by shewing [*sic*] them that it does not depend on the condition of life in which chance has placed them" (Spring, 2008: 56). Among educators, however, it was commonplace that moral instruction with the Bible as the primary text should be a cornerstone of the curriculum. The primary religious friction before 1865 occurred between devout German and Irish Catholics and the majority Protestants, over which Bible should be used in school and the basic purpose of schooling. Most notably, many Irish Catholics in the largest cities began to challenge or even resist public schooling from the 1830s on, until in the 1880s a parochial school system was created. Later sections in this chapter examine how the Irish in New York City questioned common schooling, and how Norwegians and Germans infused their religious perspectives into public schooling.

Language

Even preceding the revolution, there was concern over which language should be used in schools. Benjamin Franklin proposed that all schooling in Pennsylvania be in English because he wanted to Anglicize German immigrants, who in 1766 comprised about one-third of Pennsylvania's population. Franklin asked, in 1755, "Why should *Pennsylvania,* founded by the *English,* become a colony of *Aliens,* who will shortly be so numerous as to Germanize us instead of our Anglifying them, and will never adopt our language or customs, any more than they can acquire our complexion" (Gjerde, 1998: 72; emphasis in the original).

There were efforts to limit or even prohibit publications in the German language (Spring, 2008: 22). In spite of this pressure, many German settlers fought to maintain their own churches, schools, and cultural institutions. Germans in cities such as Cincinnati desired to be an American without being Anglicized.

Noah Webster, whose influential dictionary was published in 1828, wrote in a 1792 essay about the "Necessity for an American Language" (Johnson, 2002: 74–78). This preceded the call by German immigrants for bilingual schooling in the 1830s, and the demands by other ethnic groups to maintain and teach their language, after the major upswing of immigration in the mid-1840s. The Germans, Scandinavians, Mexicans, Chinese, and other immigrants spoke their native language at home, read newspapers and books in that language, conducted religious services in that language, and wanted their schools to incorporate that language alongside English. These groups were not monolithic, because they brought to the United States their social class, religious, and political divisions (Ramsey, 2009: 274). Regardless of these differences, however, Germans in Midwestern cities and Norwegians in their rural communities in the Upper Midwest tried mightily to maintain their native languages, in an effort to have their children be bilingual. They were successful in doing so for many decades largely because of their homogeneous isolation (e.g., Norwegians) or their urban political and cultural clout (e.g., Germans).

Mexicans in the Southwest after 1848 and Chinese in the West after 1849 also wanted their children to learn in two languages, but they were either excluded from schooling or had to establish separate schools. This exclusion or segregation occurred because of European Americans' cultural views of those groups.

Cultural Views of Immigrants

Cultural stereotypes strongly influenced Native Americans' reactions to the new immigrants. Many Americans of British ancestry, and some Germans as well, thought of the Irish, the Mexicans, and the Chinese as inferior peoples. They were said to belong to a different race, which was a term used to rank groups on the basis of intelligence, work ethic, and even cleanliness. Particularly for the Mexicans and the Chinese, this meant that public schooling would be denied them, or that their children would be segregated and taught in inferior conditions.

Many educators and political leaders rejected the idea of a multicultural society, as we might put it now. Their primary concern was that schools help to create good citizens, and they held strong opinions about the characteristics of citizenship. Noah Webster's spelling books contained a "Federal Catechism" that emphasized a patriotic and nationalistic curriculum, and a "Moral Catechism" that centered on Christian precepts such as the Sermon on the Mount. All of this was intended to maintain the hegemony of an Anglo American culture; whatever cultural patterns immigrants brought to America should be laid aside (Spring, 2008: 52–53).

Horace Mann and the Common Schools

The desire for a common understanding of what it meant to be a good citizen in this new country and beliefs about how newcomers should speak and act underlay the movement for public common schools. In the late 1830s, the common school movement began as a series of small steps. Following the Northwest Ordinance, enacted about 50 years earlier, citizens were determined that their communities should have free schools open to all students. These schools were to be locally controlled, although there were state laws and sporadic small-funding streams to support the schools.

In line with Franklin, Webster, and other revered predecessors, the reformers intended that schools impart Christian morals, promote the English language, and help newcomers to assimilate. This required a delicate interweaving of centralized policies and pronouncements at a state level, and decision making at the school district or schoolhouse level.

> Between 1837 and 1853, every state legislature in the North passed into law most of the key features of common free school systems . . . consolidating the country's culture around republican, capitalist, and Protestant values. (Kaestle, 1983: 27)

The most famous of the common school reformers was Horace Mann, who from his perch as state superintendent of schools in Massachusetts from 1837 to 1848 issued annual reports and made speeches that promoted the spread of public schools. In 1843, Mann visited Prussian and Dutch schools (Glenn, 1988: 60). His report of that trip showed a high regard for German educational ideas, which is ironic, given the backlash against German immigrants' calls for bilingual schooling in many communities. Mann's 1848 Report to the Massachusetts State Board of Education is a vital historic document that portrays well his pragmatic and idealistic vision. In it, Mann referred to education as "the balance wheel of the social machinery." Common schooling would ensure social order by muting socioeconomic discord: "It does better than to disarm the poor of their hostility toward the rich; it prevents being poor" (Johnson, 2002: 92). Mann's words were written in the context of intense European immigration to the Northeast and Midwest, new populations in the Southwest following the war with Mexico, and increasing numbers of black freedmen outside of the South. The quote can also be interpreted as a statement about the complex dynamics of the social machinery in a public school system, which would bring all children together in the same classrooms:

Reformers of all nationalities pushed for schools to be sites of "social cohesion" (Ramsey, 2009: 272). Yet, in order to entice the disparate immigrants into public schools, there needed somehow to be a balance of common values with the traditions of different cultural and religious groups. There was a constant dissonance between direction from a central authority, in the form of laws and policies, and the local people's authority over decisions related to curriculum, instruction, funding through taxation, budgeting, and school personnel. Traditional reformers thought it necessary to have a monolingual curriculum and instruction, while immigrants such as the Germans and Norwegians wanted the schools to be bilingual.

Groups in the cities and in small towns debated whether the schools should be Protestant or Catholic, and secular or religious. Mann, as other reformers of the time, wanted schools to inculcate a common moral education, which would be nonsectarian. Throughout this time period, political crosscurrents buffeted education. In Mann's own state of Massachusetts, the gubernatorial election of 1854 reflected a powerful nativist and anti-immigration strain, led by the American or Know Nothing Party. Newly elected governor Gardner asserted that the United States must "dispel from popular use every foreign language . . . ordain that all schools aided by the state shall use the same language . . . retain the Bible in our common schools . . . nationalize before we naturalize, and educate before either" (Glenn, 1988: 72–73). In the midst of these 19th-century currents, the educational experiences of people from Germany, Ireland, Norway, Mexico, and China can provide a broad geographic and cultural perspective of how immigrants swam with and against the prevailing tides of policy and public opinion.

Germans in Cincinnati

> German immigrants are generally welcome here, and as soon as they have set foot on the new continent, they are considered equals of the citizens

> (aside from political rights, which are dependent on a residence of five years). (Comments by Gottfried Duden, a German immigrant to Missouri in 1827, in Gjerde, 1998: 98)

German immigrants were the most numerous of the non-English immigrants from the Revolutionary years onward. The United States was the land of choice for Germans seeking greater economic opportunities; more than 90 percent of emigrating Germans came to this country.

Frequently, they were categorized as Church Germans or Club Germans. Church Germans had a larger rural component, tended to be more traditional, and were predominant among those who arrived in the 1830s (the 30ers). Club Germans were more urban and political, and many had emigrated after the 1848 failed revolutions in Europe (the 48ers). This division can be overstated, however; Germans were the most heterogeneous and dispersed of any immigrant group in the antebellum era. About one-fourth of them were farmers in 1870, and there were German settlements south to Texas and west to California (Daniels, 2002: 151). Germans had a reputation for being well-educated, even though the illiteracy rate as late as 1871 in Prussia was 12 percent.

Cincinnati, Ohio, became a major center for Germans who were settling in the Ohio River Valley, and it was one corner of the German Triangle formed by the three points of Cincinnati, St. Louis, and Milwaukee. By 1850, Germans numbered 30,758 in Cincinnati, which was 27 percent of the total population; by 1870 Germans made up 33 percent of the city (Tolzmann, 2005: 28). They lived first in an area dubbed "Over-the-Rhine" because it was bounded by the Miami–Erie Canal, which was seen as the Rhine River. Once someone passed over the bridge, neighborhoods fully reflected the language and culture of Germany (Tolzmann, 2005: 23, 31–33).

Germans were early supporters of the common schools, but they wanted their schools to promote the German culture and language in the curriculum. In 1837, the first law supporting German-language public schools was passed in Pennsylvania, and in 1839 a similar act came into effect in Ohio. Other Midwestern states passed school laws allowing for foreign-language instruction, although the languages were not specified. These laws both reflected extant patterns of language instruction and encouraged such instruction in new common schools (Ramsey, 2009: 276).

Cincinnati, with its large German population, became the educational model for Germans across the country. In 1840, Cincinnati became the first city in the United States to instruct students in German, largely as a means of transitioning newly arrived immigrant children into the all-English classrooms. However, by the 1850s, middle-class and well-educated Germans, especially those who had arrived after 1848, wanted the common schools to pass German literature along to all students, and to employ some of the pedagogical practices associated with German schooling. Thus, the "Cincinnati Plan" of half-day instruction in German and half-day instruction in English until Grade 4 was created. The schools even had bilingual textbooks. In high schools, German was a subject taught for one hour daily. By 1875, more than half of the city's pupils were being instructed in German (Ramsey, 2009: 278). It should be noted that there were also several hundred bilingual schools in the rural Midwest, many of them teaching in German, although such schools received little attention nationally (Ramsey, 2009: 283).

The Germans took many positions on the question of the relationship between religion and education because they came from Protestant, Catholic, and Jewish traditions. German Lutherans held varying religious views. The more conservative of them formed the Missouri Synod, which promoted parochial schools and a nonsecular education. In the 1850s and 1860s, a major clash would ensue between this group and congregations of Norwegian Lutherans, who were more liberal in religious and social orientation and who supported the abolitionist movement.

About one-third of Germans were Catholic (Daniels, 2002: 152), and they also differed on matters of schooling. Some of them agreed with the Irish immigrants who challenged the common school curriculum because it was too Protestant and too secular (at the same time); they wanted a Catholic school system for their children. Other German Catholics, the majority, willingly sent their children to the public schools so that they would learn English and readily adapt to life in their new country.

The American Jewish population was 150,000–200,000 by 1860 (American Jewish Historical Society, 1999: 35). Most Jewish immigrants from 1830 to 1865 came from states in Southwestern Germany. They spoke German and tended to settle in cities such as New York City or Cincinnati, where there were established German populations. In 1860, about 10,000 Jews lived in Cincinnati (Daniels, 2002: 155), by which time they had constructed a Jewish hospital, built a number of synagogues, and started a Jewish newspaper in English and German (Tolzmann, 2005: 47).

During the mid-19th century, German Jewish immigrants were primarily Ashkenazis, who were more educated and politically progressive than most immigrants. They intermarried with Gentiles at a greater rate than in Europe, and Jewish children attended the common schools (along with their Saturday religious schools). There were anti-Semitic attitudes among some people and occasional flares of violence, but the overwhelmingly urban Jewish immigrants of mid-century were not highly visible and had clear access to schooling.

Whatever their religion, German immigrants in cities such as Cincinnati maintained their strong cultural roots, and the schools played a large role in doing so. Irish Catholics experienced greater conflict, partly because of how they were seen by the dominant English citizens.

Irish Catholics in New York

> The mere laboring Irish, like those of the same class at home, may be seen engaged in all the humbler occupations from shouldering the hod to rag-gathering [However], the improved condition of Irishmen in America does not make them forget the soil made sacred to them by the graves of their fathers and the memories of their early loves and youthful aspirations. (Comments by James Burns about Irish immigrants, written in 1850, in Gjerde, 1998: 102)

From 1830 onward, there was an influx of Irish Catholics to the Northeast, and they faced extreme prejudice in their new land. Irish were stereotyped as "drunken" and were said to be "inferior in nature, some perhaps only behind us in development . . . a lower form . . . [consisting] of negroes, Indians, Mexicans, Irish, and the like" (Reverend Theodore Parker, in Spring, 2008: 110). Furthermore, Catholicism was portrayed as a dangerous and alien religion. In 1835, Samuel Morse wrote that "Popery is opposed in its very nature to Democratic Republicanism; and it is therefore, as a political system, as well as religious, opposed to civil and religious liberty, and consequently to our form of government" (Gjerde, 1998: 137). This anti-Catholic sentiment would undergird the Know Nothing Party of the 1840s and 1850s, which opposed open immigration and any influence by the Catholic Church. An 1837 riot between Protestants and Catholics in Boston would presage later riots and intense disagreements over school curriculum (Spring, 2008: 83).

After the onset of the potato famine in 1845, the number of Irish immigrants exploded. Nearly 1.7 million Irish came to the United States between 1841 and 1860; the total for the prior 20 years had been about 1/7 of that amount (Spring, 2008: 108). Appendix 5.2 shows that 42.8 percent of all foreign-born Americans in 1850 came from Ireland, and even 20 years later it was 33.3 percent. Together, German and Irish immigrants made up two-thirds of all immigrants from 1850 to 1870.

Irish immigrants were predominantly Roman Catholic. Most of them came from Ireland with very little formal education and low levels of income. In 1870, the percentage of Irish children with illiterate fathers was about 18 percent, a rate much higher than for any other European group emigrating at the time (Soltow and Stevens, 1981: 139). Primarily, the Irish took jobs as laborers and service workers (see Appendix 5.3). They assumed some of the lower occupational rungs in society such as building roads and canals, and performing domestic service. Most children, however, did not work until age 15 or older, and rates of school attendance for Irish children aged 5 to 19 were actually higher than for Germans and most other immigrants (Soltow and Stevens, 1981: 137). This is partly because Irish immigrants settled in urban areas such as Boston and New York that were among the earliest champions of public schooling, and most Irish children attended those schools.

Many factors influenced school enrollment of immigrant groups, and the most salient was family wealth, particularly for the Irish. Below the median wealth line, enrollment was cut by more than half, whereby there was a large increase above that line (Soltow and Stevens, 1981: 141). A simple dualism of the time differentiated shanty Irish, rural people whose children had attended irregular hedge schools in Ireland if they had been schooled at all, from lace Irish, whose children had attended urban private and parochial schools. Divisions within groups cannot be summarized so simply, of course, but social class clearly played a part in immigrants' school experiences and access to education.

Irish Catholic immigrants tended to support public education, but some did not want their children to attend a public school system. Part of the reason was a desire to have Catholic instruction and curriculum in their children's schooling, and part was due to the prejudice against them that was prevalent in the society at that time. Protestant school leaders thought that religious instruction in schools should be in nondenominational Christianity, through reading the King James version of the Bible—to which Catholic leaders objected. As early as 1830, Irish leaders had expressed concern with what they called the Protestant schools.

The great school debate of 1840 in New York City became a watershed event in the jousting between Catholic and Protestant school leaders, and presaged the eventual creation of a nationwide Catholic school system. (See Ravitch, 1974: 33–76, for a thorough account of this event.) The debate was initiated by a criticism of common school textbooks that contained passages critical of the Pope and of Catholicism. Catholics argued initially that the schools provided only a Protestant education, and later that in order to provide the appropriate religious education for Catholic children, parochial schools were necessary.

Governor William Seward of New York was concerned about Catholics deserting the public school system, and he proposed that Catholic schools be supported by public funding, yet remain under the administration of Catholic officials. Leaders of the New York Public School Society adamantly opposed that position. The outspoken and charismatic Catholic bishop John Hughes asserted that Catholic schools should be built before churches, because the public schools were anti-Catholic and at the same time lacked serious religious training. When Hughes had become bishop in 1839, there were 8 Catholic churches in New York City, and only 3,000 children attended the churches' schools. The rest of the children attended the public schools or did not attend school (Ravitch, 1974: 37). Some Catholic parents faced double taxation, since they would pay for other children in the public schools as well as for their own children in parochial schools.

The upshot of all the commotion was a public debate held on October 29–30, 1840. Hughes argued vociferously against required public schooling for Catholic children, and in favor of state support for parochial schools (Ravitch, 1974: 53–57). Following the debate, the Catholics' appeal was voted down by city aldermen and stalled in the state legislature until after the 1842 election. The bill eventually enacted was a win/lose for the ardent supporters of Bishop Hughes and the idea of parochial schools. The Public School Society was replaced by a ward-based board of education that was meant to be more responsive to citizens' concerns, and the schools were required to maintain religious neutrality. But there would be no funding for parochial schools (Ravitch, 1974: 79).

Strife around the issue of religion and schooling continued unabated. In 1842, there was a riot in New York City, and an even larger one in Philadelphia, after the public school board ruled that Catholic children could read from their Douay version of the Bible in school (Lannie, 1970: 512; Spring, 2008: 113). The seemingly inexorable movement toward a religious split was underway. The first Plenary Council was held in Baltimore in 1852, which resulted in the rejection of an un-Catholic and godless education. Subsequent plenaries in 1866 and 1884 would end with the establishment of the Catholic school system in the United States. In the schools, religious instruction would take place alongside the regular curriculum, and classes would be taught by nuns and priests. All Catholic parishes were to have a school, and all Catholic parents were duty-bound to send their children to that school.

Unlike the other immigrant groups considered in this chapter, Irish children spoke English and most of them had access to well-supported urban schools at a time when rural schooling was often underfunded. The challenges they faced were daunting, however, as they tried to overcome the social and religious biases against them. For immigrant Norwegians, language and culture were the paramount challenges they faced in their new country.

Norwegians in Koshkonong, Wisconsin

> Our countrymen who first settled on Koshkonong belonged to the industrious and thrifty people still found in Norway's mountain valleys. Accustomed to privation and physical exertion in their native land, they were peculiarly suited to tackle the frontier and clear the way for later groups of immigrants. . . . Consequently, Americans of the older generation admit that "the future belongs to the European immigrants of the present century." (Written in 1868 by Svein Nillson, a Norwegian immigrant to Wisconsin, in Gjerde, 1998: 100)

In 1825, the first Norwegian immigrants arrived in New York City on the ship *Restauration,* and two other ships brought immigrants in 1836. The Norwegians were mainly farmers who came to the United States for religious and economic reasons (see Appendix 5.3, which shows the percentage of agricultural immigrants between 1832 and 1864). Norway had an agricultural economy with insufficient resources to support large farm families, and it was under the political control of Sweden. Immigrants read or heard that there was opportunity in the United States, and after 1862 they were aware of the Homestead Act that promised cheap land in the West. Between 1850 and 1870, 77,873 Norwegians came to America (Lovoll, 1999: 16), and they constituted 50–70 percent of all Scandinavians who came to the United States during that time (see Appendix 5.2).

The earliest Norwegian settlements were in New York and Illinois, but by 1840 Wisconsin had become the largest center of Norwegian immigration. In that year, the town of Koshkonong was founded in South Central Wisconsin. Farmers there grew wheat and later raised dairy cattle. The families who immigrated came with low levels of formal schooling and few had any university education—just like their new American neighbors. What they did come with were a strong Lutheran faith (two churches were erected in 1844–1845 in Koshkonong), a desire to speak their native language, and a drive to maintain their cultural ways in more isolated areas.

In their segregated farming communities, Norwegians did not face the prejudice that many other immigrants felt. Most of them sent their children to the common schools (which they called Yankee or district schools), and they had local control of schools in a largely homogeneous rural environment. However, some Norwegians wanted to give their children religious instruction in school and opted for congregational or church-sponsored schools. Koshkonong's school opened in 1845 so that "the children of the congregation can be taught our church's pure doctrine" (Lovoll, 1999: 99–100). These schools were seen as an addition to the common schools, which were in settlements of any size. Even though all parents wanted their children to learn English, the clergy who operated the congregational schools also wanted to preserve the Norwegian language and Norwegian identity. This stance led to an internecine school debate in the 1850s and 1860s about the place and purpose of the common schools. Most Norwegians supported the common schools and wanted their children to speak English and Norwegian, and to be fully a part of the American society. Those who wanted a separate school system, as some Irish Catholics and Germans were calling for in the Northeast and Ohio River Valley, did not carry the day. But for awhile there was a compromise: The common school would be conquered from within.

> Already in the Manitowoc Declaration of 1866 a hope was expressed "to bring the English school as much as possible under the control of the congregation" by "appointing Norwegian teachers, who are good Lutheran Christians." (Lovoll, 1999: 161)

In this way, many common schools continued to teach both languages for decades. Luther College in Decorah, Iowa, was founded in 1861, as were a number of Lutheran secondary academies modeled after Norwegian schools and planned during a meeting in Koshkonong in 1869. A Norwegian-language press flourished, and Norwegians held more tightly to their native culture than did other Scandinavian groups. Like the Norwegians, Mexicans also wanted the schools to preserve their native language and a religious core, but they faced a far different historical predicament and a more daunting cultural challenge in doing so.

Mexicans in San Antonio (San Fernando de Béxar)

> Sir:—Yours of December 5, 1851, was duly received with regard to school in this County; there is not one at present. . . . A great part of the children in this County are of American fathers, but none speak the English language; which, of course, their parents are most anxious to have them learn. Hence the difficulty—that of getting a teacher who understads [*sic*] both En-

glish and Spanish. (From a clerk in San Luis Obispo County, California, in MacDonald, 2004: 82)

When independence from Spain occurred in 1821, the new Mexican government created the *Plan de Iguala,* which asserted the equality of Spaniards, indigenous people, and mestizos, including the Afro-Mexican population. The Spanish mission system, in which Catholic priests had educated the children of Mexican settlers in the Southwest of what is now the United States, was supposed to uphold this promise of access and equality. However, the idealistic language was largely empty because of unstable national governments and inadequate resources, and by the time of the war with the United States in 1845 the direction and influence of the mission schools had greatly diminished.

In 1848, the Treaty of Guadalupe Hidalgo ended the war between Mexico and the United States, after which the winner took nearly one-half of Mexico's territory. Within those lands lived around 80,000 Mexican and thousands of Native Americans who were suddenly forced to live in another country. The Mexicans were new members of the society caught in a double bind: they owned or worked the land, yet were not automatically citizens of the new U.S. territories and states forged through war. The treaty allowed for three options for the conquered Mexicans: return to Mexico, stay in the United States without becoming a citizen, or wait at least 1 year and then apply for citizenship.

U.S. census figures most certainly undercount the number of Mexican immigrants after 1848 (see Appendix 5.2 for official figures), because it is unclear how many Mexicans opted for U.S. citizenship, how many stayed on the land without benefit of citizenship in their new country, and how many returned to the now-shrunken nation of Mexico. There were about 5,000 Mexicans in Texas at that time (Daniels, 2002: 308), but thousands more, most of them laborers, came to Texas after the war (Ramsey, 2010: 81). These Mexicans, whether their families had lived there for many generations or had just arrived, faced severe discrimination from the majority white citizens who had settled in Texas and promulgated the war.

Culture, religion, and language were interconnected and vitally related to the eventual exclusion or segregation of *Tejanos* (Texans of Mexican ancestry) from public schooling. Except for the elite Mexicans who were landowners before the war and who often claimed to be Spanish to differentiate themselves from the majority *mestizos* (mixed indigenous and Spanish), Mexicans were seen as an inferior race by many Anglos (Ramsey, 2010: 78–81; Spring, 2008: 179–180). Texas was a slave state and there was strong opposition to racial mixing. A missionary teacher who arrived in Brownsville, Texas, in 1852 and later wrote about her experience, expressed the prevailing viewpoint: "I did not feel, as many others have expressed, that the *sight* of a Mexican was enough to disgust one with the whole nation." Her purpose in teaching was to save "a whole nation of souls, shut out from the light of the gospel of salvation"—this said about a population of devout Catholics! (MacDonald, 2004: 77).

Waves of complicated and discriminatory educational policies and practices arose as a result of anti-Catholic sentiment in the 1840s and 1850s, an official position that English should be the primary language of instruction, and the underlying belief that mestizos and Indians were inferior to Anglos. After the 1848 treaty, the social, economic, and even linguistic status of Mexicans declined rapidly. Spanish became a foreign language overnight, although people living in the Southwest (the North of Mexico) had spoken it for several hundred years. Language issues quickly surfaced in Texas, as the common school movement took shape there. In 1854, the "Act to Establish a System of Common Schools" was passed in Texas. Just two years later, an amendment added: "No school shall be entitled to the [monetary] benefits of this act unless the English language is principally taught therein." However, that act was frequently circumvented as Spanish and German speakers "maintained their native languages in many public schools during the transitional decades from the 1850s through 1880s" (MacDonald, 2004: 59).

Laws about language usage in schools then changed for a time during Reconstruction. Bilingual education was seen as a means of attracting Mexicans and Germans into the public schools, rather than the parochial schools (Ramsey, 2010: 83). In a ruling by the new superintendent of public instruction in 1871, teachers were permitted to teach German, French, and Spanish in the public schools, but for no more than two hours per day (MacDonald, 2004: 59; official statement on page 74). This affirmed what was already taking place: Germans and Mexicans, particularly in rural communities, were conducting much of the curriculum in their native language. A subsequent statement by another superintendent in 1886 noted the persistence of other languages and complaints about such use, and stated that English should be the sole language of instruction or "it promises much harm to public school interests" (MacDonald, 2004: 75).

San Antonio de Béxar (alternative spelling "Béjar") had been founded in 1718, and it became Texas's most populous city in the 19th century. There was strong support among the Mexicans there, whether citizens or not, for public schooling and for the inclusion of their language. *El Bexareño,* the Spanish language newspaper, openly supported public education in two languages (MacDonald, 2004: 59). Many students, though, were educated in church-sponsored institutions. Ursuline Academy was founded by nuns in 1851, to educate girls from elite families in Spanish, French, and English. The Ursuline sisters also created a free day school for poorer Mexican children, which was later operated by another religious order. Priests founded a secondary academy that soon became St. Mary's University for boys in 1852 (MacDonald, 2004: 61).

Not all Mexicans wanted their children in Catholic parochial schools. Some parents hoped that their children would learn English quickly and adapt to their new country, and their children attended free Protestant institutions such as the Presbyterian Day School, begun in the 1840s. Others held anticlerical beliefs that led them to enroll their child in the few common schools (MacDonald, 2004: 63). No matter their school preference, Mexicans wanted an education that would allow their children to be bilingual and that did not disrupt their traditional culture. Chinese immigrants to the West Coast had similar goals for their children, although their numbers were smaller and their exclusion would be even more severe.

Chinese in San Francisco

> The treatment of the Chinese in this country is all wrong and mean. . . . He cannot practice any trade, and his opportunities to do business are limited to his own countrymen. So he opens a laundry when he quits domestic service. . . . There is no reason for the prejudice against the Chinese. The cheap labor cry was always a falsehood. Their labor was never cheap, and is not cheap now. (From Lee Chew, a Chinese immigrant who came to the United States in the mid-19th century, in Gjerde, 1998: 172)

After gold was found at Sutter's mill in 1849, thousands of Chinese laborers came to California to work as miners. In the 1860s, there were 16,000 Chinese men working in the gold fields (Spring, 2008: 183). Many of them settled in cities, and later worked in large numbers to help build the intercontinental railroad system in the United States. They lived in Chinatowns and a strict cultural isolation was enforced—by the Chinese themselves, and as the result of whites' animosity toward them. Chinese were seen as aliens, and were classified in the official racial schemes as Mongols or Mongolians.

By 1870, there were 49,277 Chinese living in California, which constituted 78 percent of all Chinese in the United States (Daniels, 2002: 240). Most of the immigrants were men, and most intended to return to

China with money obtained in the United States, in order to marry and raise a family there. Although there was perhaps a 20:1 ratio of immigrant Chinese males to females, there *were* children who needed education, and a large number of them lived in San Francisco. According to the 1880 and 1890 censuses, 20 percent of all Chinese in America resided in San Francisco, and many of them lived in family units (Daniels, 2002: 242). So it was in San Francisco that "the battle for public education [of Chinese] was fought" (Ramsey, 2010: 92). Unlike the Germans, Norwegians, and even Mexicans, who were able to have bilingual instruction in private and sometimes public schools, bilingual education for Chinese children was discouraged. Chinese spoke a non-European language with a different script that seemed quite unintelligible, and therefore was suspect.

In 1860, there were only 106 Chinese children under age 16 in San Francisco, and they made up but 4 percent of the Chinese population. By 1870, the number of children had increased to 1,546, which was 13 percent of the Chinese living there (Jorae, 2009: 46). A majority of these children were males, and both girls and boys had to work to support their families, so their educational and labor circumstances were unusual. The 1870 Census recorded that 13 percent of all children in the United States between the ages of 10 and 15 were employed. The figures for San Francisco showed that 92 percent of all Chinese children were in the labor force, as domestic servants, cooks, gardeners, launderers, and factory workers (see Jorae, 2009: 79–84, for further descriptions of the labor issues).

Early on, church leaders created Sunday schools and evening schools for Chinese adults. After the late 1840s, common schools were being opened in California, which might have helped to integrate the new immigrant children. However, in 1855, the California Supreme Court ruled in the Chan Yong case that Chinese were not white and thus could not be U.S. citizens. A corresponding state law held that public funding could only be used for the education of white children. The state superintendent of public instruction believed that inferior races such as the Chinese should not mix with white children. So in response to a petition by Chinese parents, in 1859, a Chinese school was created in San Francisco, which became an evening school in 1860 because such a high percentage of children worked during the day (Jorae, 2009: 113).

There was some latitude with regard to language in the school, though, because informal and officially forbidden bilingual instruction took place. More liberal state superintendents in the mid- to late 1860s wanted the Chinese school to have a Chinese-speaking and English-speaking teacher (which did not come to pass), and parents of nonwhites were allowed to form their own segregated schools. But in the end, state and local politics would lead to further discrimination:

> In 1870 a new state segregation law provided for the creation of separate schools for black and Indian children but failed to mention the Chinese at all. This justified the decision of the San Francisco Board of Education to shut down the Chinese Public School and deny Chinese children access to even a segregated education. (Jorae, 2009: 113)

The *Report of the Commissioner of Education for the Year 1870* represented an official perspective on Chinese society and the education of Chinese children. The author was rather generous in favorably comparing the Chinese civilization to that of the United States, and dismissed "outcries against the horrors of 'amalgamation' and 'miscegenation.'" However, there was a caution about the vices of the Chinese, which were "rather moral and religious than political, as their superstition, their idolatry, their gambling propensities, their love of opium."

The way for the Chinese to gain the approval of native Americans would be to become Americanized through the adoption of the American language, adoption of American dress and habits, adoption of American homes, adoption of American manners, and eventually, admission to citizenship. The focus was on domestication of these immigrants, which meant that Chinese should meld into the American and Christian pattern of social beliefs and behavior. This "new element" would "be assimilated to the highest, completest [*sic*] form of our civilization, as intelligent, free, Christian" by being educated in the common schools (Johnson, 2002: 168–171).

Such lofty rhetoric notwithstanding from the commissioner, the popular sentiment was racist and was adamantly opposed to joint common schooling for white and Chinese children. Chinese people's legal status paralleled their educational segregation. The federal Naturalization Act of 1870 limited citizenship to "White persons and persons of African descent," so that the Chinese could not become citizens. Then the Exclusion Act of 1882 fully prohibited further Chinese immigration on the grounds that they were inassimilable. This meant that until 1943—a period of 61 years!—no Chinese person could legally enter the United States or become a citizen if already living in the country (Daniels, 2002: 245). Chinese were the only named national group that was not allowed to enter the United States. Respect for Chinese culture and access to equal schooling lay beyond the far horizon.

After 1865

At the close of the Civil War, the common school movement had taken root in the North and Midwest. It would be decades before schools for all children were available in the South, and then the schools would be separate and unequal according to one's race. The second large wave of European immigrants, led by Germans and Irish, had largely crested; the Norwegians and other Scandinavians would continue to settle in rural areas and move westward; while the third wave would begin in the 1880s, and would see Asians and Southern and Eastern Europeans enter the country in huge numbers. Thus, the long-term educational dynamics of the groups examined in this chapter were in place by 1865.

German immigrants fared relatively well throughout the 19th century and in many cases shaped the schools to their liking. However, their very gradual assimilation was speeded up by anti-German reactions during World War I. This would spell an end to bilingual schools and lead to a marked decrease in German instruction in the schools.

After 1865, there was increasing participation by the *Irish* in the urban educational and political systems, and an accompanying intermarriage with other groups, even while the separate Catholic school system developed nationwide. It would take many decades for Irish children to escape the strong stereotypes about them fostered by other Europeans in the mid-19th century.

Mexicans continued to face social and educational discrimination in states from Texas to California. A patchwork quilt of public and private schooling would hold together through the coming years of official school segregation and unofficial neglect, until the 20th century surges of immigration and court cases would finally ensure equal access to public schools.

Following the Civil War, *Norwegians* and other Scandinavians kept moving to the Midwest and West, and to cities as well as small towns. Their isolation slowly lessened, the language-specific newspapers died out, the bilingual classroom instruction ceased, and the religiously oriented high school academies closed. However, even into the 1950s, the Norwegian language was kept alive in everyday speech within certain rural areas, although its heyday as a language of instruction had long passed (Munch, 1949).

Chinese continued to experience outright exclusion and discrimination in California for many decades. In 1875, the San Francisco Board of Education integrated black children into the public school system under pressure from parents in the aftermath of Reconstruction—but kept Chinese children out. From 1871 to 1885, Chinese children could not be publicly schooled in San Francisco, which was justified in part because of the disease and immorality in Chinatown. Only after a California Supreme Court ruling in 1885 were Chinese children given access to public schooling, in the form of a new, segregated Chinese primary public school (Jorae, 2009: 114).

Many other groups made their way to the United States before the end of the Civil War, among them French and French Canadians, Swedes and Dutch, and Scotch and Italians. They, too, had stories to tell of religious, linguistic, and cultural struggles that affected their success in a new home. By 1865, most of these other immigrants had access to a common schooling; but they also had an uncommon schooling because of differences in educational experiences that depended on where they lived and on how they were perceived by others. One of the main motives of schooling was to Americanize the immigrants, but many immigrants wanted to be citizens without wholly disregarding their heritage. Here are the words of Marcus Ravage, a Romanian immigrant, writing in 1917:

> [The immigrant] has not sprung out of nowhere. Quite the contrary. He brings with him a deep-rooted tradition, a system of culture and tastes and habits—a point of view which is as ancient as his national experience. (Daniels, 2002: 102)

Many of the arguments about educational issues noted in this chapter still resonate in our society, such as the role of bilingual education or the place of religion in schools. And each person who arrives here for the first time faces the same centuries-old challenge: to find their place without losing their cultural identity.

Appendix 5.1 Size of the Population for Three Major Cities in 1850/1860, with Rank in U.S.; Percentage of Foreign-Born Population for Three Major Cities in 1850/1860, with Rank in U.S.

	New York	Cincinnati	San Francisco
1850 Popul.	515,547 (1st)	15,435 (6th)	34,776 (17th)
% Foreign-Born	45.7% (4th)	47.2% (5th)	53.4% (1st) (1852 data; 1850 records destroyed by fire)
1860 Popul.	813,669 (1st)	161,044 (7th)	56,802 (14th)
% Foreign-Born	47.2% (4th)	45.7% (5th)	50.1% (2nd)

Source: Gibson, C., and Lennon, E. 1999. Table 20: *Nativity of the Population for the 25 Largest Urban Places and for Selected Counties: 1850, 1860.* Washington, DC: U.S. Census Bureau, Population Division. http://www.census.gov/population/www/documentation/twps0029/tab20.html (1860); http://www.census.gov/population/www/documentation/twps0029/tab21.html (1850).

Appendix 5.2 Percentage of Immigrant Population, by National Origin

	Germans	Irish	*German + Irish*	Mexicans	Norwegians	Chinese
1850	26.0%	42.8%	*68.8%*	0.6%	0.6% (70.1% of all Scandinavians)	0%
1860	30.8%	38.9%	*69.7%*	0.7%	1.1% (60.6% of all Scandinavians)	0.9%
1870	30.4%	33.3%	*63.7%*	0.8%	2.1% (47.3% of all Scandinavians)	1.1%
Highest % of Foreign-Born, in 19th Cen.	1870	1850	*1860*	1880 (1.0%)	1890 (3.5%)	1880 (1.6%)

Source: Gibson, C., and Lennon, E. 1999. *Region and Country or Area of Birth of the Foreign-Born Population, with Geographic Detail Shown in Decennial Census Publications of 1930 or Earlier: 1850 to 1930 and 1960 to 1990*. Washington, DC: U.S. Bureau of the Census. http://www.census.gov/population/www/documentation/twps0029/tab04.html.

Appendix 5.3 Percentage of Immigrant Population, by Occupation

	Farmers	Laborers
1820–1831	23%	14%
1832–1846	33%	24%
1847–1854	33%	41%
1855–1864	23%	37%
Greatest Percentage	1832–1854 (led by Germans & Scandinavians)	1847–1854 (led by Irish)

Source: Cohn, R. L. 2010. "Immigration to the United States." Economic History Association. http://eh.net/encyclopedia/article/cohn.immigration.us.

References

American Jewish Historical Society. 1999. *American Jewish Desk Reference.* New York: Random House.

Cohn, Raymond L. 2010. "Immigration to the United States." Economic History Association. Available at: http://eh.net/encyclopedia/article/cohn.immigration.us.

Daniels, Roger. 2002. *Coming to America: A History of Immigration and Ethnicity in American Life.* 2nd ed. New York: Perennial.

Gibson, Campbell, and Emily Lennon. 1999. "Table 4. Region and Country or Area of Birth of the Foreign-Born Population, With Geographic Detail Shown in Decennial Census Publications of 1930 or Earlier: 1850 to 1930 and 1960 to 1990." *U.S. Census Bureau.* Available at: http://www.census.gov/population/www/documentation/twps0029/tab04.html.

Gibson, Campbell, and Emily Lennon. 1999. "Table 20. Nativity of the Population for the 25 Largest Urban Places and for Selected Counties: 1860." *U.S. Census Bureau, Population Division.* Available at: http://www.census.gov/population/www/documentation/twps0029/tab20.html.

Gibson, Campbell, and Emily Lennon. 1999. "Table 21. Nativity of the Population for the 25 Largest Urban Places and for Selected Counties: 1850," *U.S. Census Bureau, Population Division.* Available at: http://www.census.gov/population/www/documentation/twps0029/tab21.html.

Gjerde, Jon, ed. 1998. *Major Problems in American Immigration and Ethnic History.* Boston, MA: Houghton Mifflin.

Glenn, Charles L., Jr. 1988. *The Myth of the Common School.* Amherst, MA: University of Massachusetts Press.

Johnson, Tony W., and Ronald F. Reed, eds. 2002. *Historical Documents in American Education.* Boston, MA: Allyn and Bacon.

Jorae, Wendy R. 2009. *The Children of Chinatown: Growing up Chinese American in San Francisco, 1850–1920.* Chapel Hill, NC: University of North Carolina Press.

Kaestle, Carl F. 1983. *Pillars of the Republic: Common Schools and American Society, 1780–1860.* New York: Hill and Wang.

Lannie, Vincent P. 1970. "Alienation in America: The Immigrant Catholic and Public Education in Pre-Civil War America." *The Review of Politics* 32(4): 503–21.

Lovoll, Odd. S. 1999. *The Promise of America: A History of the Norwegian-American People.* Minneapolis, MN: University of Minnesota Press.

MacDonald, Victoria-María, ed. 2004. *Latino Education in the United States: A Narrated History from 1513 to 2000.* New York: Palgrave Macmillan.

Meyer, John W., David Tyack, Joane Nagel, and Audri Gordon. 1979. "Public Education as Nation-Building in America: Enrollments and Bureaucratization in the American States, 1870–1930." *American Journal of Sociology* 85(3): 591–609.

Munch, Peter A. 1949. "Social Adjustment among Wisconsin Norwegians." *American Sociological Review* 14(6): 780–87.

Ramsey, Paul J. 2009. "In the Region of Babel: Public Bilingual Schooling in the Midwest, 1840s–1880s." *History of Education Quarterly* 49(3): 267–90.

Ramsey, Paul J. 2010. *Bilingual Public Schooling in the United States: A History of America's "Polyglot Boardinghouse."* New York: Palgrave Macmillan.

Ravitch, Diane. 1974. *The Great School Wars: New York City, 1805–1973.* New York: Basic Books.

Soltow, Lee, and Edward Stevens. 1981. *The Rise of Literacy and the Common School in the United States: A Socioeconomic Analysis to 1870.* Chicago, IL: University of Chicago Press.

Spring, Joel. 2008. *The American School: From the Puritans to No Child Left Behind.* 7th ed. New York: McGraw-Hill.

Tolzmann, Don T. 2005. *Images of America: German Cincinnati.* Charleston, SC: Arcadia Publishing.

CHAPTER SIX

Political Parties and Immigration in the Early Republic

Scot J. Zentner

Introduction

The American Declaration of Independence appeals to the rights of all human beings, but it asserts the claims of a single people. This seems to imply a potential conflict between the universal principle of equality and the claims of a particular people dedicated to that principle. This same conflict is at the heart of debates over immigration. Consider George Washington's statement that we will welcome immigrants only "if by decency and propriety of conduct they appear to merit the enjoyment" (LeMay and Barkan, 1999: 10). According to Washington, the United States is in principle open to all immigrants, but as a practical matter only some may be suitable for citizenship.

The founding fathers' debate over immigration and naturalization focused on just what qualities were necessary for citizenship. The Constitutional Convention deliberated over residency requirements for federal office and set forth two broad views of the subject. On one extreme were those who argued that lengthy residency periods would allow immigrants to develop the habits and opinions necessary to be part of American social and political life. They emphasized the need for social cohesion and a shared national identity. On the other extreme were those who argued that, by their very effort to come to America, immigrants demonstrated the qualities of independence and liberty necessary for citizenship. They thought citizenship itself would induce fealty to the country and encourage civic virtue. This division between the nationalist and civic elements of citizenship has been a part of the disputes over immigration and naturalization ever since (Pickus, 2005: 1–13).

Immigration and citizenship have been recurrent issues of partisan conflict, particularly when either there is a significant foreign policy crisis or when there is a large wave of immigrants into the country. The 1790s are an example of the former; the 1850s are an example of the latter. In both of these decisive periods, the more egalitarian and liberal party won. Yet, in neither case did the victorious party claim that there were no requirements or qualities that constituted proper American citizenship. Rather, like their opponents, they maintained distinct and fairly thorough views of citizenship. Throughout U.S. history, there has been a division between a more populist party and a less populist party (Reichley, 1992). The more populist party has emphasized the civic dimensions of citizenship, the less populist party the nationalist dimensions.

In the election of 1800, the party more hostile to immigration (the Federalists) was defeated by Thomas Jefferson's Republican Party. In 1860, a significant anti-immigrant group (the Know Nothings) was largely absorbed into Abraham Lincoln's victorious Republican Party, the party dedicated to halting the expansion of slavery. Both periods culminated in what political scientists call partisan realignments, decisive national shifts in party preference and allegiance (Sundquist, 1983). The Jeffersonian realignment was distinctive principally because it was the first of its kind in history. The Lincolnian realignment was distinctive because, among other things, it overturned the first mature party system in U.S. history. Both realignments amounted to quasi-revolutionary moments. Immigration and citizenship were significant issues in both, but in each case the essentially egalitarian and republican side of American politics prevailed.

This chapter reviews the development of the parties, from the founding to the Civil War, and explores that development in connection with immigration and citizenship. First, it examines the origin and course of the first American parties in the 1790s, particularly the relationship between partisan notions of citizenship and foreign policy. Second, it examines the development of the mass party system and the rise of nativism, and the origin of the Lincolnian Republican Party out of these conditions. Throughout, the character of the citizenry remains the central issue in the partisan conflict over immigration.

Citizenship, War, and Opposition Parties

Antipathy toward partisanship has been a common sentiment throughout most of American history, especially during the founding period. In his farewell address to the nation, and in the midst of the emerging party system of the 1790s, Washington warned against the dangers of party opposition to the government (Rhodehamel, 1997: 968). Such opposition served "to make the public administration the mirror of the ill-concerted and incongruous projects of faction, rather than the organ of consistent and wholesome plans digested by common counsels, and modified by mutual interests." Under such conditions, "cunning, ambitious, and unprincipled men" would surely arise. Factionalism and demagoguery could destroy the constitutional republic. Washington thought that once a government is duly elected, it is inappropriate for citizens or particular officials to criticize it; such criticism amounting to disloyalty. At the time, most Americans agreed with him. It is not surprising, then, that the founding fathers did not consider thematically the need for or desirability of a national party system.

The question of factions or parties emerged during the debates over the framing and ratification of the Constitution. The new government was intended to blunt or control, rather than enhance, the spirit of parties. This is central to James Madison's famous argument for the extended republic in *Federalist* 10 and 51 (Rossiter, 2003: 71–79, 320–22). There he argues that factional strife, which had been a bane to the political life of the states, would be rendered benign by competition of a multitude of groups. They would, in effect, cancel out each other. Compared with state legislators, members of the new federal Congress would have to account for so many different interested and passionate groups that they would tend not to rule in the interest of any one group. Given the many pressures to which each legislator would be subject, congressional majorities typically would form only through a coalition of diverse interests. The coalescing process itself would encourage compromise and moderation. The result presumably would be the creation of laws and policies more conducive to the general interests rather than the particular interests of local factions.

The policy-making process took an unexpected turn from the outset of President Washington's administration. Treasury Secretary Alexander Hamilton began advocating a series of policies aimed at increasing the scope and power of the central government. The main elements were the federal assumption of state debts, the creation of a national bank, and measures to develop manufacturing in the United States. The objective was to secure the public credit and bind the states into a single commercial nation (Frisch, 1985: 248–75, 277–317, 331–34). To accomplish these ends, Hamilton thought, energetic and proactive leadership from the executive branch was necessary. In effect, the Congress would be led by the president.

Hamilton did not think his plan represented any real departure from the original Federalist effort to establish the Constitution. Yet it almost immediately generated opposition, most notably from Secretary of State Thomas Jefferson. As Washington tended to follow Hamilton's advice on policy matters, Jefferson increasingly felt himself distanced from the government. It became apparent to Jefferson that the formation of legislative majorities amenable to his views would require more than the deliberative process anticipated in *The Federalist.* Soon he was leading a broad public movement to stop Hamilton's program. This movement included the formation of democratic societies critical of the government and the creation of newspapers advocating limited federal power. It came to be called the Jeffersonian Republican Party, the first concerted national party in U.S. history.

Madison joined Jefferson in this effort, though he originally cooperated with Hamilton during the framing and ratification of the Constitution. While in *The Federalist* he had warned of majority faction, Madison came to realize the need to create a national majority through party leadership. He had earlier argued that majorities would indeed form, but for the most part only as coalitions of interests within the national legislature. He had not fully anticipated the problem of energy and leadership in policy-making. There was essentially a vacuum of leadership that Hamilton sought to fill through executive initiative. As early as 1791, Madison realized that the coalescing of interests within the legislature was not occurring as he had predicted. The legislature, he argued, had become captive to Hamilton's agenda (Zvesper, 1984). Along with Jefferson, Madison became concerned that the eventual result of the Federalist plan would be the consolidation of all governments in the Union under a quasi-monarchical president. A consolidation of interests throughout the nation, and by means of the Republican Party, Madison now argued, was necessary to counter this consolidation of government (Meyers, 1981: 181–83).

Madison suggested that the Republican Party was moved by more than opposition to a narrow set of public policies. The party was animated by a specifically *republican* set of principles. He argued that all societies tended to divide into two groups, those who are more and those who are less confident in the capacity of the people to govern itself. Federalists were not just proponents of different public policies; they adhered to a different conception of citizenship. The Federalists, Madison wrote, are "those, whom from particular interest, from natural temper, or from the habits of life, are more partial to the opulent than to the other classes of society; and having debauched themselves into a persuasion that mankind are incapable of governing themselves, it follows with them of course, that government can be carried on only by the pageantry of rank, the influence of money and emoluments, and the terror of military force" (Meyers, 1981: 189). Republicans are the opposite. According to Madison, they believe in self-government, hate hereditary power, and support republican forms and the general interests of the community. Of course, Hamilton and his fellow Federalists supported these things as well. But for Madison, the Federalist agenda betrayed an appreciation of monarchical forms inconsistent with genuine republicanism. To Madison, the two political parties represented something like classical regime types, one more democratic and the other more aristocratic, though each claimed to be the embodiment of true republicanism (Gerring, 1998: 257–59, 263). Republicans routinely accused Federalists of favoring monarchy or aristocracy; Federalists accused Republicans of being Jacobins or mere democrats.

As the 1790s wore on, these criticisms were couched more and more in terms of the intensifying conflict between revolutionary France and monarchical Britain (Hofstadter, 1969: 88). Jefferson suggested that Hamilton had been "bewitched and perverted by the British example." He thought Hamilton's preference for energetic government betrayed contempt for the people and a threat to their liberties. "Hamilton was not only a monarchist," he argued, "but for a monarchy bottomed on corruption" (Koch and Peden, 1944: 512–13, 126–27). The Federalist claim to moderation, Jefferson argued, was really a mask for monarchical or oligarchic aims. But Hamilton thought Jefferson "drank freely of the French philosophy, in Religion, in Science, in politics. He came from France in the moment of a fermentation which he had had a share in exciting, and in the passions and feeling of which he shared both from temperament and situation" (Syrett, 1961–1987: 11:439). According to Hamilton, the French philosophy, with its evident exuberance and imprudence, reflected a vulgarization of decent republicanism.

This partisan division translated into distinct views of immigration and naturalization. In keeping with their more democratic tendencies, the Jeffersonian Republicans generally favored less restrictive naturalization laws. The Federalists saw this openness to immigrants as evidence of Jeffersonian identification with antirepublican elements. These opposed views were evident during the debates over the nation's first naturalization law in 1790, even though the party lines were only beginning to form at that time (Cunningham, 1957: 82). Virginia Republican John Page made the strongest argument against any residency requirements for naturalization: "It is nothing to us, whether Jews or Roman Catholics settle amongst us; whether subjects of Kings, or citizens of free states wish to reside in the United States, they will find it their interest to be good citizens, and neither their religious nor political opinions can injure us, if we have good laws, well executed." He objected to the demand that candidates for citizenship provide character references for naturalization, arguing that this would lead to tests of political or partisan allegiance (*Annals of the Congress,* 1849: 1:1149, 1153). Page's arguments reflected the view that citizenship itself would tend to induce in the immigrant the loyalty and habits necessary for republican life. More so than even most Republicans, he emphasized the appeal to a certain civic humanism as the guiding principle of naturalization policy.

Massachusetts Federalist Theodore Sedgwick disagreed. He doubted that the laws, however good and well-executed, could have immediate effect on the habits and opinions of the Europeans who would come to the United States. "[T]heir sensations," he argued, "impregnated with prejudices of education, acquired under monarchical and aristocratical Governments, may deprive them of that zest for pure republicanism, which is necessary in order to taste its beneficence with that gratitude which we feel on the occasion. Some kind of probation . . . is absolutely requisite, to enable them to feel and be sensible of the blessing" (*Annals,* 1849: 1:1156). As would be the case with Federalists generally, Sedgwick emphasized the importance of a relatively long habituation into the national or political ethos of the United States. Civic engagement was not enough. The 1790 Naturalization Act as eventually adopted was quite liberal, but reflected certain nationalist concerns expressed by Sedgwick and others. It required only two years residency prior to naturalization (much shorter than most European countries), proof of good character, an oath of affirmation to support the Constitution (but no requirement to renounce allegiance to the former government), and that those naturalized were free white persons (LeMay and Barkan, 1999, Document 7: 11).

It is worth noting that the two party leaders, Jefferson and Hamilton, generally agreed on the rudimentary requirements of citizenship. Hamilton wrote: "The safety of a republic depends essentially on the energy of a common national sentiment. . . . [F]oreigners will . . . entertain opinions on government congenial with those under which they have lived; or if they should be led hither from a preference to ours, how extremely unlikely is it they will bring with them that temperate love of liberty so essential to real republicanism" (Syrett, 1961–1987: 25:496). Hamilton here is concerned that the rigorous requirements of liberty, as he understands them, may be difficult for some immigrants to meet. Jefferson, his partisan nemesis, made a very similar argument:

> Every species of government has its specific principles. Ours perhaps are more peculiar than those of another in the universe. . . . To these nothing can be more opposed than the maxims of absolute monarchies. Yet from such we are to expect the greatest number of emigrants. They will bring with them the principles of the government they leave, imbibed in their early youth; or, if able to throw them off, it will be in exchange for an unbounded licentiousness, passing, as is usual, from one extreme to another. It would be a miracle were they to stop precisely at the point of temperate liberty. (Koch and Peden, 1944: 217)

It is striking that the Federalist Hamilton and the Republican Jefferson both emphasize the need for citizens to possess temperate liberty, a habitual self-control. They both believed that citizenship in a republic required specific virtues. This was not an uncommon concern during the founding period. For example, a number of Republican Party members, Madison among them, as well as Federalists, at various times argued for property qualifications for voting. The belief was that something like personal self-sufficiency and the consequent capacity to render unbiased judgments were legitimate conditions for full voting rights. Madison would eventually decide against property qualifications, but only as it became evident that ordinary Americans were, in fact, impartial enough to justify expansion of the franchise. In the case of immigration, too, the parties agreed on the need for republican virtue. What they disagreed on was the precise meaning of that virtue and how it was to be attained.

The party conflict intensified as the foreign policy issues of the later 1790s intensified, especially the question of the American posture toward the Anglo-French war then raging. The Republicans identified with the French in that struggle, the Federalists with the British. By the middle of the decade the United States was slowly being drawn into the war, with actual clashes between American merchant vessels and the two warring powers. In 1793, President Washington issued a proclamation of neutrality in the war. Madison attacked and Hamilton defended the proclamation. In the same year, tensions arose between the Washington administration and the French government when the latter appointed Edmound Genet minister to the United States. Genet was charged with gathering privateers in America to wreak havoc on British shipping. Washington ordered Genet to cease his activities, while Genet, who was quite popular at that moment, asserted that he would take his cause directly to the American people. The following year, the Washington administration negotiated an agreement, known as the Jay Treaty, with Great Britain. The treaty, named for chief negotiator John Jay and largely orchestrated by Hamilton, resolved several disputes with the British and established smoother trade relations between the two countries. Jefferson and Madison opposed the agreement. It was ratified by the Senate in 1795, contributing to the growing agitation for war between France and the United States. Formal war was never declared, but tensions with France continued as it descended into political turmoil.

This was the context of Congress's renewed debate over naturalization in late 1794. Page and Sedgwick again traded ripostes over the question. Page reiterated his argument in favor of an open path to citizenship, but emphasized that he was not indifferent to the question of the virtues and habits of immigrants. He "thought nothing more desirable than to see good order, public virtue, and true morality, constituting the character of citizens of the United States" (*Annals,* 1849: 3:1004). But the Congress and the nation were becoming wary of the conditions in the country and the world. Sedgwick's comments reflected the new realities. He noted that a "war, the most cruel and dreadful which had been known for centuries, was now raging in all those countries from which emigrants were to be expected. The most fierce and unrelenting passions were engaged in a conflict, which shook to their foundations all the ancient political structures in Europe." He argued that the war was fought between those who believed that "personal political distinctions" were the basis of security and those who believed in a more unbridled democracy "without checks." He rhetorically asked whether it was reasonable to believe that "men who, actuated by such passions, had fought on grounds so opposite, almost equally distant from the happy mean we had chosen, would here mingle in social affections with each other, or with us? That their passions and prejudices would subside as soon as they should set foot in America? Or, that, possessing those passions and prejudices, they were qualified to make or to be made the governors of Americans?" (*Annals,* 1849: 3:1008). The changed circumstances in the country made many Americans more open to this argument. Though Sedgwick did not achieve the more extensive reforms that he wanted, the new law did increase the strictures on naturalization, including an increased residency requirement from two to five years and a requirement that applicants for citizenship not only affirm allegiance to the United States but renounce allegiance to their former sovereigns (see LeMay and Barkan, 1999, Document 8: 12).

The fear of foreign influence increased over the next three years, causing even greater partisan conflict. In early 1798, details of the XYZ Affair became known, in which French agents had demanded bribes from

American emissaries in order to restore diplomatic relations between France and the United States. The French then embarked on what has become known as the Quasi War in which hundreds of American vessels were captured at sea. The United States responded in kind. At the same time, many Federalists considered the emergent Irish Rebellion to be an added threat, particularly as many Catholic refugees from that conflict might find their way to the United States. As we shall see in the next section, the nationalist view of citizenship coincided with a certain suspicion of Catholicism. At home, the result was a wave of support for the Federalists and victory for the party in the elections later that year. It was in this heated political context that the Federalists, with John Adams as president, passed in quick succession the Alien and Sedition Acts and Naturalization Act of 1798. These were a series of laws ostensibly intended to control enemy aliens and seditious citizens, as well as to restrict or even deport any immigrants who might be hostile to the United States (see LeMay and Barkan, 1999, Documents 9 and 10: 13–16). Although passed in the flush of pro-Federalist enthusiasm, the reaction to these laws would, in turn, result in the landslide Republican victory of 1800.

The principal innovation of the 1798 Naturalization Act was the increased residency requirement for citizenship from 5 to 14 years. The act also included an earlier date for declaration of intent to naturalize, increased certification fees, and specific reporting requirements for new immigrants. The Alien Act granted the president broad discretion to deport aliens whom he considered dangerous to the peace and safety of the United States. Perhaps the most controversial of the new laws was the Sedition Act, which made it a crime for any citizen to criticize the government too stridently. These laws shared the same general impetus: Federalist fear of a coordinated effort by citizens and aliens in support of the Republican cause. Indeed, some Federalists proposed more extreme measures, including a system of surveillance and reporting to monitor supposed conspiracies against the government. Harrison Gray Otis of Massachusetts proposed allowing only native-born citizens to hold public office. Robert Goodlow Harper of South Carolina went a step further and advocated that only natives be allowed to vote (Pickus, 2005: 41). These more extreme measures were voted down, but even their having been proposed reflected the anxieties of the moment.

Some of the actions and proposals at the time were narrowly partisan. Indeed, some observers have suggested that there was a fair degree of hypocrisy on the part of Jefferson and Hamilton during this time. While Hamilton did not necessarily support the more extreme proposals of Otis and Harper, he did not oppose the Acts as passed in 1798

(Syrett, 1961–1987: 21:490, 495, 522). This tacit acceptance was perhaps in some tension with the fact that Hamilton himself was not a native-born American. It also contrasted with Hamilton's earlier views (Chernow, 2004: 600, 822). For example, in the Constitutional Convention he had argued against any residency requirements for eligibility to membership in the House or the Senate, stating that "the advantage of encouraging foreigners is obvious. . . . Persons in Europe of moderate fortunes will be fond of coming here, where they will be on a level with the first citizens" (Bowen, 1966: 208). Jefferson's actions during the 1790s likewise may be interpreted as more partisan than principled. He earlier expressed serious doubts about the wisdom of granting citizenship to just anyone. Yet he would support Republican attempts to remove virtually all conditions on naturalization.

The height of the party battle occurred with passage of resolutions in the Virginia and Kentucky state legislatures condemning the Alien and Sedition Acts. The resolutions, drafted by Madison and Jefferson, asserted that the acts were unconstitutional extensions of federal power and encroachments on the states. Jefferson's original draft of the Kentucky Resolutions asserted that nullification of congressional acts was a justifiable exercise of state power (Peterson, 1986: 286). Madison did not go that far in the Virginia Resolutions; he eventually authored a report on the Resolutions detailing his argument for a more moderate expression of protest. This report was adopted in early 1800 and became an important part of the election campaign that year. "The Virginia Report," Marvin Meyers has noted, "became the classic statement of Republican opposition principles. Stepping delicately between the duties of national loyalty and the ultimate right of revolution, Madison emphasized the legitimate constitutional means of 'interposition' open to the states" (Meyers, 1981: 230). Madison's argument for interposition outlined a notion of national political parties, using states as their platforms, as quasi-revolutionary organizations occasionally necessary to oppose federal power (Zentner, 2005). He argued, in effect, that political parties were justifiable vehicles necessary to watch over and even warn governments not to overstep their proper bounds.

Fortunately, the conflict between Federalists and Republicans did not devolve into revolution or civil war. The immediate threat to the United States from France began to wane in 1800 as Napoleon Bonaparte consolidated his power. The Irish Rebellion passed as well. The reactionary pro-British feeling thus began to recede and the sentiments of the American people reverted to the Republican Party. After the party's historic victory in 1800, President Jefferson famously remarked in his first inaugural address: "We have called by different names brethren of the same principle. We are all federalists—we are all republicans" (Peterson, 1986: 291–92). This apparently meant that the party dispute was not so great as to prevent the two sides from coming together. This new unity was perhaps symbolized by the 1802 repeal of the 14-year residency requirement for naturalization (see LeMay and Barkan, 1999, Document 11: 16–18).

However, Jefferson also would note elsewhere that: "The Revolution of 1800 was as real a revolution in the principles of government as that of 1776 was in its form" (Lipscomb and Bergh, 1903–1905: 15:212). The divide between the parties had become intense. They had begun to think of themselves, for a while at least, almost as if they were opposed peoples. Republicans likened Federalists to the British. Federalists likened Republicans to the French. Their views of immigrants followed accordingly. But the Federalists would eventually cease to exist as an organized force in American politics, much as the Loyalists did after the Revolution. With the success of the Revolution of 1800, it seemed, parties were no longer necessary. In truth, for Jefferson, Americans were not all Federalists and Republicans; they were now really only Republicans. In this sense, the party battle of the 1790s was something like a nonviolent civil war. The conclusion of that war seemed to bring with it the end of important differences, including differences over who was and was not suited to become an American.

Nativism, Slavery, and Mass Parties

By the early 1820s, the Federalists were no longer a viable national party. Virtually every major political figure claimed to be a Republican. However, because every prominent leader acted under the same party label, public understanding of the principles and policies of the candidates became problematic. The result was a situation in which politicians, in effect, nominated themselves for public office, with only their personal prestige or affiliations to recommend them. This came to a head in the presidential contest of 1824, in which four candidates eventually received votes in the Electoral College. Even though Andrew Jackson gained a plurality of the vote, the House of Representatives appointed the runner-up John Quincy Adams president. Many considered his presidency as less than fully legitimate.

The most perceptive prominent critic of this state of affairs was New York Senator Martin Van Buren. He discerned two basic problems. First, without a significant opposition party, the electorate could not discern which candidates favored the Jeffersonian Republican agenda, which Van Buren supported. Second, he realized that without a coherent electoral process, especially the nomination of candidates, the country was threatened by a new form of demagogic politics centered on personalities and factions. Van Buren thought that these two problems could be mitigated by a more disciplined national system of two parties permanently competing with one another. Against the prevailing view, he argued that parties are "highly useful" and even "inseparable from free governments" (Van Buren, 1918: 125).

Van Buren believed that the party system in his home state of New York provided a model for the country. The Republican Party operation there, known as the Albany Regency, was a disciplined organization defined primarily by the subordination of individual politicians to the party. Acting in 1828 as the de facto chairman of the national Democratic Party, the successor to the Jeffersonian Republicans, Van Buren set about transforming the party system. His principal achievement, along with presidential candidate Andrew Jackson, was to bring the variety of state and local organizations and groups broadly dedicated to Jeffersonian principles under the umbrella of the national Democratic label. This was done typically by promising to those organizations local autonomy in exchange for support of the intentionally broad agenda of the national party (Aldrich, 1995: 106–19). In the decades that followed, this organization would be centered on the national conventions, which would be made up of delegates from the state and local parties and whose main task would be the nomination of the national party's presidential candidate. As a result of this challenge from the Democrats, the Whig Party, the successor to the Federalists, eventually developed by 1840 the same kinds of institutions and practices.

The new organizational discipline would serve to moderate individual politicians. This new party, Richard Hofstadter has explained, "would create opportunities for nominations, patronage, careers, in return for the loyalty it demanded of its members" (Hofstadter, 1969: 244). In such a system, demagogues would be less likely to emerge. Silas Wright, a prominent Albany Regency man, captured the discipline of the new party. In 1824, he said of prospective party careerists that "they are safe if they fear the enemy, but that the first man we see *step to the rear,* we *cut down* . . . they *must* not falter, or they perish" (Garraty, 1949: 40). While some observers may object to this kind of party, Van Buren, Wright, and others believed that precisely discipline of this kind was necessary to check the abuse of personal power (Van Buren, 1918: 125).

Van Buren (1867) believed that party discipline would be especially important for Democrats. This was so because as the more democratic or popular the party, it would need greater organization to bring together its disparate supporters. Such a party needed, he wrote, "an extraneous means to secure harmony in its ranks" (Van Buren, 1867: 5). The Federalists and later Whigs, he thought, were more aristocratic and, thus, less in need of strict organization. The new party structure came to be called the mass party. The organization would not be centered in an elite located in the nation's or the state's capital, but would emphasize participation in politics throughout the country. This extension of the party corresponded with the steady expansion of the electorate in the first decades of the 19th century, partly due to a continuous flow of new immigrants to the country.

In order to wed individual politicians and activists to the party, the use of the patronage and other material incentives took on new dimensions, particularly at the local level. This resulted in the rise of the party machines, organizations that tended to emphasize such incentives as much as or even more than the ideological or policy prescriptions of the party. William Marcy, noted member of the Albany Regency, infamously stated the guiding principle of this partisanship: "to the victor belong the spoils of the enemy" (Spencer, 1959: 60). The party loyalty of ambitious political figures would therefore have an additional, concrete support.

Ordinary citizens would also benefit from the largesse of the political party. The goal of party leaders was to use their various connections in government, business, and the churches to provide benefits for, and thereby induce loyalty from, ordinary citizens. Absent the modern welfare state, the parties in this period were a principal source of social assistance to the poor and dispossessed (McSweeney and Zvesper, 1991: 108–11). More generally, the party would become a medium through which the ordinary citizen would engage civic life. This would occur not only through material assistance, but also through parades, holiday celebrations, and the like, which emphasized broad participation in politics rather than deference to a political elite (Aldrich, 1995: 97–98).

These changes in the organization and methods of the parties were particularly important with respect to immigration. New immigrants to the United States often found themselves in a vulnerable situation, particularly given the cultural and language barriers they encountered. Such immigrants were open to influence from the party machines. As William Crotty (1994) notes:

> The political machine helped acculturate generations of immigrants into American society. It figuratively and literally met people at their boats, helped them settle in ethnic neighborhoods, provided them with gift baskets of food or clothing or coal for heating at Christmas and Thanksgiving . . . , occasionally got them jobs, and acted as an intermediary with

> government agencies. The political machine gave these newcomers a political voice and, over time, a helping hand in moving up in American society. (137)

These activities were especially pronounced within the Democratic Party, which, given its more populist stance dating from the 1790s, remained the party more open to immigrants. This did not mean that all Democrats were accepting of immigrants. As one scholar notes, "whatever negative dispositions were manifested toward immigration at the rank-and-file level, these were overridden by the Democratic Party's overwhelming organizational interest in recruiting the new arrivals" (Zolberg, 2006: 139).

This dimension of mass party organization took on greater significance as the 19th century progressed. There was an enormous increase in immigration to the country in the two decades before the Civil War. This increase largely resulted from Irish immigrants leaving their native land in the wake of the great potato famine. But there were also many Germans and others who came in search of greater economic opportunity and, in some cases, political freedom. More people came to the United States in the decade from 1845 to 1855 than in the previous seven decades combined.

There were relatively mild attempts in the first decades of the century to restrict immigration to the United States, principally through passenger shipping regulation and land policy (Zolberg, 2006: 140–53). But the rapid increase in immigration starting in the mid-1840s triggered a sharp nativist reaction in the country. This led to the formation of new anti-immigrant and anti-Catholic organizations, the most important of which was the Order of the Star Spangled Banner, a secret society started in New York State. Members of the Order would disavow any knowledge of the organization and, thus, came to be called Know Nothings.

The nativist reaction was especially intense against Catholic immigrants, a great number of whom were Irish. The antagonism toward Catholics had been a long-standing fact in the predominantly Protestant United States. German immigrants, too, especially those of Catholic persuasion, were looked down on by the majority. Germans were fond of brewing and drinking beer, which was frowned on by the more puritan native Protestants. This reflected the popular temperance movement of the time, with Protestant clergymen often warning of the dangers of Irish whiskey and German beer.

The religious objection to alcohol only reflected a more basic political difference with Catholicism. Indeed, the importance of Catholicism as the chief object of nativist scorn, as opposed to hostility to immigrants generally, cannot be underestimated. "The cornerstone of our Republic," a Know Nothing editorialist maintained, "is political, mental and social liberty, and in direct antagonism with these principles, stands Romanism. It denies the liberty of free inquiry, the liberty of speech, and thus saps the fountain of freedom. . . . There can be no republicanism where Catholicism bears sway" (Anbinder, 1992: 105). With its emphasis on church authority, deference to priests, and openness to alcohol, Catholicism was thought by many Protestants to breed servile habits and opinions at odds with the needs of republican citizenship.

The chief policy goal of the nativists was a 21-year waiting period for citizenship, an increase from the 5 years that was first adopted in 1795. The Know Nothings, however, were somewhat more successful at achieving their goals at the state rather than the federal level, where they advocated literacy tests and language qualifications for voting. Their greatest success was achieved in Massachusetts, where in 1859 a two-year delay on voting rights for naturalized citizens was adopted (Zolberg, 2006: 160). These policies were more extreme versions of those expressed by the Federalists in the 1790s, the animating principle of which was the nationalist dimension of citizenship. Millard Fillmore—1856 presidential nominee of the American Party, the Know Nothings' organized national party—expressed the traditional view that immigrants from foreign lands were not prepared for republican citizenship: "Americans should govern America. I regret to say that men who come fresh from the monarchies of the old world, are prepared neither by education, habits of thought, or knowledge of our institutions, to govern America" (Fillmore, 1856: 10–11). The idea was that just as a native-born citizen typically could not vote or hold office until the age of 21, so should immigrants not be able to participate in politics for the same length of time. Henry Gardner, nativist governor of Massachusetts, captured this sentiment when he succinctly stated that we should "nationalize before we naturalize" (Anbinder, 1992: 121).

Given the Democratic Party's interest in immigration, the nativist reaction to a great extent manifested itself as criticism of that party. The Know Nothings included in their indictment of Catholic immigration criticism of the methods and practices of the mass party form. As historian Tyler Anbinder (1992) has explained:

> Know Nothings charged that by cutting red tape, paying court fees, and finding judges who looked the other way if the immigrant could not prove five years' residence, Democrats were bribing immigrants to vote their

> ticket. Because these naturalization drives usually took place just weeks or days before elections and were usually conducted in private, Know Nothings concluded that the naturalization process had been corrupted into a systematic procedure to produce the votes necessary to keep unscrupulous demagogues in office. (122)

This Know Nothing attack on political machines coincided with the more general Protestant instinct for reform exhibited in the temperance and abolition movements. Van Buren had intended the mass party form to moderate or defuse political passions, but the Know Nothings saw the activities of the mass party as just more examples of political corruption. "By focusing attention on the evils of antebellum political parties," Anbinder (1992) notes, "Know Nothingism became the first national movement to repudiate Van Buren's assertion that parties were beneficial and desirable" (123).

While their antiparty sentiment manifested itself primarily as opposition to the Democratic Party, the Know Nothings posed a challenge to the Whig Party as well. The Whigs had come into being to oppose Jackson and the Democrats, eventually capturing the presidency in 1840. But the Whig Party would eventually dissolve in the 1850s in the midst of the nativist movement and the great crisis over slavery. Historians argue over just what led to the demise of the party, but there are at least two general reasons. First, the Whigs had difficulty assimilating the newly assertive nativists into its electoral coalition. The party had long been associated with business concerns interested in keeping open the supply of cheap immigrant labor. Second, and more important, the Whigs found it difficult to negotiate the political waters regarding slavery, especially in light of the party's attempt to remain a political force in both the North and the South. Like the Democrats, the Whigs were an intersectional party, that is, they were more or less competitive in both the free states of the North and the slave states of the South. As slavery became more divisive, the incentive for the parties to become sectionalized increased (Holt, 1999). This eventually happened with the Democratic Party, which by 1860 essentially became the party of the South and of slavery. The new Republican Party would become the party of the North and antislavery.

The intersectional basis of the parties before the 1850s was in keeping with Van Buren's original design for a party system that would moderate political activity. He thought that a permanent party system, based on the original ideological divisions between Jeffersonian Republicans and Federalists, would blunt or transcend the tendency toward sectionalism. The old partisan feelings regarding the tariff, internal improvements, and the national bank, for example, actually had salutary effects. If these feelings were suppressed, he wrote, "geographical divisions founded on local interests or, what is worse, prejudices between free and slaveholding states will inevitably take their place. Party attachment in former times furnished a complete antidote for sectional prejudices by producing counteracting feelings" (Ceaser, 1979: 138). In this way, the party system would help to prevent the issue of slavery from escalating into a sectional crisis or even civil war.

This system eventually gave way to those sectional pressures. The political debate over slavery intensified just as nativist reaction to the immigrant wave was reaching its peak. The issue had been growing in importance throughout the first half of the century, but became increasingly important during the Mexican–American War and the debate over whether slavery would be permitted in territories acquired during that conflict. In 1848, Van Buren himself would be the presidential candidate of the Free Soil Party, which emerged in opposition to the extension of slavery into the territories. The Compromise of 1850, intended to mollify interests on both sides of the slavery issue, did so only temporarily. The problem emerged into a truly dangerous sectional crisis with the passage of the Kansas–Nebraska Act in 1854, which repealed the 1820 Missouri Compromise and effectively opened every U.S. territory to slavery. In opposition to this law and the growing power of proslavery interests more generally, the Republican Party was formed.

Northern opposition to the extension of slavery had several causes, from moral indignation at the injustice of the institution to the belief that slave labor was an unfair threat to free labor. The critique of slavery was also rooted in egalitarian criticism of antirepublican influences. It echoed the claims of the Jeffersonian Republicans. "In some Northern eyes," Michael Holt (1978) explains, "slavery had created an aristocratic society in the South dominated socially, economically, and politically by a small oligarchy of planters in defiance of the republican principle of majority rule." The slave power in the South not only violated the rights of enslaved blacks, but schooled its white citizens in the ways of tyranny. "In republican ideology, power itself was evil, the natural antagonist of the freedom and independence it had been the purpose of the Revolution to protect. To prevent the extension of slave society, therefore, was to insulate Northerners from that privileged, powerful, and antirepublican aristocracy" (Holt, 1978: 51–52).

While this critique of slavery had a Jeffersonian flavor, it also corresponded to the Know Nothing view of republicanism. Antislavery and anti-immigrant sentiments tended to coincide. This overlap may seem confusing to modern observers of the politics of the 1850s. As David Potter (1976) suggests, because of their ideological moorings, modern historians often have difficulty coping with "the fact that anti-slavery, which they tend to idealize, and nativism, which they scorn, should have operated in partnership" (252). For many participants in the political fights of the 1850s, however, this partnership seemed quite sensible. This was especially the case with the predominantly Protestant members of the Know Nothing society. Their objection to slavery was rooted in egalitarianism, but also in a more complicated religious and political view of liberty, equality, and citizenship. Stated bluntly, they believed that slavery and Catholicism were both threats to republicanism.

It is worth noting a similarly unusual relationship between slavery and immigration that occurred during the founding period. There is evidence that the free white clause was included in the original 1790 Naturalization Act not primarily to prevent people of color from immigrating to the United States (though it certainly had that effect as well), but to make the emancipation of the slaves politically viable. Noah Pickus (1995) argues that many white Americans who opposed slavery were nevertheless wary of creating a racially mixed society after emancipation. "The clause," Pickus notes (1995), "was consistent in their minds with ensuring that citizens possessed the proper character and shared sense of nationhood and with protecting themselves against the dangers posed by freed slaves who might demand greater retribution than simple political equality would allow" (61). Similarly, many opponents of slavery extension in the 1850s, most notably Abraham Lincoln, at least rhetorically opposed political and social equalities for blacks after emancipation. However wrong opponents of slavery may have been about the possibility of a racially diverse society, both of these episodes highlight the practical problems that immigration and slavery posed.

It was unclear just how the party turmoil of the 1850s would be resolved. Van Buren's strong party system was collapsing under the pressure of events. The 1852 election turned out to be the last presidential election in which the Whig Party had a prominent role. In 1854, the fledgling Republicans were just emerging as an organized party and attracting some immigrant support, especially from Scandinavian and German Americans who adamantly opposed slavery. The Know Nothings were technically not an organized political party at all, but a society whose members could be Whigs or Democrats or Republicans, and thereby could infiltrate or affect any of these parties (Holt, 1999: 849). Many congressmen with Know Nothing affiliations would eventually embrace the nativist American Party label, but the immediate outcome of the 1854 congressional elections was confusing. What was clear was the general hostility to the Democratic Party both for its pro-immigrant and proslavery positions. But it was unclear just what new major party would emerge to oppose the Democrats. As Potter (1976) has noted, the results of the 1854 elections, "although in some respects ambiguous, seemed to indicate the possible triumph of Know-Nothingism rather than of antislavery. At that juncture, there seemed to be a likelihood that the Catholic or immigrant question might replace the slavery question as the focal issue in American political life" (249–50).

The uncertainty of the situation was evidenced in Lincoln's strategic political thinking at the time. He was personally opposed to Know Nothing bigotry against Catholics and immigrants, but he understood the political importance of the nativists, particularly given that so many of them in the North were opposed to slavery. Building a new political party in such circumstances was a very delicate matter requiring the utmost prudence. He captured every dimension of the problem in an August 11, 1855, letter to fellow Republican Owen Lovejoy:

> Not even *you* are more anxious to prevent the extension of slavery than I; and yet the political atmosphere is such, just now, that I fear to do anything, lest I do wrong. Knownothingism has not yet entirely tumbled to pieces—nay, it is even a little encouraged by the late elections in Tennessee, Kentucky & Alabama. Until we can get the elements of this organization, there is not sufficient materials [*sic*] to successfully combat the Nebraska democracy with. We can not get them so long as they cling to a hope of success under their own organization; and I fear an open push by us now, may offend them, and tend to prevent our ever getting them. About us here, they are mostly my old political and personal friends; and I have hoped their organization would die out without the painful necessity of my taking an open stand against them. Of their principles I think little better than I do of those of the slavery extensionists. Indeed I do not perceive how any one professing to be sensitive to the wrongs of the negroes, can join in a league to degrade a class of white men. (Basler, 1953: 316)

To form a successful opposition to the extension of slavery, it was necessary to ally with antislavery advocates wherever they might be found. Lincoln's own objection to slavery was based on a reasoned account of the natural equality of all human beings, which he would articulate most fully in his famous debates with Democratic Senator Stephen Douglas in 1858. But the reality was that a significant number of Americans were opposed to slavery for religious reasons that were not entirely reconcilable with the rationalism that informed Lincoln's argument. He was fully aware of this and understood that it would be impolitic to alienate the nativists because of their bigotry if their support were necessary to combat the greater evil of slavery (Miller, 2002: 316–24).

Some historians argue that the eventual success of the Republicans depended to a significant degree on nativist support (Gienapp, 1987: 421; Silbey, 1985: 127–65). As Lincoln anticipated, many with ties to the Know Nothings eventually found themselves drifting to the Republican Party. Other historians argue, however, that while nativism was a factor, the slavery issue dwarfed it (Foner, 1995: 226–60; Anbinder, 1992). Even though antislavery and anti-immigrant sentiments often coincided, in the North at least it became clear that opposition to the extension of slavery was the more important issue. Lincoln had counted on this. And by the 1856 election, this had become clear even among the Know Nothings. As with the political parties, the Know Nothings were split between northern and southern wings. In 1856, the American Party presidential nominee Millard Fillmore sided with the southern wing's support of the Kansas–Nebraska Act. Part of the reason for this was that the anti-Nebraska movement in the North had come to be seen by some as a counterpart to the disunionist, proslavery advocates in the South. Fillmore's move outraged many northern Know Nothings who opposed slavery as much as or more than they opposed Catholics and immigrants. As it was, Fillmore and the Republican nominee John C. Freemont split the anti-Democratic vote, resulting in the election of James Buchanan to the presidency.

The Know Nothings and their American Party organization soon after dissolved, leaving most nativists in the North to join the Republican Party (Potter, 1976: 259). The result was a consolidation of the antidemocratic vote for Lincoln in 1860. By that time, the sorting out of parties and issues was complete, with nativism no longer able to place significant constraints on Republican leaders. In fact, the 1860 national Republican Party platform opposed any state or federal law that treated native and naturalized citizens unequally. Republicans did not openly reject the nativists, but were not forced to make major concessions to them either. Doubtless, part of the reason why this was possible was the drop in rates of immigration into the country after 1855, the drop being due to potential emigrants in Europe learning of the nativist reaction in the United States and due to economic and political factors around the world (Zolberg, 2006: 161). In part, too, Republicans reacted to and benefited from the support of immigrant naturalized citizens, particularly Scandinavian Americans and German Americans, both heavily residing in Wisconsin, birthplace of the party, and in Illinois, Lincoln's home state. German Americans claimed a strong role in the party's emergence and success, exemplified by German-language newspaper endorsement of Lincoln, and under the leadership of prominent 1848ers, such as Carl Schurz, who went on to be the first secretary of the interior, and Civil War General Franz Sigel (LeMay, 1987: 24, 27).

Conclusion

The calming of the nativist issue after 1855 was like the calming of the alien issue in 1800. Both were largely driven by external events. In the late 1850s, the receding of the immigrant wave gave those with nativist proclivities less reason to be fearful of foreign influences. In 1800, the reduction of tensions between the United States and France made the fear of foreign intrigues less plausible. Anti-immigrant ire failed to provide a basis for a lasting majority party coalition in either case, though nativism clearly was a significant political factor in both periods. That ire appeared in large measure to be a transitory phenomenon, though a general prejudice toward immigrants was common even during the less volatile political periods from the founding to the Civil War.

The decline of nativist rancor did not represent a resolution of political turmoil. In the case of 1860, national two-party competition had been restored on a new sectional basis coinciding with the free and the slave states. Van Buren's durable party system blunting the sectional divide was gone. With the South's secession from the Union in the wake of Lincoln's election, the nascent possibility of civil war implied by party conflict became real. The underlying sectional tendency of the parties dated back to the 1790s. Federalists dominated the New England states, Republicans the South. The Republican victory in 1800 was largely the result of New York, Van Buren's home state, switching its support from Adams to Jefferson. Had that not happened and the Federalists retained power, it is uncertain what course events would have taken. Calls for nullification or even secession from southern Republicans might have resulted, though it would seem that an issue as profound as slavery might have been necessary to make that possible.

Immigration and nativism can cause the most divisive kinds of partisanship. Nativism would become more intense in the decades following the Civil War, with more stringent policies adopted to limit immigration. And it remains to be seen whether immigration policy will become, in our time, the central issue dividing political parties. This is more likely to happen if, as was hoped for by the Know Nothings, cultural or ethnic distinctions were to become the very bases of the parties themselves. We might recommend Jefferson and Lincoln as useful examples of the kind of party leaders needed to avoid such an eventuality.

References

Aldrich, John. 1995. *Why Parties? The Origins and Transformations of Party Politics in America.* Chicago, IL: University of Chicago Press.

Anbinder, Tyler. 1992. *Nativism and Slavery: The Northern Know Nothings and the Politics of the 1850s.* New York: Oxford University Press.

Annals of the Congress of the United States. Washington, DC: Gales and Seaton.

Basler, Roy P., ed. 1953. *The Collected Works of Abraham Lincoln.* 9 Vols. New Brunswick, NJ: Rutgers University Press.

Bowen, Catherine Drinker. 1966. *Miracle at Philadelphia.* Boston, MA: Little, Brown and Company.

Ceaser, James. 1979. *Presidential Selection: Theory and Development.* Princeton, NJ: Princeton University.

Chernow, Ron. 2004. *Alexander Hamilton.* New York: Penguin.

Crotty, William. 1994. "Urban Political Machines." In *Parties and Politics in American History: A Reader,* eds. L. Sandy Maisel and Willaim G. Shade. New York: Garland Publishing.

Cunningham, Noble. 1957. *Jeffersonian Republicans: The Formation of Party Organization: 1789–1801.* Chapel Hill, NC: University of North Carolina Press.

Fillmore, Millard. 1856. *Speeches of Millard Fillmore, at New York, Newburgh, Albany, Rochester, Buffalo, &c.* Washington, DC.

Foner, Eric. 1995. *Free Soil, Free Labor, Free Men: The Ideology of the Republican Party before the Civil War.* New York: Oxford University Press.

Frisch, Morton J., ed. 1985. *Selected Writings and Speeches of Alexander Hamilton.* Washington, DC: American Enterprise Institute.

Garraty, John A. 1949. *Silas Wright.* New York: Columbia University Press.

Gerring, John. 1998. *Party Ideologies in America, 1828–1996.* New York: Cambridge University Press.

Gienapp, William E. 1987. *The Origins of the Republican Party, 1852–1856.* New York: Oxford University Press.

Hofstadter, Richard. 1969. *The Idea of a Party System: The Rise of Legitimate Opposition in the United States, 1780–1840.* Berkeley, CA: University of California Press.

Holt, Michael F. 1978. *The Political Crisis of the 1850s.* New York: John Wiley & Sons.

Holt, Michael F. 1999. *The Rise and Fall of the American Whig Party.* New York: Oxford University Press.

Koch, Adrienne and William Peden, eds. 1944. *The Life and Selected Writings of Thomas Jefferson.* New York: Modern Library.

LeMay, Michael. 1987. *From Open Door to Dutch Door: An Analysis of U.S. Immigration Policy since 1820.* New York: Praeger.

LeMay, Michael, and Elliott Robert Barkan, eds. 1999. *U.S. Immigration and Naturalization Laws and Issues: A Documentary History.* Westport, CT: Greenwood Press.

Lipscomb, Andrew, and Albert Bergh, eds. 1903–1905. *The Writings of Thomas Jefferson.* Washington, DC: Jefferson Memorial Association of the United States.

McSweeney, Dean, and John Zvesper. 1991. *American Political Parties.* London: Routledge.

Meyers, Marvin, ed. 1981. *The Mind of the Founder.* Hanover, NH: University Press of New England.

Miller, William Lee. 2002. *Lincoln's Virtues: An Ethical Biography.* New York: Alfred A. Knopf.

Peterson, Merrill D., ed. 1986. *The Portable Thomas Jefferson.* New York: Penguin.

Pickus, Noah. 1995. *Immigration and Citizenship in the 21st Century.* Chapel Hill, N.C.: University of North Carolina Press.

Pickus, Noah. 2005. *True Faith and Allegiance: Immigration and American Civic Nationalism.* Princeton, NJ: Princeton University Press.

Potter, David M. 1976. *The Impending Crisis, 1848–1861.* New York: Harper & Row.

Reichley, A. James. 1992. *The Life of the Parties: A History of American Political Parties.* Lanham, MD: Rowman & Littlefield.

Rhodehamel, John, ed. 1997. *Writings.* New York: Library of America.

Rossiter, Clinton, ed. 2003. *The Federalist Papers.* New York: Signet Classics.

Silbey, Joel H. 1985. *The Partisan Imperative: The Dynamics of American Politics Before the Civil War.* New York: Oxford University Press.

Spencer, Ivor Debenham. 1959. *The Victor and the Spoils: A Life of William L. Marcy.* Providence, RI: Brown University Press.

Sundquist, James L. 1983. *Dynamics of the Party System: Alignment and Realignment of Political Parties in the United States.* Washington, DC: Brookings Institution.

Syrett, Harold C., ed. 1961–1987. *The Papers of Alexander Hamilton.* 27 Vols. New York: Columbia University Press.

Van Buren, Martin. 1867. *Inquiry into the Origin and Course of Political Parties in America.* New York: Hurd and Houghton.

Van Buren, Martin. 1918. *The Autobiography of Martin Van Buren.* Annual Report of the American Historical Association.

Zentner, Scot. 2005. "Regimes and Revolutions: Madison and Wilson on Parties in America." In *The Progressive Revolution in Politics and Political Science,* ed. John Marini and Ken Masugi. Lanham, MD: Rowman & Littlefield.

Zolberg, Aristide R. 2006. *A Nation by Design: Immigration Policy in the Fashioning of America.* New York: Russell Sage/Harvard University Press.

Zvesper, John. 1984. "The Madisonian Systems." *Western Political Quarterly* 37: 236–56.

CHAPTER SEVEN

Naturalization Law, Immigration Flow, and Policy

Carla L. Reyes

Introduction

The law of naturalization from the founding of the United States until 1865 developed a sort of symbiotic relationship to the immigration flow and to immigration policy and set precedents for many subsequent revisions in immigration law. Initially, naturalization law sought to encourage emigration and simultaneously cultivate productive, responsible additions to the national citizenry. With property rights linked to immigration status, the enactment of naturalization law essentially set immigration policy. Although specific eligibility requirements varied over time and among the colonies and later the states, hallmark elements of naturalization law during this early period include restrictions based on race, residency, good moral character, and fealty—taking a specific oath of loyalty—to the United States. Notably, many of these early requirements remain stalwart prerequisites for present day naturalization.

In contrast to current immigration policy, which is fraught with disagreement, policy makers during this early period generally agreed that the young nation should commit to an open-door policy of immigration, with virtually no restrictions on immigration. Practically, all who sought entrance were admitted, and governmental policy was to reach out and seek immigrants (LeMay, 1987: 6–7). One congressional official explained this early approach to naturalization as follows: "the reason for admitting foreigners to the rights of citizenship amongst us is the encouragement of emigration, as we have a large tract of country to people." (Pfander and Wardon, 2010: 396). This early phase of policy-making was guided by an asylum view of naturalization, articulated by President George Washington:

> The bosom of America is open to receive not only the opulent and respectable stranger, but the oppressed and persecuted of all Nations and Religions; whom we shall welcome to a participation in all our rights and privileges, if by decency and propriety of conduct they appear to merit the enjoyment. (LeMay and Barkan, 1999: 10, Document 6, Letter of General George Washington on America as Asylum)

With the successful establishment of an independent nation and then its newly revised Constitution in 1789, official policy was to keep its gates open to all. Data from that time period suggests that the policy was successful—an estimated 250,000 immigrants arrived between the end of the Revolutionary War and the passage of the 1819 Act. The years 1819 to 1829 saw another 125,000 immigrants enter the United States, and then from 1830 to 1860 nearly another 4.5 million newcomers arrived (Aleinikoff et al., 2003: 149; LeMay, 2006: 14–15).

This influx presented its own set of policy problems, from language-based prejudice to ethnic and religious rivalry. The immigrant population responded to these difficulties in a variety of ways, with some groups giving into their own nativist sentiments, and others seeking refuge in geographical enclaves of similarly situated immigrants. Ultimately, however, naturalized immigrants engaged the American political process in order to advance the same causes for which they first immigrated: social and religious freedom, economic opportunity, and equal property and labor rights. The 18th- and 19th-century immigrant struggle to overcome opposition and prejudice in order to pursue those values that first propelled them to come to the United States foreshadows the primary and continuing struggle that immigrants continue to confront in the present day.

Overview of Naturalization Law from Founding to 1865

This early period of immigration policy is commonly referred to as the open-door period, because naturalization law was generally used as a factor to encourage emigration from Europe, particularly from the British Isles and Germany, and immigration to the United States. As a result, naturalization policy from the end of the Revolutionary War to 1865 reflects the colonial desire to populate the nation and enhance its prosperity.

Preconstitutional naturalization policy therefore involved competition among states to attract the most desirable newcomers. Colonial Americans, who often viewed strangers as legitimate objects of suspicion, cautiously allowed settlers but were wary of those of religious differences, or those who might become public charges. The influx of Quakers and Germans in the early 1700s led to specific colonial immigration laws that served as models for later state and national laws. Similarly, the enactment of a uniform federal naturalization law, in 1790 (Act of March 26, 1790; 1 Stat. 103), set fairly relaxed eligibility requirements (e.g., only two years of residency) that dominated the policy landscape, with some amendments, until the 1860s, and indeed beyond that period.

Colonial Naturalization Policy

As colonies, the legal rules of England applied generally to the new lands in America. The colonies thereby inherited the common law rule that, at death, a foreign national forfeited his property to the Crown (Zolberg, 2006: 33–34). Acquiring English citizenship through naturalization represented the only path to secure property rights. Unfortunately, naturalization occurred only by grant of Parliament, which involved high costs and extended periods of processing time (Pfander and Wardon, 2010: 379). Furthermore, English naturalization required an applicant to take communion in the Protestant tradition and to swear allegiance to the Crown, effectively preventing Catholics, Jews, and other non-Christians from eligibility (Zolberg, 2006: 34; Pfander and Wardon, 2010: 380). England also offered denizenship, a lesser immigration status that provided foreign nationals the rights to own land and trade; however, only the Crown could grant such status (Carpenter, 1904: 290). The Crown sought to extend such policies to its American colonies with the enactment of the Plantation Act: the British Naturalization Act of 1740 (summarized in LeMay and Barkan, 1999: 6–9, Document 4).

The colonies, however, recognizing the importance of prospective landownership in encouraging emigration to their shores, interpreted their colonial charters to allow them to independently extend citizenship to newcomers through their own legislation. Rights granted to foreign nationals in this manner, however, did not extend beyond the borders of the colony (Carpenter, 1904: 296–97). Generally speaking, such legislation required applicants to be free persons, did not impose residency requirements, did not require an oath to the Anglican church, and permitted the extension of naturalization rights to some Jews, but generally prohibited the extension of such rights to Roman Catholics (Zolberg, 2006: 34). Concerns over immigration of the poor, sick, impotent, or infirm who might become a public charge was a theme often reflected in colonial legislation. Take, for example, the Provincial Law of Massachusetts, enacted March 12, 1700, and as amended on June 29, 1722, which required poor immigrants to provide townships with security that they would not become a public charge. A further example can be found in the Massachusetts colonists' desire to provide incentives for Protestant settlers to enter the colony and encourage French-speaking Protestants (the Huguenots) to settle in the Province (Act of April 2, 1731, or as amended in June 1756) (LeMay and Barkan, 1999: 2–10).

After some time, England worried about the heightened rigidity of its own naturalization law as compared to the colonial eligibility requirements, fearing the disparity would negatively impact its economic situation. King George responded by imposing restrictions on the colonies' power to enact naturalization laws (Carpenter, 1904: 294). Such actions eventually played a prominent role in the founders' demand for independence. Specifically, the Declaration of Independence charged King George with having "endeavoured to prevent the Population of these States; for that purpose obstructing the Laws for Naturalization of Foreigners; refusing to pass others to encourage their migration hither, and raising the conditions of new Appropriations of Lands" (Declaration of Independence, para. 7). Many argue that this seventh charge against the English Crown reflected the founders' objection to (1) a 1773 order prohibiting colonial governors from approving any new colonial naturalization acts, (2) a veto of a 1771 North Carolina law giving tax breaks to new settlers from Europe, and (3) a 1773 order prohibiting continued westward expansion of the colonies into lands obtained from France (Zolberg, 2006: 25–26; Pfander and Wardon, 2010: 381–82).

This colonial battle with the Crown regarding the power to regulate naturalization would shape both the policy approach of individual states under the Articles of Confederation and the constitutional framers' approach to both the naturalization clause in the Constitution and the early naturalization laws flowing from the same. The experience left the founders specifically determined that naturalization law would be generally applicable to everyone under United States' jurisdiction, available to all free people—regardless of wealth or class, and be wielded as a tool to shape policy prospectively rather than be used as a method to impose retroactive protections for government actors.

Naturalization Policy under the Articles of Confederation

After the Revolutionary War, the Articles of Confederation left the power of naturalization and denization in the hands of each individual state. The

Articles of Confederation did, however, contain a clause instructing, "The free inhabitants of each of these States . . . shall be entitled to all privileges and immunities of free citizens in the several States" (Articles of Confederation, November 15, 1777, Art. IV). The newly independent states began competing with one another to attract new citizens. For example, Pennsylvania admitted any foreign national that would vow to purchase land in the state and could demonstrate good moral character to become a denizen within one year and a naturalized citizen within two years (Pfander and Wardon, 2010: 383). Similarly, Virginia decided that all white persons demonstrating two-year residency in the state were eligible for citizenship. Other states, such as South Carolina, tended to be more restrictive, requiring the passage of private bills for granting naturalization.

While intended to provide some measure of uniformity throughout the states, the Articles' Privileges and Immunities Clause had the opposite effect. Immigrants tended to game the system by initially immigrating to a state with lenient eligibility requirements, naturalizing, and then moving to the state of their choice, possibly one with more stringent naturalization law. The Privileges and Immunities Clause bound the new state to honor the privilege of naturalization bestowed on the newcomer by its sister state (Pfander and Wardon, 2010: 384–85). Such antics became the source of significant tension between state governments. These difficulties reached their peak in the late 1700s due to the large influx of immigrants. By 1776, more than one-third of American citizens were nationals of countries other than England (West, 2001: 166). In 1786, the framers unveiled a solution—the Naturalization Clause of the Constitution (Article 8, Clause 4). The clause endows the national government with the power "to establish a uniform rule of naturalization." In one deft stroke, the framers resolved the privileges and immunities problem while simultaneously addressing their long-standing grievances from the colonial era—accessibility to and retroactivity of the Crown's naturalization policy.

The Naturalization Act of 1790

Congress first exercised its power under the Naturalization Clause in 1790 (Act of March 26, 1790; 1 Stat. 103). As the first federal law to address naturalization requirements, the Naturalization Act of 1790 imposed three basic requirements. An immigrant could become a United States citizen if he or she (1) was a free white person, (2) had resided for at least two years in the United States and for at least one year in the state of application, and (3) could demonstrate good character and allegiance to the U.S. Constitution. Importantly, it also included a provision regarding the children of the immigrant: "And the children of such persons so naturalized, dwelling within the United States, being under the age of twenty-one years at the time of such naturalization, shall also be considered as citizens of the United States."

Because only citizens could own land, the Naturalization Act of 1790 was viewed as intimately tied to land policy. The residency requirement, for example, was designed to prevent absentee landowners and encourage real additions to the community (Pfander and Wardon, 2010: 396). It was also thought that naturalization law could be used to help shape the type of citizenry from which the new nation would be formed. For example, the law's requirement regarding proof of good moral character, a requirement that persists in present day naturalization law, reflects the belief of "Americans of every party . . . that 'the national government had a legitimate interest in controlling the character of potential citizens' through naturalization policy" (West, 2001: 166).

This first federal naturalization law also reflects the two limitations placed on Congress by the founders with respect to immigration policy. First, the founders limited Congress to the enactment of "public laws of general applicability," such that Congress was thought to be prohibited from enacting private bills that naturalized immigrants on a selective basis (Pfander and Wardon, 2010: 393). This requirement reflected the colonial reaction to the process in England whereby naturalization could only be obtained by a private bill from Parliament—a procedure that, by its expensive and selective nature, inherently limited opportunities for naturalization to the wealthy and well-connected. Second, the power of congress to bestow any immigration status short of naturalization would be bound by the requirements of uniformity and general applicability (Pfander and Wardon, 2010: 402). However, because the Constitution simply bestowed the power "to establish a uniform rule of naturalization," and because few immigrated to the United States unless they would be eligible for citizenship, Congress relied on naturalization policy to encourage or discourage emigration, and did not enact legislation regarding other immigration status until much later (West, 2001: 166).

The Naturalization Act of 1795

By 1795, tensions over naturalization policy increased, such that most policy makers agreed that foreign nationals "bring with them, not only attachments to other countries, but ideas of government so distinct from ours, that in every point of view they are dangerous" (Steinfeld, 2001: 649). As a result, it was generally thought "that foreigners needed a longer period of acculturation and closer scrutiny before entering America's political arena" via voting rights through citizenship. Therefore, in January 1795, Congress revised the Naturalization Act to require a five-year residency period, with a requirement that an immigrant declare the intent to become a citizen after three years, along with renunciation of any title or order of nobility. The new law also included a stronger oath requirement (Act of January 29, 1795; 1 Stat. 414).

Notably, these changes reflect the politics of the age as much as any actual policy concerns. The Federalists dominated Congress in 1795 and were largely responsible for the passage of this second naturalization law. The Federalist concern with tightening the naturalization requirements reflects their belief that new immigrants were more likely to vote for the Democratic Republican Party (Pfander and Wardon, 2010: 359).

The Alien, Sedition, and Naturalization Acts of 1798

In 1798, reacting to the hostilities with France, Congress again heightened the bar for becoming a naturalized citizen. The Naturalization Act of 1798 imposed a 14-year residency requirement, with 5 of those years spent in the state of application, and with a declaration of intent to naturalize required after five years, assessing fees, and stipulating a more detailed naturalization process and imposing penalties for various failures to comply with the law (Act of June 18, 1798; 1 Stat. 566—cited in LeMay and Barkan, 1999: 13–15). Congress also imposed the first requirement that foreign-born aliens register with a federal officer. The Alien Enemies Law and the Alien Law (Act of June 25, 1798; 1 Stat. 570) together gave the executive sweeping power to deport citizens of hostile nations during war and to expel any foreign national suspected of treason (Powell, 2005: 7):

> That it shall be lawful for the President of the United States at any time during the continuance of this act, to order all such aliens as he shall judge to be dangerous to the peace and safety of the United States, or shall have reasonable grounds to suspect are concerned with treasonable or secret machinations against the government thereof, to depart out of the territory of the United States. (LeMay, 2006: 18)

The Sedition Act completed the series of restrictive measures by curtailing freedom to criticize the government (Powell, 2005: 8). The 1798 acts had a two-year enforcement limitation.

Again, politics internal to the young United States may have had as much to do with the passage of the new eligibility requirements as the

Quasi War (1798–1800) with France. At this time, the vying political factions generally worried about the increasing strength of the Jefferson Republican Party (Powell, 2005: 7). Irish, German, and other new immigrants were more likely to support the Jeffersonian party than the Federalists, and restricting naturalization eligibility was viewed as one means of obtaining an advantage in the voter's pool (Powell, 2005).

Naturalization and Immigration Laws from 1802 to 1859

The stringent requirements of the 1798 Act and its sister laws were short lived, as the Jeffersonians repealed them in 1802, or otherwise allowed them to expire (Powell, 2005: 200). As president, Thomas Jefferson urged the passage of a new, less stringent, naturalization law, stating "under the 'ordinary' chances of human life, a denial of citizenship, under a residence of fourteen years, is a denial to a great proposition of those who ask it" (Powell, 2005: 200). Ultimately, the Jeffersonian-controlled Congress enacted the Naturalization Act of 1802 (Act of April 14, 1802; 54 Stat. 1172). This act reinstated the five-year residency requirement, with one-year residency required in the state of application, and required a declaration of intent to naturalize after three years residency (Powell, 2005: 200). The Act of 1802 retained the requirement that aliens arriving after the effective date of the law register with a federal officer.

Congress amended the law on March 26, 1804, to exempt foreign nationals who had entered the United States before the law took effect from the declaration requirement. The declaration provision was further amended in 1824, requiring the declaration after two years, rather than three (Powell, 2005: 200). Finally, the act included a section (2168) that provided for the naturalization of widows and children of the declarant if he should die before the naturalization was completed, upon their taking the oaths proscribed by the law (34 Stat. 603). In the Act of March 3, 1813 (45 Stat. 1514), Congress reaffirmed the five-year residency requirement for the naturalization process, a stipulation that, with certain exceptions, continues to the present day (LeMay and Barkan, 1999, Document 12: 19).

In 1819, the Congress enacted the first immigration law—the Act of March 2, 1819 (3 Stat. 489), often referred to as the "Manifest Act." Consistent with precedent established by colonial provincial law, its purpose was simply requiring the enumeration of passengers by ship captains or shipmasters and the collection of data on immigrants and immigration, which was to be given to customs officials at the ports of entry. As such, it marks the beginning of formal federal immigration law. It required "that each and every collector of the customs, to whom such manifest or list of passengers as aforesaid shall be delivered, shall, quarter yearly, return copies thereof to the Secretary of State of the United States, by whom statements of the same shall be laid before Congress at each and every session" (LeMay and Barkan, 1999: 20). This first federal immigration law nonetheless left a major role for the state governments in immigration policy. State governments at the various ports of entry promulgated rules and regulations and state officials inspected ships. State officials also checked arriving passengers against the manifest and processed, on the wharfs, the arriving immigrants.

Congress amended the naturalization process again in 1824, providing for the naturalization of alien young adults arriving unaccompanied by a parent (who not uncommonly may have died at sea during the voyage that typically took a month or more at the time). It was a common enough occurrence since as many as nine percent of emigrants died in passage. The law provided that any alien, under the age of 21, who had arrived unaccompanied by a parent and had resided 3 years in the state, and who continued to reside there at the time of application could be admitted a citizen of the state of residence, and, upon achieving the age of 21 and residing in the United States for 5 years, could be naturalized (Act of May 25, 1824; 934 Stat. 603). Finally, mention should be made of the law granting citizenship to women married to citizens. The Act of February 10, 1855: Citizenship of Married Women (39 Stat. 889) stated that any woman married to a citizen of the United States might be lawfully naturalized, except for prostitutes.

The 1848 Treaty of Guadalupe Hidalgo

Although not undertaken specifically to address naturalization policy, in its Article VIII, the Treaty of Guadalupe Hidalgo did provide nonwhite foreign nationals the opportunity to become naturalized U.S. citizens. Under the terms of the treaty, Mexican nationals living in the territory Mexico ceded to the United States would become U.S. citizens unless they affirmatively chose to remain a Mexican national within one year (Johnson, 1998: 127). The treaty also promised those who became naturalized citizens under its terms that they would receive full citizenship rights under the U.S. Constitution (Johnson, 1998: 128). As a result of the treaty, between 75,000 and 100,000 Mexican foreign nationals became U.S. citizens (Powell, 2005: 189).

Putting Naturalization to Use: Overcoming Opposition and Prejudice

Despite the open door policy undergirding the technical requirements of naturalization law during the early period, the sheer number of immigrants arriving to the United States began to cause agitation and fear among existing U.S. citizens. As one writer explains,

> From the beginning, Americans had a double-sided view of immigrant and immigration. On the one hand, they frequently saw immigrants as a critical source of future prosperity. On the other, they were concerned that only the right sort of immigrants should come into the country. (Steinfeld, 2001: 648)

As a result, states frequently enacted legislation targeting Catholic, German, and Irish immigrants, among other groups. The early period was therefore marked as much by immigrants' struggle to overcome opposition and prejudice as it was by the open door policy. Each group faced different opposition and reacted in unique ways. Their stories parallel some of the struggles faced by modern-day immigrants, despite the different demographics that characterize modern day immigration.

German Immigrants

During the colonial period, many German immigrants congregated in the colony of Pennsylvania (Powell, 2005: 104). During colonial times, German immigration was distinguished by the movement of entire communities bound together by religious creeds not accepted in their homelands. They came in groups as Mennonites, Dunkers, Lutherans (from Catholic-dominated German states), Calvinists, and Jews. Geographically, they were Palatines, Salzburgers, Wurttenburger, and Hanoverians. They sought out and cultivated some of the richest farmlands in colonial America. Indeed, their granaries served as the breadbasket of the Revolution. Initially scattered thinly among the native stock, they were united only by their language. They exercised little political clout and showed little interest beyond their local and private affairs.

That was changed by the Revolutionary War. Though scattered widely, they still comprised the largest single nationality group after those from the British Isles. They felt no loyalty to the Crown and were often unfriendly toward the Tories, who favored continued union with England. They were easy converts to the revolutionary cause and several German regiments were raised and fought prominently and well in the war. Their wartime service was widely recognized and their general social and economic conditions improved, leading to their taking a more active role in public affairs. Politically, they tended to affiliate with the Democrats, reflecting their small-farmer backgrounds. They were less at home with the "Eastern seaboard establishment" (LeMay, 1987: 22–23).

However, during the 1800s, many more German immigrants arrived as farmers eager to ply their skill to their own land, and German settlement patterns shifted, with many German immigrants settling in the Midwest, where they anticipated a greater likelihood of finding farmland (Powell, 2005: 106). German immigration to the United States peaked in the 1850s with nearly one million Germans fleeing political unrest and social or religious persecution, and the economic recession brought on by the potato blight, for the safety promised by the shores of the United States (Powell, 2005: 106). By the time of the Civil War, they numbered more than 1.5 million. German immigrants were recruited by state governments in the Midwest, by railroads and shipping lines, and by various manufacturers.

Naturalized German Americans played an active role in the American political landscape, viewing such activity as another avenue for shaping their destiny in the new country. They did not do so without significant opposition, however. German immigrants faced discrimination for reasons of language and culture. German Americans consistently fought accusations centered on their supposed "failure to assimilate," accusations they were susceptible to as a result of their tendency to group together geographically (Aleinikoff et al., 2003: 147).

From Andrew Jackson's presidency until the 1840s, naturalized citizens of German origin, especially those with Roman Catholic Church affiliation, generally maintained close ties to the Democratic Party (Trommler and Shore, 2001: 24). During the 1850s, that party alignment shifted. Increasing numbers of German immigrants were coming from the northern states of Germany and were Protestant in their affiliation (primarily Lutherans). These German immigrants, and the many German American citizens who were 1848ers, were heavily influenced by ideals of Republicanism and liberal democracy. Their influence far exceeded their numerical strength of some 10,000, because the Forty-Eighters, as they came to be known, became leaders of the German American communities. They started German-language newspapers, reading societies, theatres, and related cultural activities. They disapproved of the way slave-owning Southern Americans began slowly taking over the Democratic Party (Trommler and Shore, 2001: 24). German Americans lacked meaningful alternatives for some time, however. The Whig Party began declining at this time due to divisions regarding how to approach the North–South slavery divide. While Northern Whigs tended to be antislavery, which appealed to

German Americans, the Northern Whigs "also harbored nativists, temperance advocates and Sabbatarians, and thus was not a welcoming place for Germans" (Trommler and Shore, 2001: 24).

The other prominently rising political party during that time, the Know Nothing Party, was similarly a nonstarter for German Americans, given its intense nativist focus. The Know Nothing Party was "committed to placing a curb on immigration itself and to ensuring that foreigners not be permitted to participate in the nation's political affairs" (Aleinikoff et al., 2003: 150). As the Know Nothing Party continued to attack German Americans (and other immigrants) in the 1840s, many Germans shifted their allegiance to the Free Soil Party, or the new Republican Party (Adam, 2005: 240). The Free Soil/Republican Party propounded an antislavery platform while also appealing to German American ideals of equal property and labor rights (Trommler and Shore, 2001: 25). Despite their struggle to overcome opposition and prejudice, German Americans played a significant role in shaping the political landscape of the country, especially as a wave of new German immigrants arrived in the early 1850s (Trommler and Shore, 2001: 25). German Americans used their influence to pursue a middle-class agenda of freedom and equality in property and labor rights.

The German wing of the Republican Party (founded in Ripon, Wisconsin in 1854) was important to President Lincoln's election in 1860. Carl Schurz, an 1848er, served on the party's platform committee. There were some 265 German-language newspapers in circulation in 1860, such as the *Illinois Staatsanzeiger,* nearly all of which endorsed the Republicans and Lincoln specifically. Only 3 of the 265—all in the South—favored the secession cause. The shifting tides of German American political allegiances also demonstrate that when Congress undertook changes to the naturalization laws in order to affect politics, their suspicions that new immigrants would lean toward one party over the other were often correct. Carl Schurz was appointed to a diplomatic position in Lincoln's administration before serving as a major general in the Civil War. He later was appointed as the nation's first secretary of the interior.

In 1862, the Lincoln administration led Congress to enact two laws that had significant impact on immigration and on naturalization. Congress enacted the Homestead Act (Act of May 20, 1862: 392–393). It became an important incentive attracting immigrants to the United States with its abundant land of deep topsoil. Tens of thousands were drawn to the Midwestern states. Similarly, Congress set an important naturalization precedent that had wide-ranging impact. In the Act of July 17, 1862 (40 Stat. S46), it passed the Honorably Discharged Soldiers Act. Section 2166 of the act stipulated that

> Any alien, of the age of twenty-one and upward, who has enlisted, or may enlist, in the armies of the United States, either the regular or the volunteer forces, and has been, or may be hereafter, honorably discharged, shall be admitted to become a citizen of the United States, and upon his petition, without any previous declaration of his intention to become such; and he shall not be required to prove more than one year's residence within the United States previous to his application to become such citizen; and the court admitting such alien shall, in addition to proof of residence and good moral character, as now provided by law, be satisfied by competent proof of such person's having been honorably discharged from the service of the United States. (LeMay and Barkan, 1999: 30)

This act had immediate, far-reaching results. More than 200,000 German-born served in the Union Army. They provided 10 divisions each of volunteers from New York and Ohio. More than 516,000 German Americans served in the war, comprising 23.4 percent of all Union soldiers. New York State alone supplied 36,000, Missouri 30,000, and Ohio 20,000, and the Union Army conducted major recruiting efforts aimed at German Americans in heavily German-populated cities such as Baltimore, Cincinnati, Milwaukee, New York, and St. Louis.

The German-speaking divisions served with distinction. Noted German American officers of the Civil War include Major General Franz Sigel, the highest-ranking German American in the Union Army, and the aforementioned Major General Carl Schurz, whose unit served as bodyguards at Lincoln's inauguration and at his funeral in April, 1865. Brigadier generals who were German-born include August Willich, Louis Blender, Max Weber, and Alexander Schimmelfennig. Other German American officers of note were Godfrey Weitzel, Adolph von Steinwehr, Edward Salomon, Frederick Salomon, August Kantz, Felix Salm-Salm, and Peter Osterhaus. In addition to these German-born officers, German-born volunteers fought with such distinction that several were awarded the Congressional Medal of Honor for Valor in the Civil War.

Indeed, the granting of speedy naturalization for military service became an important inducement in all subsequent U.S. wars. Of more than 3,400 Medal of Honor recipients, the nation's highest award for military heroism created in 1861, awardees were born in 33 countries (U.S. Senate Committee on Veterans' Affairs Report, 1979). Irish-born head the list at 258, with German-born being second at 128. German-born immigrants who were awarded the Medal of Honor in the Civil War include Private Frederick Alber, Corporal William Archinal, Sergeant Richard Binder, Sergeant Major Abraham Cohn, Captain Hubert Dilger, Sergeant Richard

Enderlin, Private Peter Kappesser, Private Henry Klein, Private J.C. Julius Langbein, Lieutenant Theodore Schwan, and Quartermaster William Wells. Like the Homestead Act land grants, after the war Congress awarded land grants to Civil War veterans, and this incentive drew many thousands of German immigrants to the Midwest after the war.

Irish Immigrants

Irish immigrants came to the United States in large numbers in the 18th and 19th centuries to leave poverty, the restrictive rule of the British Crown, civil unrest, and famine behind (Powell, 2005: 152). At the outset, Irish immigrants prominently settled in large cities, including New York City, Boston, and Philadelphia. By 1800, Philadelphia hosted 6,000 Irish immigrants, and from 1820 to 1840 more than one-third of all immigrants arriving in the United States were Irish, with an increasing proportion of those being poor Irish Catholics (Powell, 2005: 154). The rate of Irish immigration grew exponentially, with 1.7 million Irish arriving to the United States between 1845 and 1860 (Powell, 2005). Irish emigration rose exponentially during the period of the Great Famine (1847–1852), when the island lost half its total population, about 25 percent due to death by starvation, and accompanying pandemic disease outbreaks, like cholera and typhoid fever. Another 25 percent loss was due to emigration. An estimated 1.2 million came to the United States (LeMay, 1987: 25).

Irish immigrants encountered difficulty as early as the colonial period. The largely Protestant Irish that settled in Boston, for example, constantly encountered hostility from Puritan city leaders on account of religious differences, while also fending off complaints from other citizens regarding their poor economic situation upon landing (Ural Bruce, 2006: 8). By 1850, two-thirds of the domestic laborers in Boston—mostly women—were Irish-born (Dinnerstein and Reimers, 1975; Handlin, 1979). Irish immigrants provided a huge pool of indigent manual labor and comprised the first large unskilled labor class, precisely when the nation was developing its class consciousness (O'Grady, 1973: 65).

Even before Boston and New York City began posting "No Irish Need Apply" signs in the 1850s, colonial governments had set precedents for using the law to discriminate against the Irish immigrant. For example, the Quaker-led government in Pennsylvania imposed harsher taxes on the Irish population (Ural Bruce, 2006: 8). As the Napoleonic Wars (1796–1815) and the War of 1812 rendered international migration more dangerous, the Irish began to experience a period of relative quiet and peace with their neighbors (Ural Bruce, 2006: 9). Unfortunately, this lasted only until the next wave of Irish immigration began in 1815.

By the 1820s, this new wave of Irish immigration would be dominated by Irish Catholics, rather than Irish Protestants, provoking a frustrated response from across the young nation, which heavily disfavored Catholicism (Ural Bruce, 2006: 10). This frustration ultimately erupted in violence between 1820 and 1840 with mobs, protests, and violent attacks aimed at the Irish born, whether naturalized or not, in Boston, Philadelphia, Kensington, and New York, among other areas (Ural Bruce, 2006: 11–13). Facing this oppression directly translated into Irish political interests, as it "taught them to protect their own interests, and their support for a cause would, by necessity, depend on how it affected their homes, their families, and their dreams for Ireland or America, or both" (Ural Bruce, 2006: 13).

The third wave of Irish immigration began after the Great Famine, around 1845, just as the Know Nothing Party was on the rise. Notably, the Know Nothing Party experienced its largest successes in areas with large Irish Catholic populations, such as Massachusetts (Ural Bruce, 2006: 18). The Know Nothing Party went so far as to link the proslavery movement with Catholicism and the fact of being foreign born, saying "Americanism and Freedom are synonymous term. . . . Foreignism and Slavery are equally so, and the one is antipodes of the other" (Ural Bruce, 2006: 19). The Irish, for their part, did not allow themselves to be politically trampled, but fought back through the political system itself.

For reasons similar to those of German Americans, naturalized Irish Americans initially supported the Democratic Republican Party, and later its successor, the Democratic Party. The Federalists, and later the Whigs, continuously called for stricter naturalization laws. The Democratic Party, on the other hand, actively recruited the Irish to increased political participation (Ural Bruce, 2006: 20–21). Naturalized Irish Americans cunningly used the invitation to seize low-level civil service jobs and thereby accomplish two things: obtain employment, and gain access to power and political and economic favors in order to work up the social stratosphere (Ural Bruce, 2006: 20).

As with the German immigrants, Irish immigrants used the Naturalization Act of the Civil War, and their service in the war, to speed up their acceptance and their acculturation. More than 144,000 Irish immigrants served in the Civil War. They enlisted as volunteers in great numbers from the states that likewise drew so many German-born immigrant volunteers: New York State provided more than 51,000 Irish; Pennsylvania sent more than 17,000; Illinois enlisted more than 12,000; Massachusetts enrolled more than 8,000; Missouri more than 4,000, and even Wisconsin, at the time more sparsely populated with Irish immigrants who had often arrived there after helping construct the railroads from the east heading west, sent nearly 4,000. The Irish Brigade served with heroic distinction and was commonly known as "the Fighting Irish," and as the "Irish Legion."

The Irish Brigade was led by a number of notable Irish officers: Brigadier General Thomas Francis Meagher, Brigadier General Thomas Reade Cobb, General Thomas Smyth (killed in action), General Robert Nugent, Colonel Michael Corcoran, Colonel Patrick Daniel Kelly (killed in action), Colonel Richard Byrnes (killed in action), and Major—later Colonel—Richard Enright. From the Irish Brigade alone, 961 soldiers were killed in the war. Numerous units suffered heavy casualties: the 63rd NY Infantry lost 156 killed in action, the 69th NY Infantry 259, the 88th NY Infantry 151, the 28th MA Infantry 250, and the 116th PA Infantry 145. Like the Germans, a number of Irish volunteers were awarded the Congressional Medal of Honor: Private Peter Rafferty of the NY 69th; Lieutenant John Tobin of the 9th, Coxswain John Cooper of the USS *Brooklyn,* Surgeon William Blackwood of the 48th PA Infantry, and Private George Platt of the 6th U.S. Cavalry.

Scandinavian Immigrants

Immigrants from Norway, Sweden, and Denmark were also drawn by the liberal naturalization provisions. Scandinavians were among the first European people to explore North America, with Viking explorations and minute settlements dating back to the period of 800 to 1050, nearly 500 years before Columbus discovered the Americas.

In the mid-1600s, several settlements from the region were established in Delaware, and a smattering continued to come during the colonial era. Total Scandinavian immigration to the United States eventually reached 2.5 million. On the whole, they were a successful group of immigrants and before the Civil War were able to reach and settle in the Midwest, particularly in Michigan, Wisconsin, and Minnesota (where a rune stone evidence has been found dating them back to around 1150). They naturalized quickly, and concentrated in farming and the timber industry. In the Midwest settlements, however, Scandinavian immigrants also went into business, commerce, manufacturing, finance, and other professions. Like the Germans, by the time of the Civil War they were mostly affiliated with the Republican Party (LeMay, 1987: 26–27).

Dutch Immigrants

Total immigration from the Netherlands was just over 350,000. Their presence was strong during colonial times and early independence years in New Jersey and New York. Brooklyn, the Bowery, and the Bronx, for example, all take their names as derivatives of Dutch words. Religious dissenters from the Netherlands founded colonies in Michigan and Iowa in 1846. Their emigration from the Netherlands coincided with the potato blight and resulting economic depression that struck their homeland, as it did much of Western Europe, in the late 1840s. These religious separatists established a settlement in Holland, Michigan that became the prototype for a new wave of settlers from the Netherlands in Wisconsin and Illinois as well as Michigan and Iowa. Dutch immigrants were particularly attracted to these areas because they found the soil and climate so favorable and reminiscent of their homelands.

The unifying force among Dutch immigrants was religion. Schisms resulted in the formation of the Dutch Reformed Church, the Christian Reformed Church, and the Netherlands Reformed Church. The Holland, Michigan settlement was particularly successful. Dutch settlers there achieved a high social status, and they founded Hope College there. Not to be outdone, the Christian Reformed Church, a more conservative group, emulated their example by forming Calvin College in Grand Rapids, Michigan (LeMay; 1987: 27–28).

Mexican Nationals Naturalized under the 1848 Treaty of Guadalupe Hidalgo

The naturalization provisions of the 1848 Treaty of Guadalupe Hidalgo caused some controversy, given the large population of Mexican nationals living in the ceded territory. Despite numbering nearly 100,000 strong, "the rapid influx of Anglo settlers in the wake of the gold rush of 1848 and the building of transcontinental railways from the 1860s ensured that Mexican-Americans would lose almost all political influence until the latter part of the 20th century" (Powell, 2005: 190). Mexican Americans attempting to vindicate their rights under the treaty would later argue that "While rights to property, especially land, were safeguarded by the provisions of the Treaty of Guadalupe Hidalgo, in practice Mexicans and Mexican-Americans were cheated of most of their properties in a short while" (Griswold del Castillo, 1992: 147).

The charge is not without merit. For example, in 1849, just one year after the treaty's adoption, Mexican Americans working the Northern California goldfields faced a wave of violent opposition. The very next year the Foreign Miners' Tax of 1850 "effectively forced Mexican-Americans out of the gold-fields (even though they were not 'foreigners')" (Murrin et al., 2007: 671). Mexican Americans in California also lost their land to debts taken during the droughts of 1860 and to pay legal fees incurred in defending their land from Anglo-Americans attempting to obtain the land by adverse possession (Murrin et al., 2007: 671–72). Although Mexican Americans residing in New Mexico enjoyed a more robust freedom than their Californian counterparts due to the reduced numbers of Anglo-Americans there, Mexican Americans residing in Texas also faced significant social and legal oppositions (Murrin et al., 2007: 672).

In fact, some Texans even took action to prevent Mexicans from naturalizing, despite the treaty's guarantees, based on an argument that as nonwhite persons, Mexicans were ineligible. In *In re Rodriguez,* 81 F. 337 (1897), however, a federal court in the Western District of Texas held that, at least for naturalization purposes, the Treaty of Guadalupe Hidalgo compelled the court to classify Mexican nationals as white. Despite this advantage over other immigrant classes, many scholars assert that U.S. naturalized citizens of Mexican ancestry were never able to fully capture the promises and benefits of citizenship (Johnson, 1998: 129; Powell, 2005: 190; Griswold del Castillo, 1992: 146–148). Indeed, Latino immigrants continue to struggle for political and social empowerment akin to immigrant groups of other nationalities (Thorpe, 2009).

Conclusion

Current naturalization law continues to reflect the policy set out by the early lawmakers from founding to 1865. Eligibility for naturalization continues to be predicated upon residency requirements, good moral character, and the taking of an oath to support the U.S. Constitution, among other factors (Kurzban, 2006: 1080–92). Although naturalization is no longer limited to free white people, immigrants continue to struggle both for (1) the right to naturalize and (2) acceptance and welcome once naturalized—that is, acculturation and incorporation into U.S. society.

Similarly, the way purely political considerations affected naturalization law reflects modern-day polarization over immigration policy. Simply put, once the young United States achieved its goal of populating its vast lands, naturalization regulation became messier, with future impact on voting trends gaining as much consideration as mainline immigration policy issues such as assimilation, landownership, moral character, and allegiance to the United States. The entrance of such political considerations into the naturalization regulatory debate at such an early stage foreshadows the political labyrinth posed by modern immigration law and policy, including considerations of amnesty, earned legalization, and border security provisions in current proposals to reform U.S. immigration law.

References

Adam, Thomas. 2005. *Germany and the Americas: Culture, Politics, and History—A Multidisciplinary Encyclopedia.* Santa Barbara, CA: ABC-CLIO.

Aleinikoff, Thomas Alexander, David A. Martin, and Hiroshi Motomura, eds. 2003. *Immigration and Citizenship: Process and Policy.* 5th ed. Eagan, MN: Thomson West.

Carpenter, A.H. 1904. "Naturalization in England and the American Colonies." *American Historical Review* 9(2): 288–303.

Dinnerstein, Leonard, and David Reimers. 1975. *Ethnic Americans.* New York: Harper and Row.

Griswold del Castillo, Richard. 1992. *The Treaty of Guadalupe Hidalgo: A Legacy of Conflict.* Norman, OK: University of Oklahoma Press.

Handlin, Oscar. 1979. *Boston's Immigrants.* Cambridge, MA: Harvard University Press.

Johnson, Kevin R. 1998. "An Essay on Immigration, Citizenship, and U.S./Mexico Relations: The Tale of Two Treaties." *Southwestern Journal of Law & Trade in the Americas* 5: 121.

Kurzban, Ira J. 2006. *Kurzban's Immigration Law Sourcebook.* 10th ed. Washington, DC: American Immigration Law Foundation.

LeMay, Michael. 1987. *From Open Door to Dutch Door: An Analysis of U.S. Immigration Policy since 1820.* New York: Praeger Press, 1987.

LeMay, Michael. 2006. *Guarding the Gates: Immigration and National Security.* Westport, CT: Praeger Security International.

LeMay, Michael C., and Elliott Barkan, eds. 1999. *U.S. Immigration and Naturalization Laws and Issues: A Documentary History.* Westport, CT: Greenwood Press.

Murrin, John M., Paul E. Johnson, James M. McPherson, and Gary Gerstle. 2007. *Liberty, Equality, Power: A History of the American People, Compact.* Stamford, CT: Cengage Learning.

O'Grady, Joseph D. 1973. *How the Irish Became Americans.* New York: Twayne.

Pfander, James E., and Theresa R. Wardon. 2010. "Reclaiming the Immigration Constitution of the Early Republic: Prospectivity, Uniformity, and Transparency." *Virginia Law Review* 96(2): 359–441.

Powell, John. 2005. *Encyclopedia of North American Immigration.* New York: Facts on File.

Steinfeld, Robert J. 2001. "Subjectship, Citizenship, and the Long History of Immigration Regulation." *Law and History Review* 19(3): 645–53.

Thorpe, Helen. 2009. *Just Like Us: The True Story of Four Mexican Girls Coming of Age in America.* New York: Scribner.

Trommler, Frank, and Elliot Shore. 2001. *The German American Encounter: Conflict and Cooperation between Two Cultures, 1800–2000.* Brooklyn, NY: Berghahn Books.

Ural Bruce, Susannah. 2006. *The Harp and the Eagle: Irish-American Volunteers and the Union Army, 1861–1865.* New York: New York University Press.

U.S. Senate Committee on Veterans' Affairs Report. 1979. *Medal of Honor Recipients, 1863–1978*. Washington, DC: U.S. Government Printing Office.

West, Thomas. 2001. *Vindicating the Founders: Race, Sex, Class and Justice in the Origins of America*. Lanham, MD: Rowman & Littlefield.

Zolberg, Aristide R. 2006. *A Nation by Design: Immigration Policy in the Fashioning of America*. Cambridge, MA: Harvard University Press.

CHAPTER EIGHT

Colonial Borders, New World Orders: Servants, Slaves, and the Founding Divisions of Labor in the Nation of Immigrants

Mark N. Hoffman

Introduction

Contemporary debates about U.S. immigration policy tend to reflect investments either in pluralist narratives of nation-building immigrant labor and melting-pot assimilation or in nativist narratives of enduring ethno-racial American identity and justified exclusion (Buchanan, 2006; Huntington, 2004). These apparently opposing narratives function to obscure the enduring imperial and colonial dimensions of immigration discourse in the United States. In so doing, they obscure the enduring practices of *social control* through which European and Euro-American discourses *both* (1) incorporate migrant groups as workers into their expansionist projects by organizing them into ethno-racial hierarchies *and* (2) exclude immigrants from domains of full citizenship. Drawing on prominent theories and histories of racial identity formation, this chapter foregrounds continuities that link contemporary practices of immigration management to the bordering practices and racial conceptions of national identity that emerged during the period of European and Euro-American expansion in the 17th and 18th centuries, prior to the recording of official immigration statistics. Focusing on the institutions of slavery and servitude, it identifies the colonial origins of some aspects of modern immigration discourse. Whereas many prominent theories of immigration to the United States treat these institutions as aberrant or relegate them to a distant past, I argue that the *forced* migration and superexploitation of European and African bonded labor should be regarded as foundational practices in the history of Euro-American immigration management.

Popular historical literature on post-abolition immigration to the United States tends to reinforce narratives of American exceptionalism by focusing on the relatively successful struggles of voluntary immigrants from Western Europe, and on the temporary, race-based restriction of immigration from Asia and Latin America between the late 19th century and the Kennedy-era reforms of the mid-1960s. With some notable exceptions, this literature relies on a progressive narrative of American inclusiveness and tolerance. Scholars of race, class, and gender have made substantial contributions to a growing body of critical literature attending to the often neglected racial and colonial dimensions of immigration policies and practices that existed in various forms throughout the 19th and 20th centuries. Drawing on the seminal works of W.E.B. Du Bois and others, theorists of racial identity formation have studied the bordering practices that secure the "wages of whiteness" (Roedinger, 1999) privileges distributed through political and legal mechanisms on the basis of socially legitimated racial hierarchies and divisions of labor. This literature helps to explain enduring patterns of socioeconomic inequality and racial subordination in the ostensibly colorblind era of universal civil rights. Other authors have deepened our understanding of these patterns by identifying their origins in practices of European imperial expansion and colonialism in the Americas (see, for instance, Toderov, 1999; Inayatullah and Blaney, 2004).

What follows seeks to contribute to this conversation by offering an expressly postcolonial analysis of the exploitation of immigrant groups, including African American slaves, before and after the American Declaration of Independence. By colonial, I mean administrative *practices* developed to advance imperialist projects of domination and expansion in *peripheral* spaces located both in foreign lands and *within* established national territories (Young, 2001: 17). Following the historian Mai Ngai, I call the latter form of domination internal colonialism (Ngai, 2004: 301). By postcolonial, I mean a critical orientation that draws attention to the enduring practices through which colonial relationships of domination are produced and maintained among would-be rulers and those they seek to rule, notably the social construction of racial subjects and the policing of boundaries between dominant and subordinate social groups (Young, 2001).

I proceed both chronologically and thematically, focusing on events and developments that demand postcolonial analysis. The chapter begins by situating forced migration to the American territories within a European imperial context. The first section discusses negotiations and settlements of early British, French, and Spanish colonialists in their encounters with indigenous peoples in Ireland and the Americas. The second section discusses the production of colonial subjects that preceded the profitable forced migration and exploitation of the English, Scottish, and Irish poor. I focus on the colonization of Virginia because of the important social and economic roles it played in founding the American republic. Continuing to analyze the Virginia case, the third section addresses the origins of institutionalized African slavery, plantation slavery, and chattel slavery and the construction in America of what W.E.B. Du Bois has termed the "color line." Here, I examine the ruptures that produced American colonial subjects, white and black, foreclosing the possibility of interracial solidarity among bonded laborers. The fourth and final section discusses the legacies of these foreclosures in the postindependence development of race-based immigration policies and practices. I conclude by reflecting briefly on the possible significance of these observations for the study of contemporary immigration discourse in the United States.

Rupture and Repetition 1: Imperial Expansion, Colonial Encounters, and Unsettling Settlements

Although their objectives differed significantly, European powers shared many of the same imperial imperatives. Among these were the need to secure newly established territories in foreign spaces inhabited by indigenous peoples with strong attachments to the land; the need to increase the profitability of trade by lowering costs of production and distribution; and the need to sustain the allegiance of a critical mass of subjects in far-flung regions of the New World. As historians and postcolonial theorists have shown, careful attention to the first of these imperatives reveals the extent to which European colonial practices, including the forcing and restricting of migration, were shaped by encounters, conflicts, and alliances with various Native American peoples (see Toderov, 1999; Inayatullah and Blaney, 2004). When considered in the context of European colonial adventures in Africa, the transatlantic slave trade, and the forced migration and forced labor of the European poor, this fact demands postcolonial reflection and analysis.

In order to outcompete their European rivals in a new global domain, colonial producers and traders experimented with a range of exploitative practices and institutions, from the coercive expropriation of Native American land and resources and the enslavement of indigenous people, to exploitative planter-tenant farming, to indentured servitude and other term-limited bond labor, to lifelong, hereditary chattel slavery and racial domination. Novel forms of migration and social control accompanied new modes of fur trading in French Louisiana; sugar production and mineral extraction in the Spanish West Coast and Florida; and monoculture tobacco, sugar, rice, and cotton production in the American South and the British West Indies. In part to advance the interests of the European and Euro-American bourgeoisie, and in part to ensure the allegiance of Euro-American property owners to capital and the Crown, colonial officials adapted old-world ethno-racial justifications for use in New World contexts.

In order to exploit subordinated colonial subjects as low-wage laborers in the New World, those subjects had first to be *produced* through ideologies and technologies of domination. When European colonial officials arrived in North America, they had already developed a complex lexicon to describe peoples they deemed inferior both to the old European aristocracy and to the emerging capitalist class. Indeed, the language used by British, Dutch, French, and Spanish officials to justify the conquest and exploitation of American Indians strikingly resembles descriptions of poor people in their home countries as well as to some British descriptions of French Catholic papists and French descriptions of British Protestant heretics. Naeem Inayatullah and David Blaney (2004) have shown how state-centric ways of dealing with difference by drawing and policing ethno-racial borders developed in conjunction with the emergence of the modern nation-state in late-medieval Europe. Imperialists developed ethnic and racial conceptions of national identity both to justify war between European powers and to justify the conquest, incorporation, subordination, forced labor and migration, and annihilation of supposedly inferior populations within European nations and empires. While practices of war-making involved the mutual recognition European powers as relatively worthy competitor-enemies, colonial regimes recognized indigenous and indigent populations primarily as useful instruments in the production of surplus wealth and as dangerous threats to the emerging capitalist order.

Historians of imperialism and the transatlantic slave trade have examined the connections between the emergence of the nation-state and capitalism and the corresponding mass migration of indigent and indigenous workers. Transformations in agricultural and industrial technologies combined with laws of private enclosure in the 16th, 17th, and 18th centuries displaced peasant farmers and produced a floating population of nomadic unemployed and underemployed paupers and vagabonds (Coldham, 1992; Allen, 1997). These vagrants roamed the countryside and moved, or were forcibly moved, to European cities and towns and to settlements and plantations in the New World. Containing, controlling, and exploiting Europe's volatile indigent population became a central concern of power- and profit-seeking sovereigns, large landholders, and state-endorsed companies (Coldham, 1992; Morgan, 2003).

The intensifying demand and supply of cheap convict labor empowered actors from sovereigns, who could order increased surveillance, sweeps of city streets, and the enforcement of draconian Poor Laws; corrupt judges who frequently took bribes both from merchants seeking slaves and from brothels seeking protection; and criminal bounty hunters and kidnappers (Coldham, 1992). Merchants and planters encouraged the tactic of emptying overcrowded British prisons and brothels by transplanting undesirables to the Virginia colony. Snatching and selling street urchins and vulnerable beggars, kidnappers, or spirits emerged as important agents of forced colonial migration during the 17th and 18th centuries. In some ways, their work resembles the work of illegal human traffickers today. Although officially illegal, kidnapping was lucrative because it provided planters with a cheap source of labor. Coldham (1992) notes that one was punished more harshly for stealing a horse than stealing a person (47).

As we shall see, English officials justified the draconian treatment and mass deportation of the English poor using many of the same disparaging stereotypes that were used to define the people colonized by the British in Ireland, the Americas, India, and the Middle East. The poor were idle, dirty, uncivilized, lazy, promiscuous, and barbarous (Coldham, 1992). They were a threat to public order and thus had to be executed or banished and put to work for the greater good of the empire. Like the fear of African slaves and the fear of subsequent waves of new immigrants to the Americans, it was precisely the constructed threat these forced migrants posed that transformed them from people with rights into exploitable bodies. Later generations of Anglo-Americans would express concern over the importation of undesirables from Europe, just as those same undesirables transformed the American South into an economic powerhouse.

In the case of convicts, the transportation and borderline enslavement of the English could be achieved through near total martial law, which was indeed the mode of governance in the early-17th-century British colonies

(Flaherty, 1969: 9–25). For convict subjects, colonial Virginia was a virtual prison. However, as Coldham (1992: 26) notes and Morgan (2003) explains more fully, even the poorest of Englishmen had some sense of their rights as English subjects. While the state of martial law might work to suppress a small group of convicts in a work camp, such camps would not support the long-term, sustainable productivity of the colonies. A critical mass of colonial settlers had to develop a stake in the future of the colony in order for it to thrive as a productive, self-sustaining power. Over the course of the 17th century, English and Anglo-American colonists established a complex, multiclass system of colonial rule that would allow Virginia to become the economic engine of the early American republic. This system was founded on colonial racism, and had its roots in earlier British colonial adventures.

Producing Colonial Migrant Subjects in the Old and New Worlds: The Irish and the Native Americans

The British presence in Ireland and Scotland provides instructive illustrations of distinctively colonial population and migration control in the era of early capitalism. Indeed, out of the colonial experiments in Ireland, Scotland, and the British countryside emerged ideologies and practices that were later deployed to control social groups in the American colonies including Irish immigrants—both bound and free. As early as the 13th century, English rulers, in true colonial fashion, sought to incorporate its neighboring island into its sphere of influence while at the same time denying Ireland's inhabitants the privileges afforded to full English subjects. Through surrender and regrant policies, Henry VIII expropriated Irish Catholic land and redistributed it to Protestant Englishmen (Henderson and Olasiji, 1995: 61). Producing basic foodstuffs and raw materials for absentee English landlords and ruled by discriminatory laws, Irish herders and farmers had neither legal standing in English courts nor political representation in English assemblies (Henderson and Olasiji, 1995: 62; Allen, 2002: 31). Backed by the Crown, English legislators, landholders, and soldiers delegitimized Irish social and economic structures, including tribal relations and customs, subsistence agriculture, the communal use of land for grazing, and Irish laws of primogeniture (patrilineal inheritance) (Henderson and Olasiji, 1995: 62). By the 17th century, native Irish Catholics were, like many Africans and Native North Americans would become, a subordinated class within the British political economy.

Also like Africans and Native Americans, the Irish were *racialized* subjects within British colonial discourse. Theodore Allen (2002) argues that

> the forms of essential elements of discrimination against the Irish in Ireland and against the African Americans, which gave these respective regimes the character of racial oppression, were those that destroyed the original forms of social identity, and then excluded the oppressed groups from admittance social identity normal to the colonizing power. (82)

The subordination of Irish natives was justified on the basis of innate British Protestant supremacy and Irish Catholic inferiority, not merely on the basis of religious affiliation or economic inequality, both of which could be overcome. As early as the 12th-century Norman invasion, English conquerors began to develop elaborate justifications for the oppression of the native Irish. The 13th-century *History and Topography of Ireland,* which would serve as a manual for subsequent generations of colonialists, summarizes the representations of these barbarous natives (Gerald of Wales). To British imperialists, the Irish were a backward people, unfit for full membership in civilized society. The prominent theorist and conservative anticolonialist Edmund Burke wrote in a letter against the 18th-century Penal Laws that colonial supremacists viewed the Irish natives as "a race of bigoted savages who were a disgrace to human nature" (Allen, 2002: 31; Burke, 2006).

The racial status of the native Irish is apparent in the fact that they were prevented from integrating themselves into British Protestant society *even when they aspired to assimilate.* Social restrictions and laws prevented the conversion of Irish Catholics to the Anglican faith or from marrying Protestants. Native Irish Catholics were prohibited from owning land in their home country. Moreover, English laws systematically denied them access to the British education system and barred them from earning positions within the British ruling class (Allen, 2002). These restrictions combined with a series of draconian legal measures, culminating in the infamous 17th- and 18th-century Penal Laws, at once stripped the Irish of their cultural and social identities and barred them from entering British society through assimilation. Their coercive incorporation into the British economy and systematic exclusion from British body politic were rooted in many of the same disparaging stereotypes through which British colonialists later classified Native Americans and Africans as inferior races.

As in most cases of colonial domination, constructing racial hierarchies meant strictly policing the boundaries of sexual, social, and political intercourses.

Racial oppression in Ireland functioned to curb miscegenation and potentially rebellious interracial alliances. Many of the efforts to separate colonial subjects emerged as responses both to unanticipated mixing of cultures and people and unexpected collective campaigns on the part of Irish Catholic and Irish Protestant rebels. Cromwell's efforts to exterminate the Irish and Sir Humphrey Gilbert's dream of starving them out of the country were in many ways reactions to Irish resistance. The Poor Laws and Penal Laws, in turn, served further to segregate and subordinate native Irish from the Protestant ruling class. These juridical and coercive mechanisms foreshadowed the separation of poor white bond laborers and tenants from African Americans, slave and free. Indeed, it represents a familiar colonial pattern that one can identify in the segregation of immigrant workforces today.

As David B. Quinn (1949) has noted, English constructions of Irish backwardness and barbarity provided a framework through which English colonialists interpreted the foreign behavior of Native Americans. Colonial tropes justified the forced labor and migration of Native American and of native Irish populations and later of Africans. Sir Humphrey Gilbert and Sir Walter Raleigh, the half brothers who earned colonial credentials in their role as settlers of Ireland and, in Gilbert's case, the brutal slaughter of French Catholics in the mid-16th century, sought to apply what they learned in their Irish experiments to their North American colonial expeditions. Sponsored by Queen Elizabeth, they sought to civilize and cultivate the wildlands north of Spanish Florida in the late 16th century. Consulting the Spanish colonial model, Raleigh identified two types of Indians before his arrival in Roanoke. The Spanish classified the good Indians as noble savages who could be civilized through submission to European colonial forces and disciplined through European modes of profitable production. Bad Indians were voracious cannibals who had either to be expelled from colonial holdings or annihilated. The English colonialists expected to find indigenous peoples who would welcome the benevolent rule of planters in return for the benefits of civilized life beyond bare subsistence and for protection both from raiding tribes of cannibals and from tyrannical Spanish and French colonists to the South and the West (Morgan, 2003: 44–45).

What Raleigh and his successors found did not meet these expectations. Native Americans in what was to become Virginia and the outlying areas had already developed advanced agricultural and hunting practices. They desired neither to work for the English nor to eat them. In fact, the earliest English colonial tenant farmers and indentured servants found themselves dependent on Indians for their survival (Morgan, 2007: 90). Specifically, they needed Indian-produced corn, which they acquired both through trade and through pillage. In their efforts to extract raw materials for profitable English commodities, early colonialists had neglected to ensure the basic subsistence needs of their settlers. In what became a dire condition of desperate dependence, it would have been impossible to recruit or to enslave en masse the ostensibly savage people that surrounded them, as some merchants and governors such as the famous John Smith would have liked (Morgan, 2007: 77). Although many Native Americans were captured and bound to work for English interests for set periods in the 17th century, the vast majority remained independent. Managing to maintain their ways of life through adaptation and strategic alliance, they engaged with the English primarily as hospitable allies or hostile enemies in the European scramble for American territory and resources.

Despite the failures of efforts to employ or enslave Native Americans en masse, the subordination of Indians as a racially distinct and inferior group foreshadowed the forced migration and enslavement of Africans. As C. S. Everett points out, Indian captives from campaigns of westward expansion were bought and sold by colonists both within Virginia and to the British West Indies. As opposed to the de jure term-limited servitude of European immigrants, Native Americans were often subjected to lifetime, hereditary servitude (Everett in Gallay, 2009: 76). As Everett argues, armed conflict between colonists and Indians served as proof of Indian savagery and rationalized their capture, forced migration, and enslavement.

New Means of Production, New Colonial Relations

Unable to secure a stable labor force among native populations before the flourishing of the transatlantic trade in African slaves, English colonial officials and company men had to rely on colonial subjects from their homeland, namely, the Irish, Scottish, and indigent English. Short- and long-term royal investors in the early American colonies, along with those of the emerging European planters (who ventured to the New World) and adventurers (who funded the project but stayed home), expected high rates of return in short order (Allen, 1997). Early failures to find precious minerals, such as in Raleigh's lost Roanoke colony, intensified demand for low-cost labor to aid in the production of cash crops. As mentioned earlier, the demand for labor in the new colonies dovetailed with new imperatives of population control in Europe. In England, the privatization and enclosure of land and replacement of tenant farmers with grazing sheep produced a massive army of idle, poor people, many of whom became wards of the state. Successive sovereigns beginning with Queen Elizabeth agreed with the ruling classes that the threat posed by these indigents to public order and private property called for a radical response. Queens and kings—taking their lead from vanguard merchants such as Gilbert and Humphrey—promoted supposedly humanitarian efforts to clear the

English streets of vagabonds, thereby saving them from idleness, poverty, thievery, and the gallows.

As Allen and Morgan point out, in the early years of the Virginia colony the demand for cheap labor was not so great that it trumped English tenant-farming customs. Before the full conversion from failed efforts at mineral extraction to tobacco cash-crop production, more than half of the original bands of laborers in Virginia were officially tenant farmers who worked for wages, farmed for themselves, and produced tobacco for the Virginia Company. By the mid-17th century, the overproduction of tobacco in Virginia had the effect of lowering its value. The Virginia Company resolved the problem of falling prices by transforming tenant farmers into bond laborers, by recruiting indentured servants, and by importing British criminals and colonial subjects from abroad.

This servant industry was simultaneously colonial, in the sense that it imposed European rule on supposedly backward people and undercultivated land, and capitalist, in the sense that it was driven by stakeholders in private companies seeking profits. It was in many ways these companies themselves that ruled large sections of English colonies around the world. In the early 16th century, English merchants and planters worked with jurists, kings, and queens to produce joint stock companies that could weather the storms of colonial experiments and recruit masses of exploitable workers from around the empire. As Jordan and Walsh explain, it was an English judge, Lord Chief Justice Pompham, who spearheaded efforts to arrest masses of English vagrants and send them to America. The express purpose of this initiative was both to rid England of its undesirables and to profit from their labor.

In 1618, the Virginia Company introduced a head-rights system that would grant land to every nonindentured settler. Head-rights encouraged investment by granting 50 acres of land per servant to those who paid for the servants' passage. From the standpoint of English rulers, these incentives increased the power of the state by promoting the exile of threatening undesirables and by increasing state revenue through the taxation of tobacco. From the standpoint of profit-seeking merchants, the incentives to buy and sell bonded laborers had the effect of transforming people into commodities.

The first bonded laborers sent to the American colonies fell into several categories: free-willers, convicts, indigent children, women, and Catholics. Merchants seduced dislocated and impoverished workers in the first category with promises of a better life across the sea. In the case of landless Irish Catholics, indentures were essentially forced into servitude, as they had no other means of survival in Ireland. In exchange for their Atlantic passage, hopefuls were asked to sell their labor power for anywhere from three to seven years. As Don Jordan and Michael Walsh have written, it is in many ways more accurate to say that these voluntary emigrants sold *themselves*. Colonial laws provided indentures with few rights or protections against masters who commonly abused, beat, and killed them or worked them to death in the service of a capitalist enterprise. Planters could and frequently did extend the terms bondage of indentured servants for alleged violations of strict colonial laws or simply to increase productivity. Those who survived their bond period were often denied their promised freedom dues, which may have included land and livestock, and were thus thrust into debt peonage or forced to sell themselves to another master (Jordan and Walsh, 2007).

Against the odds, many indentured servants from England did manage to survive their terms of servitude and realize the dream of owning and cultivating land in British colonies. If they were lucky enough to be bought by a generous master, they would collect freedom dues and go to work planting and harvesting their own plots once they had completed their term. As the colonial justice system developed independently from England, a small but growing percentage of English servants who had served their original terms won their freedom through court battles (Jordan and Walsh, 2007).

By contrast, convicts offered the chance to work in Virginia to escape incarceration or execution in England had less of a chance of independence than their free-willing counterparts. On the servant ships and upon their arrival in the colonies, they were chained and packed in rows and treated much like African slaves would be treated in the years to come. They were advertised as commodities in colonial newsletters alongside cattle and trade goods, and sold at markets and off the backs of merchant trailers in practices that resembled the auctioning of African slaves (Coldham, 1992; Jordan and Walsh, 2007). Like African slaves, they were deemed threatening enough to public order to be frequently whipped by plantation overseers. While they were more expensive than regular indentured servants, they were cheaper than African slaves and could be forced to work longer than free-willers.

Adding to the ranks of bond laborers were masses of young children and, more and more, women sent to serve as maids and wives of servants. Merchants seeking quick profits made a business of kidnapping poor urchins from the streets of English towns and cities and of convincing parents to give up their children to allow them to escape a life of poverty. The bond period of children ranged from 12 to 18 years depending on the age at which they were captured and transported. Like convicts and free-willers, children bond laborers were often sold to the highest bidder and worked without adequate rest, food, or medicine. Working in harsh conditions in a foreign climate, many of these children did not survive their childhood, much less their term of bondage.

The systematic dislocation and transportation of Irish Catholics to the new colonies testify to this exportation of colonial systems of rule along with readymade colonial rulers and subjects. Cromwell's invasion of Ireland in the mid-17th century, and the draconian anti-Catholic policies that followed in its wake, inflicted such devastation on the Catholic population that transportation seemed a welcome escape from debilitating repression and poverty. Many of those who were not forcibly removed to the slave colony of Barbados voluntarily bound themselves to a merchant master as a means of escape. Colonial rulers moved with them, adapting methods of control. Prior to the influx of African slaves, Catholics were marked for especially harsh treatment. Until 1660, the Irish natives were often forced to serve longer terms than their English and Scottish counterparts. In Maryland, they were forced to conform to Anglo-Protestant cultural and religious norms, but denied full inclusion in the political community.

The different treatment of different bond laborers and tenant farmers may have served as a mechanism for social control in the years before the massive influx of African slaves. However, given the oppressive conditions faced by all immigrants to the new colonies, one might have expected massive uprisings against colonial masters who did relatively little work and reaped the bulk of the rewards of tobacco sales. Evidence suggests that the threat of rebellion was a near-constant concern of the ruling-class planters and merchants in the colonies (Morgan, 2003; Allen, 1997). As the tobacco industry grew exponentially, so did the demand and supply of exploitable workers. As more workers survived their bondage and began farming their own land, planters began to seek a new source of superexploitable labor. As we shall see, the incorporation of African slaves into the colonial economy did not initially diminish the danger of rebellion. A new system of colonial control had to be produced to secure a new colonial hierarchy.

Rupture and Repetition 2: Resistance, Rebellion, and Racial Domination

What happened in the peripheral spaces of the colony always complicated imperial ambitions and designs generated in European power centers. As in Ireland, unanticipated alliances, rebellions, and migrations in the Euro-American colonies disrupted the smooth extraction of wealth by merchants and rulers. The unforeseen economic effects of monocrop production exacerbated the obstacles posed by resistance and by alliances among different racialized classes of immigrant workers. Bond laborers defied their masters, and planters and merchants defied revenue-generating European legislation and royal decrees. The reduction of tenant farmers to bond labor status produced a system in which a superexploited working class vastly outnumbered their colonial masters. Without what Allen (1997, 2002) calls a secure "buffer zone" or "intermediate stratum" of social control, that is, a social class of workers who share with their rulers a stake in the colonial political economy, the center would not hold. The sticks of colonial oppression and the carrots of liberty held just out of reach created a structure that ultimately proved untenable. The problem of labor solidarity and immanent rebellion had to be resolved in order for the colonial appropriation of surplus to endure. For a variety of reasons, American colonialists resolved this problem through a system of racial oppression.

Roads to Rebellion and Racial Slavery

As prominent historians have noted, the early years of colonial bond servitude in British America were governed primarily by mechanisms of violent coercion and open military dictatorship (Allen, 1997: 75). Once plantations were firmly established in Virginia, a new generation of Euro-Americans elites asserted their authority by creating relatively autonomous local governments to replace the system of English direct rule. Acting through the newly established General Assembly, Colonial Council, and General Court, Virginian elites secured and expanded the powers they and their predecessors had been granted by royal charters and the Virginia Company. To increase profits by lowering labor costs and to block competition with tenant farmers and freed former servants, these elites systematically dismantled the ladders of socioeconomic mobility.

As Allen notes (1997: 93), the first immigrants to Virginia were officially divided into five classes: (1) gentlemen (who reaped profits but were exempted by law from any physical labor), (2) freemen (a petty bourgeoisie of independent farmers and self-employed artisans), (3) tenants-at-halves (who enjoyed half the fruits of their agricultural labor), (4) hired indentured servants, and (5) apprentices. Allen subdivides these classes further into owners of property (the first two classes) and nonowners. One of the most notable accomplishments of the property owners was their temporary reduction of the laboring classes to the state of bond servility and the corresponding reduction of labor costs, for example, through the extension of the working day and the reduction of wages.

A series of attacks by Native American tribes provided justification for austere measures to restrict tenants' production of corn. Colonial officials argued that corn production served as an enticement to marauding bands of Indians. That colonists had for many years depended on Indians for corn was omitted from the official justification of restrictions. Partly in order to prevent further mixing among immigrant servants, freedmen, and Indians on the frontier, legal restrictions and armed frontiersmen prevented Indian tribes from entering colonial territory. In 1646, Governor Berkeley played a crucial role in establishing what in time became one of the first border control regimes on Virginia's eastern frontier. Under the terms of their submission to the colonial order, members of the former Powhatan confederacy agreed to ask the Governor for permission before selecting their own rulers.

These restrictions combined with the collection of fixed rents and the reduction of tobacco production (to raise its price) forced immigrant tenants into debt and effectively blocked freed servants from entering the class of independent farmers. Forbidden from producing anything but tobacco for English merchants, tenants and aspiring independent farmers had to buy corn from English profiteers who sold the staple at exorbitant prices. In lieu of money or trade goods, property owners accepted years of bonded service in exchange for room and board. To survive, first-generation tenants and farmers from England, Scotland, and Ireland often had to sell themselves into bondage.

The decline of tobacco prices, manufactured shortages of corn, and Indian raids served to increase the leverage of the property-owning class. Through local government and appeals to the Crown, planters managed to convert these crises into advantages. The transformation of tenants and freeman into bonded laborers effectively increased the concentration of land in the hands of large plantation owners. In addition to the acquisition of land through the head-rights system, the acquisition of laborers became an important source of wealth. The trade in, or renting out, of immigrant servants became standard practice toward the end of the 1620s (Morgan, 2003). Colonial officials appropriated destitute tenants, apprentices, and shipments of new farmers as commodity-servants. New shipments of immigrants, it was argued, lacked the capital and the skills to sustain themselves in the colonies, and therefore had to be attached to wealthy planters for their own sake and in order to avoid becoming a public charge or nuisance. Bond or free, their survival depended on owners of the means of tobacco production. Advocating the need to increase productivity and sustain population growth, planters secured legislation that extended the terms of bondage of already-indentured servants. In addition, the House of Burgesses enacted harsher penalties for those who resisted longer workdays for little or no wages or sought to flee bondage to live with hospitable neighboring Indian tribes. Dependent laborers in this early period were rarely defended by the courts in cases of abuse (Allen, 2002; Morgan, 2003). Penalties for minor infractions of decidedly un-English colonial regulations increased workers dependence on the local bourgeoisie.

Still, many indentured servants finally won some degree of freedom, and as the numbers of freedman rose, so did the demand for more land. Planters anticipated this development and bought large tracts to rent out to freedmen at high prices. In this way, they were able to sustain profits by continuing to exploit their former bonded laborers. New poor immigrants in the 17th century were locked into this vicious cycle. How they would fare was determined in part by the luck of the draw. If their masters made good on their promise to free them after their term of service, and if they granted their freedom dues, and if they were able to find a decent plot of land, they could begin the hard life of independent farming. Just how rare was this level of success is evidenced by the fact that very few tenant farmers or indentured servants went on to play any role as elites in the planter class or in colonial governing bodies (Allen, 2002).

The obstacles to independence faced by a growing number of tenant farmers and freedmen led to rising discontent among first- and second-generation immigrant workers from Britain. Anger and frustration over restrictions on land acquisition and corn and tobacco production were often directed at Indians as opposed to colonial governments. Because freedman could not acquire land already bought by large plantation owners, they were forced to find what they could on the border that separated them from the former Powhatan Confederation of Native American nations. The Virginian colonial government frequently intervened on the side of Euro-American immigrants against the so-called savage natives and endorsed their efforts to expand westward. The recognition of Euro-Americans of whatever class as fundamentally superior to the natives established a racial barrier similar to the one that separated British settlers in Ireland from Irish Catholic natives. The redirection of anger and frustration toward Native American and French competitors undermined the cultivation of solidarity among the immigrant poor, not to mention between Euro-American workers and Native Americans.

Nevertheless, as in Ireland, frustration over oppressive working conditions and discriminatory laws eventually boiled over into violence.

Although Bacon's Rebellion of 1676 was directed at securing land from the Powhatan Indians, it defied Berkeley's oppressive colonial government's orders on behalf of those suffering most under his rule. Moreover, it represented the colonial government's worst fears of interclass alliance. Bacon's supporters included not only indentured servants, tenants, and freedmen, but also scores of African slaves. As Allen notes, despite its apparent racial animus, it raised the specter of working-class racial solidarity against the colonial elite. Even after its brutal suppression, it left a chilling effect that was apparent in royal concessions to Virginia colonial subjects that bypassed the local legislature, and in renewed local efforts to establish a new colonial system of social control.

The enduring Anglo-Irish and Euro-Indian antagonisms had demonstrated the advantages of systems of racial oppression over the superexploitation of an increasingly unified class of servile colonial subjects. The rebellions in Ireland and then in Virginia also displayed the threat posed collectively by the losers in colonial systems of social control. The more conspicuous was the gap that separated the promise of freedom from the reality of seemingly unending servitude and debt peonage, the greater the danger to the colonial hierarchy and the system of accumulation and appropriation of wealth. As the ranks of freedmen and would-be freedmen rose, their demands for relative rewards and freedoms had to be acknowledged. The challenge for the ruling elite became how to satisfy these demands while at the same time preserving a system in which profits could be secured through the exploitation of docile, nonwaged workers. Racial, hereditary chattel slavery began to serve this function in the 18th century.

Rupture and Repetition 3: Slavery and Revolution

A great deal has been written on the radical transformation of the status of Africans in the American colonies in the 17th and 18th centuries. I offer a brief account here for the purpose of illustrating both the continuities and the profound changes represented by the turn to racial slavery. In the wake of Bacon's rebellion and subsequent expressions of freedmen's discontent in Virginia, creating "a society that would nourish the freeman's freedom and at the same time make possible the unlimited exploitation of labor" became a paramount goal of colonial governance (Morgan, 2003: 292).

Resistance and rebellion had demonstrated that the enslavement of Euro-Americans would be impractical if not impossible, especially given the promises of land and freedom dues that motivated many of them to make the treacherous Atlantic voyage and to work under life-threatening conditions for little or nothing. As Morgan notes, while the ruling class in Virginia may not have had moral qualms about enslaving the entire nonpropertied population of the colony, to do so would require a series of conspicuously deliberate legislative and policing initiatives designed to reduce aspiring independent farmers to the status of inferior colonial subjects. Although this had been achieved in Ireland and, in a limited way, in the case of indigenous populations in the Americas, to enslave a population of Euro-Americans convinced of their superiority and of their corresponding right to freedom would have required an untenable, brutal system of martial law. Rising life expectancies and expectations of indentured servants erected limits to capital accumulation that racial slavery could break down.

Of course, as Native American resistance and the participation of African Americans in Bacon's rebellion demonstrated, it would not be an easy task to enslave non-Euro-Americans either. The 16th-century Native Americans and African Americans had, in different ways, asserted their own rights to freedom from oppressive colonial laws. Many of the first Africans transported to Anglo-American Virginia were considered servants and shared hopes of freedom with Euro-American indentures and poor farmers (Henderson and Olasiji, 1995: 242). Although many served longer terms than their Euro-American counterparts, a significant number bought their freedom or became free after their terms of bondage expired (Allen, 1997).

The relatively higher prospects for the successful mass enslavement of blacks was initially revealed not in a deliberate campaign, but in a series of successful, local legal decisions that recognized blacks as an undeserving racial group. The significance of the case of John Punch as a turning point is well known, but is worth mentioning here. Punch was an African American servant convicted of running away from his master with two European indentured servants in 1640. The General Court extended the terms of bondage of the two Euro-American servants by four years. By contrast, they sentenced Punch to a lifetime of servitude, arguing only that he was a non-Christian and a negro to justify his enslavement (Allen, 1997: 178–80). As in Ireland, the designation "non-Christian" would not be a decisive mark of inferior status, as it defeated the purpose of Britain's ideological civilizing mission to Christianize both Africans and Indians, and opened the possibility, attempted by many new slaves, of self-liberation through conversion (Allen, 1997: 196–98). To appease missionaries and reconcile the English civilizing mission with the enslavement of Africans, courts subsequently ruled that baptism could not change the status of a slave, and that the legal status of slaves was different than Christian *white* servants (Morgan, 2007: 331).

In a series of decisions from the 1660s to the turn of the century, the Virginia courts institutionalized the differential treatment of white servants and black slaves. Extreme forms of punishment were legally reserved for blacks, as were prohibitions against taking abusive white masters to court. By the turn of the 17th century, the property of bonded African Americans was systematically expropriated, whereas white servants were allowed to keep their meager belongings, such as livestock. Over time, these laws both produced white contempt for blacks, and more demand for African slaves as a superexploitable labor force (Morgan, 2007: 332–33). Slaves were officially recognized as a category of worker in 1661. From that time on, whites increasingly played a police function in suppressing black resistance. Although ownership of black slaves was concentrated in the hands of rich landowners, the structural position of servitude they occupied ensured a position of privilege for poor whites. For their part, wealthy planters, concerned about black insurrection as the numbers of black slaves rose, began to invest more in whites as privileged protectors of private property (Morgan, 2007: 379).

As in Ireland, several laws and practices maintained the hierarchical separation of whites and blacks by controlling sexual relations. Perhaps the most important was the 1662 act that legislated matrilineal hereditary servitude. By enacting that "all children . . . should be held bond or free according to the condition of the mother," Virginian legislators allowed masters who raped their slaves to remain the masters of their own children. A series of antimiscegenation laws followed, targeting unions between black or biracial and white women, and reestablishing distinctions between black slave and white servant that were blurred by these unions (Law Library of Congress, online).

Even with the development of a legal system of racial subordination, poor whites and enslaved blacks still joined together in rebellion in the 17th and 18th centuries (Henderson and Olasiji, 1995: 244). By this time, however, the white investment in and commitment to a system of racial, hereditary chattel slavery had reached a critical level. Royal charters increased this investment by subsidizing the emerging British slave trade. At war with the Dutch and determined to curb Dutch profiteers who would sell slaves in exchange for goods produced in the English colonies, the Crown sought to replace the Dutch slave trade with its own (Morgan, 2007). As kings, queens, and colonists like Raleigh and Gilbert had done in Ireland, the Royal African Company established an elaborate set of practices for the acquisition, commodification, and transportation of African bond laborers to the English colonies. This initiative combined with the increasingly productive employment of slaves in Virginia, and then in South Carolina, effectively *produced* both slave societies and the slave market (Smallwood, 2008).

As Stephanie E. Smallwood has shown, the deliberate institutionalization of the slave trade relieved American planters of the burden of subduing and commodifying diverse cultural groups of Africans. The physical and social technologies of violence necessary to ensure the relatively smooth transportation of Africans were founded on scientific calculations of the maximum degree of pain and poverty their human bodies could withstand. To avoid collective rebellions and the death of African cargo, traders in the Royal African Company, along with independent English interlopers, had to isolate Africans from their cultural frames of reference (e.g., by loading ships with people from different language-speaking groups) and reduce them to a state of abjection (e.g., by chaining them and depriving them of all but bare-subsistence provisions with no cultural significance) (Smallwood, 2008). As Smallwood explains, the process of commodification could not be achieved all at once. Rather, the transformation of cultural agents into colonial subject-commodities was achieved through a series of violent incarcerations and forced migrations from capture (usually by Africans at war or working for European colonial agents) in the African interior, to incarceration centers and auction blocks at the coast, to the well-documented horrific death traps that were the slave ships, again to auction blocks in Anglo-America, and finally to plantation servitude. As scholars of the slave trade have noted, African slaves were often bought or sold several times before arriving at their final destination.

Despite disorienting dislocation, violent abuse, and dehumanizing confinement, Africans frequently acted in concert and rebelled against captors, traders, colonial agents, overseers, and planters (Smallwood, 2008; Allen, 1997). As in Ireland, efforts to reduce African people into instruments always failed to remove the threats of African solidarity and insurrection. Colonial officials and slave traders tried to represent these rebellions as indications of African barbarity, thereby reinforcing colonial justifications for their subordination and enslavement. As their numbers increased in the American colonies relative to white planters and servants, and as laws and practices of subordination established a new racial hierarchy in the 18th and 19th centuries, fears of black–white servant solidarity dissipated. Confronting the specter of black insurrection, relatively privileged whites joined with planters to secure their position of superiority in the new colonial order.

As both Morgan and Allen point out, many of the colonial tropes used to justify the subordination of the Irish and Scottish were transported along with Irish and Scottish indentured servants to justify their subordination in the colonies. These tropes often took the form a proto-nativism expressed as fear of the criminal, idle and undisciplined, violent, thieving, dishonest, promiscuous and sexually deviant, murderous, disobedient, and otherwise barbarous element that these immigrants introduced. Of course, the unrelenting demand for low-cost, superexploitable labor outweighed these fears, which were transformed into brutal practices of subordination to suppress the threat of disorder and rebellion. While African slavery introduced a racial ingredient based on phenotypical associations with the aforementioned colonial stereotypes, it is important to note that representations and fears of Africans resembled those of Irish, Scottish, and English poor servants. Indeed, the transfer of these colonial representations from the Irish to the Africans required a reconfigured investment in the racial category of whiteness, if not, as Allen's polemic suggests, the invention of this category. As is evidenced by the English and French consultation of the Iberian models, whiteness and blackness were already available as colonial categories when the English entered the transatlantic slave trade. As Bacon's rebellion demonstrated, however, the category had not yet been effectively reconfigured to recruit impoverished Euro-Americans and to exclude Africans. To ensure a superexploitable labor force, the beneficiaries of superexploitation mobilized Irish and Scottish servants and would-be independent farmers as white subjects worthy of the rights and benefits of citizenship.

White Republican Revolution: Equality, Liberty, Racial Slavery, and the Colonial Ordering of Immigrant Workers

As Allen argues, the recruitment of oppressed whites required a veritable sea change of colonial sensibilities and allegiances. The first volume of Allen's *Invention of the White Race* details the transformation of Irish servants' anticolonial sentiment from rebellious resistance to British colonial oppression to active acceptance and even encouragement of white supremacy and the institution of racial slavery. As a testament to the successful recruitment of Irish servants and settlers as whites, leaders of Irish immigrants adamantly defended slavery against charges of hypocritical collusion advanced by the Irish anticolonial leader, Daniel O'Connell. Having won a degree of freedom and independence in the American colonies by the mid-19th century, especially once the trade in African slaves was in full swing, first- and second-generation Irish immigrants appeared unwilling to risk sacrificing their superior status by allying with O'Connell and Africans as fellow-oppressed colonial subjects. Although meager relative to early American dreams of land, freedom, and independence and to the exorbitant profits of the ruling bourgeoisie, the benefits of whiteness and the stigmas associated with blackness, it seems, were enough to dissuade most poor Irishmen from making common cause with Africans.

Perhaps the most important of the benefits associated with whiteness was the status of not being slaves. As Morgan notes, poor whites in the American South lived in dangerously close proximity to brutal forms of lifetime chattel slavery. Many of them escaped from a condition similar to that of African slaves on the Barbados sugar plantations. In Virginia, the institution of slavery opened enough of a gap in socioeconomic status between Africans and an increasing number of small, poor, quasi-independent white freeholders to create a decisive impression of shared interests with southern white patricians and a shared stake in the peculiar institution. Republican ideologues encouraged this identification by valorizing the figure of the landowning yeoman farmer and encouraging his acquisition of small plots (50–100 acres). The ostensibly independent, armed yeoman was, of course, the central character in Thomas Jefferson's republican vision. The patrician's manifestos ironically, but understandably, decentered the interests of his own class, which were reflected in the concentration of wealth conspicuously on display at Monticello and Mount Vernon. The bedrock of the new republic would be the self-made immigrant man of honest means, *not* a decadent gentleman and *not* a slave.

Lingering frustration and anger over enduring obstacles to independence directed at local colonial government were thus redirected toward the meddling English Crown. Without the taxes and restrictions imposed by this increasingly distant, oppressive power, republicans began to argue, yeomen would be able to realize their birthright as Euro-American freeholders, namely, the right to own property including slaves. The fact that colonial officials and settlers defied the Crown did *not* mean that they defied the colonial order. In many ways, the revolution was an effort to *preserve* this order for the sake of a reconstituted set of white beneficiaries. As Morgan points out, Anglo-American patricians, and many middling settlers, clung to their British identity. They opposed the backwardness and barbarity first of the poor immigrants from beyond the pale, and then to African immigrants and their descendents. As Morgan points out, the fact that Revolutionary soldiers were granted 50 acres and a slave for their service is not an aberration. It was, in fact, a realization of an original American dream.

Histories of the American Revolution that represent the transition from British to American identity as an absolute rupture obscure the continuity represented by the transition from civilized English identity, defined by its negation of an imagined barbarity, to civilized Anglo-American white identity, as opposed to purportedly barbaric African slaves. This erases the continuities that link prerevolutionary forced migration and servitude to postrevolutionary racial and socioeconomic oppression, both of slaves and, in different but consequentially significant ways, of new immigrants. It leads, in short, to major blind spots in most arguments and debates about contemporary immigration policy and practice. One could reasonably argue that immigration management in the United States was and remains a distinctively European colonial project.

New Frontiers: Post-Abolition Internal Colonialism and Contemporary Continuities

Just as it would be a mistake to assume that the American Revolution produced an absolute rupture in Anglo-American colonial discourses of immigration management, it would be equally misleading to assume that the abolition of the slave trade and then of slavery ended the colonial ordering of immigrant workforces. As W.E.B. Du Bois, among others, has proven, the problem of the color line survived abolition, as did the mechanisms of racial oppression, although in different forms. Following Du Bois's lead, historians have shown how the practices of Reconstruction rehabilitated and entrenched colonial hierarchies without the benefit of constitutional sanction (Foner, 2002). Sharecropping and convict labor were throughout the late 19th century at least another form of racial oppression, and in many ways "slavery by another name" (Blackmon, 2009). As in 17th-century Virginia, local courts produced and protected the superior social and legal status of all whites, including recent immigrants, over all blacks. To reinforce their sense of superiority, whites were employed as policemen and protected as supremacist vigilantes. The Klan emerged to protect white racial superiority against the threats of black integration. They endured through ages of mass immigration and nativist restriction as the self-identified guarantors of racial hierarchy and purity.

Meanwhile, the pattern of inclusive exclusion of racialized groups of new immigrants—of their incorporation into the American economy and exclusion from the American polity—has continued in a variety of forms. Large corporations continue to recruit massive numbers of immigrant workers who are denied full legal status as members of the American political community. Waves of German, Scandinavian, Irish, Italian, Eastern European, and Latin American immigrants have all occupied forms of this racialized position in the Euro-American political economy. Corporate profits have depended on the social and political marginalization of these groups. Just as American republicanism reinforced both the demand for superexploitable labor *and* the demand for the exclusion of threatening African immigrants from the polity, postrevolutionary American patriotism reinforced the demand for cheap labor from Asia, South America, and Eastern Europe, *and* the exclusion of those groups from domains of citizenship.

It is a mark of colonial immigration management that xenophobic (now nativist) investment in racial superiority empowers the exploiters of labor by further marginalizing subordinated groups of new immigrants. Fear of and contempt for new immigrants, like the fear of and contempt for Africans displayed by whites in the 17th century, produces a hostile environment in which employers can play the role of a benevolent protector. The fact that both nativist ideology and legal discourse now refers to countries of origin as opposed to class or race in its articulation of criteria for inclusion and exclusion may reconfigure the boundaries that organize different groups of immigrants into hierarchies does not fundamentally alter the Euro-American colonial pattern. Students of U.S. immigration policy and practice would benefit from studies that emphasize the continuities that link practices of immigration management today to their not-so-distant colonial origins.

References

Allen, Theodore W. 1997. *The Invention of the White Race: The Origins of Racial Oppression in Anglo-America.* New York: Verso.

Allen, Theodore W. 2002. *The Invention of the White Race: Racial Oppression and Social Control.* New York: Verso.

Blackmon, Douglass A. 2009. *The Re-Enslavement of Black Americans from the Civil War to World War II.* New York: Anchor.

Buchanan, Patrick. 2006. *State of Emergency: The Third World Invasion and Conquest of America.* New York: St. Martin's Press.

Burke, Edmund. 2006. *The Works of the Right Honourable Edmund Burke.* London: B and R Samizdat Express (e-book).

Coldham, Peter Wilson. 1992. *Emigrants in Chains.* Surry, NC: Genealogical Publishing Co.

Du Bois, W.E.B. 1998. *Black Reconstruction in America.* New York: Free Press.

Du Bois, W.E.B. 2010. *The Souls of Black Folk.* London: Aziloth Books.

Flaherty, David, ed. 1969. *Laws Divine, Moral, and Martial Compiled by William Strachey.* Charlottesville, VA: The University Press of Virginia.

Foner, Eric. 2002. *Reconstruction: America's Unfinished Revolution.* New York: HarperCollins.

Gallay, Allen. 2009. *Indian Slavery in Colonial America.* Lincoln, NE: University of Nebraska Press.

Henderson, George, and Thomson Olasiji. 1995. *Migrants, Immigrants, and Slaves: Racial and Ethnic Groups in America.* Lanham, MD: University Press of America.

Huntington, Samuel P. 2004. *Who Are We: The Challenges of American National Identity.* New York: Simon and Schuster.

Inayatullah, Naeem, and David Blaney. 2004. *International Relations and the Problem of Difference.* New York: Routledge.

Jordan, Don, and Michael Walsh. 2007. *White Cargo: The Forgotten History of Britain's White Slaves in America.* New York: New York University Press.

Law Library of Congress. *Slavery and Indentured Servants.* Available at: http://memory.loc.gov/ammem/awhhtml/awlaw3/slavery.html.

Morgan, Edmund S. 2003. *American Slavery, American Freedom.* New York: Norton.

Morgan, Kenneth. 2007. *Slavery and the British Empire.* New York: Oxford University Press.

Ngai, Mai. 2004. *Impossible Subjects: Illegal Aliens and the Making of Modern America.* Princeton, NJ: Princeton University Press.

Oakes, James. 1990. *Slavery and Freedom: An Interpretation of the Old South.* New York: Norton.

Quinn, David B. 1949. *Raleigh and the British Empire.* New York: The MacMillan Company.

Rawley, James A. 1981. *The Transatlantic Slave Trade: A History.* New York: Norton.

Roedinger, David R. 1999. *The Wages of Whiteness.* New York: Verso.

Smallwood, Stephanie E. 2008. *Saltwater Slavery: A Middle Passage from Africa to American Diaspora.* Cambridge, MA: Harvard University Press.

Toderov, Tzvetan. 1999. *The Conquest of America: The Question of the Other.* Norman, OK: University of Oklahoma Press.

Wales, Gerald of, John O'Meara Translator. 1982. *The History and Topography of Ireland.* New York: Penguin Classics.

Young, Robert J. C. 2001. *Postcolonialism: An Historical Introduction.* Malden, MA: Blackwell Publishers, Inc.

CHAPTER NINE

A Holy Experiment: Religion and Immigration to the New World

Sharon Kornelly

Introduction

The history of religion in the United States is closely tied to American ideals of freedom and independence. In 1620, the first colony of Puritans fled religious persecution in England to settle in the New World. Through their search for a Promised Land, the Puritans launched an American story and created a model for all people seeking refuge to express their beliefs. The Puritan's eventual success encouraged other religious communities to immigrate to the growing American colonies. More by accident than by intentional design, however, the influx of so many different religious communities compelled the founding fathers of the United States to create a nation built on the premise of separating political governance from religious conviction, thus establishing the foundation for a very American belief in religious freedom. This chapter describes and explains the linkage between immigration and the religious freedom principle so integral to American society. It uses examples of religious groups who moved as entire communities from the Old World to the New in search of a new Jerusalem for themselves, for a place where they could practice their faith and exercise their religious freedom unfettered by constraints placed on them by a central or, eventually even, a state government. The story of the quest reverberates throughout American history, from the earliest colonial times through the early foundation period. Indeed, it continues beyond the time of the Civil War, the time focus of this volume, as new religious community groups arose, or fled from Europe to America between the Civil War and World War II.

The search for religious acceptance was clearly the main reason motivating many of the first European immigrants to the New World, yet the history of religious tolerance in the young colonies is fraught with contradiction. For example, Puritans escaped religious tyranny in England but their own intolerance of other religions often led to the imprisonment, whipping, exiling, and even hanging of non-Puritans. Ironically, the severity of these punishments was the precise cause for the establishment of new colonies, such as Rhode Island and Pennsylvania, which were founded with the specific goal of supporting religious tolerance. Other colonies, such as Virginia and the Carolinas, were directly sponsored by the English Crown, so they maintained strong ties with the Church of England. By the 1700s, dozens of ethnic groups and their respected religious denominations populated the North American colonies. Rather than serve as a barrier to their unification, however, the acknowledgement of religious diversity ultimately became a unifying force for the fledging nation.

Even though the Puritan's role in establishing religious freedom is often overly romanticized, it is true that they established an immigration pattern for religious communities seeking the Promised Land. Many early immigrants to the American colonies fled religious intolerance in Europe. The seemingly open, unhindered land of the New World offered tremendous opportunity to people throughout Europe whose prospects were often determined by class discrimination and religious instability. Through the 17th century, most European kingdoms were closely bound to the Roman Catholic Church. The notable exception to this is England, which by 1539 had completely separated from the Pope and burned its Catholic monasteries. The English Crown established its very own Church of England, but this move only separated the monarchy and its citizenry from the Roman Catholic Church. It decidedly did not sever the bond between politics and religion. In England and elsewhere in Europe, the king or queen served as both the highest political and the highest religious authority of that kingdom.

Europeans who held spiritual beliefs that differed from the ruling class were more than just religious dissenters. They were actually considered extreme political radicals capable of undermining God and the Crown. People faced punishment and discrimination for not following their government's religion, particularly in England. This initial push factor set a tone for religious immigration to the American colonies. In turn, European perceptions of America's religious tolerance and unlimited opportunities provided a pull factor to the new land (LeMay, 1987: 2). By the time the

American colonies had grown into a young nation in the mid-1700s, much of Europe was engulfed in civil war, religious unrest, and a continent-wide famine that caused economic instability. As a result, America's immigration pull factors of religious freedom and opportunity for all ultimately became a significant and increasingly symbolic part of the nation's history.

European Origins

When Christopher Columbus first landed in the American Caribbean in 1492, many of the major events that would trigger European immigration to this New World had not yet occurred. All of Europe's monarchs were still part of the Roman Catholic Church, which united Christian kingdoms against the rest of the world. Yet the European discovery and subsequent establishment of colonies on the American continents also came during a moment of tremendous change in attitudes toward religion and its role in governing individuals. In that same year, Columbus's sovereign, Queen Isabella of Spain, completed the Last Crusade against Islam by removing the Moors from Southern Spain and Portugal. European principalities slowly began to position themselves as distinct empires in a quest to further build their international powers. A mere 25 years later, Martin Luther made his official protest against the Roman Catholic Church, which ultimately created the great division between Europe's Protestant and Catholic nations, and led to a century of warfare on the European continent. Kingdoms and Crusades hardly seem modern, but the consequences of the events that took place in 16th-century Europe had a lasting impact on American immigration and the settlements of Old World religions in the new frontier.

The first religious immigrants to the New World were Catholic missionaries charged with bringing salvation to the land's indigenous populations. Throughout the 16th and 17th centuries, missionary work, fueled by the closing chapter of the Crusades and later reenergized by the zeal of the Reformation, played a central role in Europeans' first interactions with Native American tribes. While only a small chapter in the early European immigration to America, missionaries operating throughout the Spanish territories established and maintained a strong Roman Catholic presence in the North American southwest, and throughout South and Central America. Protestant colonies also shared an interest in saving the souls of Native Americans. Most English colonies included missionary work within the provisions of their charters. These missions had an incalculable impact on native populations, with far-reaching implications for culture loss and revival, as well as on migration patterns through the 21st century.

Secondly, Protestant and Catholic empires vied for power in the New World. When European empires demarcated their territories on maps, they essentially designated which regions of the New World would be open to Protestant settlement and which would be sympathetic to Catholicism. Until the mid-1700s, it was simply not possible to conceive of life without religion, and to a large extent, most people did not think about the spiritual realm as being separate from less lofty beliefs or daily activities. Religion and governance were intertwined, as were understandings of spiritual matters and daily life. Belief in God and loyalty to one's monarch were directly equated with personal duty and pride. The expansion of the empire's wealth and territory, whilst curbing the growth of others, was a driving force for many European explorers and traders. Even people who were not religiously devout maintained the intense rivalries between empires, and thus pursued goals that were deeply rooted in religion.

The Catholic empires of Spain, Portugal, and France were first to establish missions and trade routes in the New World. By the time English and Dutch Protestants settled in the North American colonies, during the early 17th century, they had to protect themselves from French Catholic territories to the northwest and Spanish Catholic holdings to the south. Protestant suspicion of the Catholic Church lingered for centuries in the North American ethos. In the 1830s, the influx of Irish Catholic immigrants led to violent protests in Baltimore, Boston, New York, and Philadelphia. Protestant Americans feared that the newly arrived Catholics would follow the governance of the Pope and undermine the democracy of their adoptive nation.

Finally, the division between Catholic and Protestant empires further reinforced ethnic and linguistic differences, eventually leading to separate national and cultural identities in Europe. Though no part of the European continent was unaffected, the impact of the Protestant Reform movement was most widely felt in German-speaking principalities, Scandinavia, and England. In addition, while these Protestant denominations were united by a central Christian philosophy and a distrust of the Roman Catholic Church, they often had little else in common. Slight theological distinctions between Protestant groups were often intensified by significant cultural, linguistic, and geographic barriers. Once in America, European immigrants often moved to areas where they shared both the ethnic and religious heritage of other members of that community. As a result, migration patterns in the New World initially reinforced Old World ethnic divisions and helped develop distinct regional cultures in the American colonies.

The Protestant Reformation

Several independent Protestant Reform movements developed simultaneously across Europe during the early 16th century. These movements were a reaction to significant philosophical and societal changes that affected the entire continent. As we shall see, they fueled extensive migration, both internal migration within Europe and emigration from the European continent to the Americas. The Reformers' gravest concerns stemmed from their rejection of the overt corruption of the Roman Catholic clergy and the Pope's nearly total control over European monarchies. The emergence of small principalities that were somewhat disconnected from medieval feudalism coincided with a growth in commerce, producing a noble class that was determined to override the Vatican's theocracy. These economic and political influences clearly served as the primary impetus for the various Protestant Reform movements that unfolded throughout Europe. In addition, however, the dawn of the Renaissance spurred interest in scholarship and scientific exploration that ultimately changed how people viewed the world and their role within it. Shifting attitudes regarding the importance of the individual encouraged the spiritually devout to read biblical scriptures for themselves. The development of the printing press made the scriptures and other religious writings widely accessible. This led to a religious awakening that focused on understanding one's personal relationship to God rather than on the religious rituals of a liturgical-based church.

The underlying causes of the Protestant Reformation united the movement against the Catholic world, but the diversity of Protestant denominations and the significant controversies that arose amongst various groups should not be overlooked. The Protestant emphasis on personal study of the scriptures led to vastly different interpretations of the relationship between God and human beings. These theological debates often centered around different interpretations of predestination and salvation, baptism, the inherently sinful nature of mankind, transubstantiation,[1] and the following of divine law during religious rituals. Collectively, these questions created the momentous theological rift between Catholics and Protestants, and divided various Protestant groups. To today's population, these differences may seem like relatively minor details, but they had profound implications on how various people perceived themselves, and how they interacted with people who opposed their religious philosophies. This pressured certain religious communities to leave Europe, which eventually led to the development of religious pluralism and religious tolerance in North America.

Lutheran and Reform Churches had the strongest influence throughout Europe and, therefore, constituted the majority of the Protestant immigrants to North America. In spite of their separate beginnings, the early differences between these religions were relatively small. Lutherans based their beliefs in the teachings of Martin Luther, a former Catholic monk who openly opposed the corruption of Germany's Catholic clergy. His theology emphasized the primacy of God's word, Christ's presence in the sacrament, and predestination. Lutheranism spread throughout German-speaking Europe and into Scandinavia. Reform Churches were initially similar to Lutheranism in almost all aspects except the sacrament. John Calvin, a French theologian based in Switzerland, was instrumental in energizing Reform movements throughout Europe. By the mid-1500s, Calvinism was prevalent throughout German-speaking Europe including Switzerland, the Netherlands, Hungary, Austria, and Poland. The Calvinist Reform movement also had a strong influence on French Huguenots, Scottish Presbyterians, and English Puritans.

In most places where the Lutheran or Reform Churches were firmly established, they were sponsored by the reigning government of the principality. Local politics and minor regional distinctions often intensified the religious differences between European Lutherans and Reformers. This situation was reversed in North America, however, where relative similarities in language and cultural heritage softened the religious differences between Lutheran and Reform Churches. Throughout the 18th century, German immigrants to Pennsylvania regularly established Union Churches that could be shared between Lutheran and German Reform congregants.

Once the Catholic Church was no longer held supreme, hundreds of independent religious groups flourished throughout Europe. These radical Protestant groups formed a small but significant alternative to government-sponsored Lutheran or Reform Churches. Other than sharing a loose adherence to Protestant beliefs, these groups were extremely diverse and many totally rejected formal establishment. By the mid-17th century, Pietism, which emphasized inner-spiritual development, was a significant component of the beliefs of many radical Protestant groups. While many of these communities no longer remain, collectively, they consistently challenged the tenets of mainstream Protestantism, particularly with respect to understanding God's relationship with humans, interpreting God's law for religious rituals, and predestination. Anabaptists (rebaptizers) and Quakers made the particularly provocative claim that religious practice should be separated from civil governance. Other groups, such as the Schwenkfelders and the Mennonites, were comprised of closely knit communities that followed the spiritual principles of a revered teacher. The implicit political nature of radical Protestant groups caused them to be particularly vulnerable to persecution, as they defied the authority of both the Roman Catholic Church as well as the more dominant and conservative forms of Protestantism, which retained a liturgical and ritual emphasis. As a result, many radical Protestant groups migrated to North America where they were able to reestablish their communities in entirety and forge the American frontier according to their beliefs.

The Protestant Reformation in England

The effects of the Protestant Reform in England posed a different set of circumstances than those on the European continent, and deserve particular attention because of their direct impact on religious immigration to the American colonies and to the United States in the 1840s. In 1531, King Henry VIII forced the church clergy into accepting him as the "Singular Protector, only Supreme Lord, and, as far as the law of Christ allows, even Supreme Head" of the Church of England (Ahlstrom, 1972: 85). With this, he clearly separated himself and the Anglican Church from the Pope's authority. Three years later, the Act of Supremacy made the English monarch the unequivocal ruler in all matters of political and religious governance. These actions alone, however, did not make England a Protestant nation. Henry VIII's departure from the Roman Catholic Church was primarily a political statement, rather than a spiritual one.

King Henry's gesture, however, guaranteed that the turbulence of the Protestant Reformation engulfed English life for the next two centuries. As a Protestant sympathizer, King Henry VIII ensured that his son and immediate successor, Edward VI, had Protestant tutors and advisors. As a result, the Protestant influence on the English monarchy increased during the mid-16th century. This sense of religious constancy was short-lived. From King Edward's young death in 1553 to the end of James II's reign in 1688, the religious policies of the English empire changed under each ruler. English Puritans, who wanted to return to a pure Christian religion, were regularly persecuted. When the possibility of chartering a settlement in America emerged in the early 1600s, the first small group of Puritans saw this as an opportunity to leave this instability and actually implement their beliefs in a spiritually empty world.

"As a City upon a Hill"[2]: The Religious Geography of the New World

Religious tensions caused by the Protestant Reformation were readily apparent throughout the New World. They were particularly striking, however, in the early English colonies, where government-sponsored churches that regulated religious worship frequently clashed with colonists' spiritual beliefs. The first English colonies were established either through a proprietary grant given by the reigning monarch or through buying a charter from the Crown. As such, even though some colonial charters were purchased specifically so that people could escape England's religious tyranny, they were still not completely free from the royal crown or the Anglican Church. Colonists had to ask permission to establish their own religious belief as their colony's prevailing church. The English monarchy could revoke colonial charters—and sometimes did—often causing significant changes in the colony's religious laws. Still, this instability was far less profound than what many religious immigrants had encountered in Europe.

All English colonies were Anglican by default, but charters that specifically sponsored Puritanism or the Roman Catholic Church established those religions as dominant and provided them with government funding. Most colonies also enacted strict laws against religious dissenters, referred to as Nonconformists, who opposed the colony's official church. While punishment differed throughout North America, it was usually more severely enforced against the so-called radical Protestants, such as Quakers and Anabaptists. The dominant religion of each colony, along with colonists' attitudes toward religious acceptance or intolerance, ultimately served as critical factors in shaping the religious character of each region that persisted well after Independence.

In the early colonies, religion held an extremely important role in peoples' daily lives and cannot be neatly separated from their cultural, economic, political, or social concerns. Noting the pervasive aura of religion during the early settlement of America does not mean, though, that all colonists shared the same perspective toward spirituality, religious practices, or the role of the church. While many settlers continued to behave with the religious fervor that is often associated with the first Puritans, it is noteworthy that not even all of the people brought by the Mayflower were among the pious. Arguably, religious devotion helped to unify settlers when they experienced the particularly inhospitable conditions of their first years in North America. As more settlements were established and more people immigrated to the fledging colonies, however, attitudes regarding the role of religion became more divergent. Many still sought a transcendental spiritual encounter with God, but it is clear that others simply attended church to socialize with far-flung neighbors and reaffirm their role within the community (Ulrich, 1991: 108).

The Mayflower Compact and the Massachusetts Bay Company

While not the first English settlement in North America, the Mayflower passengers who eventually landed at Plymouth Rock in 1620 hold a mythological place in the history of the United States. Clearly, their story of persecution, their desire for independence, and their ability to overcome adversity embody the American spirit. That they were able to establish a continuous settlement in the New World, after so many others had been abandoned, is truly remarkable. Whether their success was due to their resolute piety is debatable, but there is no doubt that Puritan fundamentalism played an important part in the development of the Plymouth colony and the larger adjacent colony of Massachusetts Bay, which was chartered in 1630.

In spite of the tremendous hardships faced by early settlers in New England, the English colonies in North America were by far the most established and successful throughout the 17th century. Several factors—including the English Crown giving a New World charter to almost anyone with proper funding or stature, and the political instability caused by the English monarchy's ambition to dominate the world's empires—resulted in an enormous influx of immigrants to New England between 1620 and 1650. By 1643, more than 20,000 people had migrated to the Holy Commonwealth of Massachusetts Bay, where they developed an independent, self-sustaining community based in Puritan beliefs. Their success encouraged other religious groups, whose spiritual and political ideologies clashed with the European ruling classes, to also come to North America.

While many of these colonists were English Puritans who sought spiritual refuge in the New World, few actually desired to completely separate themselves from either the English monarchy or the Church of England. Instead, most viewed themselves as independent, yet loyal, subjects of the Crown and aimed only to establish pure Christian worship, grounded in Anglican principles. In fact, many Puritans viewed Separatists—those who wanted a clear division from the Anglican Church, and thus from England—as holding dangerously radical political views.

Even more extremist were some Quakers who suggested that religious beliefs and political affairs should be completely separated. For most Puritans, what now seems a very-American idea regarding the division between church and state was simply untenable. Religious piety and political authority were fully integrated in the Holy Commonwealths. The colonies used taxes to fund the Puritan Church. Men had to be full church members in order to vote in the colony's public community affairs, and, to be a full member of the church, a person had to recount the divine circumstances of his or her religious transformation.

Puritan emigration from England to the New England colonies waned after 1649, when Puritan revolutionaries led by Oliver Cromwell overthrew the monarchy. Ironically, in 1649, Maryland, a proprietary colony of England, enacted the Act of Toleration, outlining greater religious freedoms than existed within the two Puritan colonies of Massachusetts and Connecticut. When the English monarchy was restored in 1660, the development of other successful North American colonies presented fleeing Puritans with a multitude of options for establishing a new home.

Rhode Island

In the winter of 1636, several well-renowned exiles from the original Holy Commonwealths founded Providence, Rhode Island as their own refuge from religious intolerance. This group of previously unaligned radical Protestants, which included Separatist Roger Williams and Pietist Anne Hutchinson, petitioned for the first colonial charter to explicitly grant the freedom of religious conscience to its inhabitants. While rarely an initial destination for early immigrants, Providence became a safe-haven for those who found that they clashed with the strict religious and political regulations enforced in the other New England colonies. Quaker missionaries, in particular, often sought refuge in Rhode Island when persecuted elsewhere. In addition, several new and radical religious ideas were tested and reconstituted in Rhode Island.

Most early colonists of Rhode Island, however, did not explicitly hold these more radical religious beliefs prior to leaving Europe. Rather, they were sympathetic to these ideas and, in Rhode Island, they found solace in a community of people who shared them. Even though Rhode Island's religious charter more closely resembles our present-day American understanding of religious freedom and diversity, the colony itself was an idea ahead of its time and had little impact on immigration to the New World.

Jamestown and Virginia

Unlike the New England colonies, the Virginia charter was not a response to religious intolerance. Instead, as England's first colony in the New World, Virginia was directly aligned with the Anglican Church. The Virginia colony was initially chartered during the reign of Queen Elizabeth, the English monarch who was arguably most influential in pushing the Anglican Church toward Protestant theology. Robert Hunt, an Anglican priest, was hired to accompany the first ship of colonists, which landed at Jamestown in 1607. As the New World's first Anglican priest, he established the Church of England in America and served the spiritual needs of the colonists. Hunt was also responsible for establishing Protestant missionary efforts among local Native Americans—an endeavor that was explicitly outlined in Virginia's charter. Virginia's first governors used religious conviction to create civil order and to motivate disheartened settlers during the bleak years of Jamestown's early history.

In spite of the decidedly non-Puritan religious foundation of the colony, Virginian laws regarding its settlers' adherence to religion were equally as ruthless as those established in the North. Similarly, the Anglican Church was government-run and subsidized by local taxes. In 1661, Virginia enacted strict regulations against Baptists and Quakers. These laws were somewhat successful in immediately curbing the activities of Nonconformists, but had little long-term effect in enforcing religious devotion among most Virginians. Instead, full membership in the Anglican Church became associated with the elite gentry. The relationship between church membership and social status was further reinforced by the great distances between Virginian plantations, which made regular church attendance difficult. While the seemingly lax religious commitment among Virginia's lower classes meant little during the 17th century, it created a fertile atmosphere for the massive evangelical conversion events of the Great Awakening that characterized American religious life throughout much of the 18th century.

Shortly before the Revolutionary War, Virginia became home to many converted Baptists and Baptist sympathizers. Considered an extremely radical Protestant group, Baptist preachers were regularly fined and imprisoned throughout the colonies. In spite of the threat of harsh punishment, Baptist brothers, Shubal Stearns and Daniel Marshall, were very successful in evangelizing the settlers of Virginia's frontier. Their efforts increased the number of Baptist Churches from 5 to 34 in a matter of five years, which caused the Virginia assembly to take increasingly repressive measures against Nonconformists. As a young lawyer, Thomas Jefferson saw the plight of Baptists and advocated for their rights within the colony. This experience later influenced his views in outlining religious rights for all American citizens, and was explicitly written into the Virginia Statute for Religious Freedom (Hening, 1823: 84–86).

Like Rhode Island, Virginia's role in religious immigration is indirect, as there was not a singular religious pressure that pushed or pulled people to come to the colony. The environment, however, allowed men like Jefferson, Stearns, and Marshall to thrive. Their impact, profound and revolutionary as it was at the time, helped to develop a uniquely American attitude toward religion, the effects of which could only truly be understood in later decades and centuries.

Maryland

In 1632, King Charles I granted Cecelius Calvert, known as Lord Baltimore, a proprietary charter to the colony of Maryland. As a devout Roman Catholic who had previously been exiled from Virginia, Lord Baltimore ensured that Catholicism was the dominant government-sponsored religion in the colony. Initially, the Anglican Church was present in name only. In order to ensure the religious tolerance of Roman Catholics, the colony passed a religious Toleration Act in 1649, which also attracted a large population of Nonconformists and religious dissenters into Maryland. In spite of a few organized Puritan uprisings throughout the 17th century, most colonists remained unaffiliated with a formal church.

King William III revoked Lord Baltimore's charter in 1691, making Maryland a royal colony. On numerous occasions, the royal governor and assembly attempted to establish the Anglican Church as the colony's only acceptable religion. These laws were initially rejected because they violated the Toleration Act. The Maryland assembly placed restrictions on Anglican Nonconformists, and eventually was able to enforce the legal founding of the Anglican Church in 1702. The Maryland charter was returned to the Calvert family in 1715, after they converted to Anglicanism. This intensified the Anglican Church's stronghold on the colony while simultaneously enforcing distinct social class divisions between the Anglican ruling elites and the Nonconformist settlers. While a beacon of religious dissent at its inception, in less than a century, Maryland became the most vigilant colonial supporter of the Church of England.

The Carolinas

The proprietors of the Carolina charter mainly aspired to develop large noble estates and demonstrated a relative lack of interest in the colony's religious affairs. The original founders were mildly sympathetic to the Anglican Church, but the charter included a provision for the freedom of religious conscious. A veritable lack of economic and religious regulation in the Carolinas encouraged many Nonconformists and rebellious types from the other colonies to settle in the Carolinas. Though it was almost completely uninhabited by Europeans until 1670, the colony grew to a population of more than 4,000 in less than 30 years.

While the population steadily expanded, formal religion developed more slowly in the Carolinas. South Carolina's first Anglican Church was established in 1681. By 1704, Anglican parishes surrounding the urban areas of South Carolina were considered among the most orderly and well-maintained in the colonies, even though religious Nonconformists still comprised the majority of the colony's population. Throughout its colonial history, South Carolina continued to boast a substantial number of Puritans and Baptists who had immigrated from New England, French Huguenots, and Quakers.

Similarly, North Carolina attracted many dissenters, particularly Quakers who migrated south to escape religious intolerance in Virginia. Unlike South Carolina, however, the Anglican Church was unable to take a firm hold in the region. Scattered settlements and extensive wilderness areas made it difficult to establish any form of centralized church. Members of the colony's assembly repeatedly tried to enact laws to make the Anglican Church the official religion in North Carolina, but each of these proposals was rejected.

In the Carolinas, the establishment of the Anglican Church was significant insofar as it formalized social class divisions. The relative attitude of religious tolerance combined with the difficulty of establishing formal churches across the vast territory allowed evangelism to become a powerful spiritual force during the 18th century. Unencumbered by civil laws or parishes, the openness of the Carolinas was also appealing to the growing number of German-speaking Pietist communities who migrated into the southern frontier following the American Revolution.

Georgia

A group of missionaries, doctors, and other professionals who were deeply involved in the humanitarian movements of the early 18th century procured the Georgia charter from King George II in 1732. The Crown tasked them with creating a buffer between already established English colonies and the territories claimed by France and Spain. The proprietors' goal, however, was to create a socially idyllic colony that provided England's poor with an alternative to debtors prison. In addition to these destitute colonists, Georgia's proprietors invited persecuted religious communities to settle in the colony. In 1735, a group of Moravian Brethren accepted this offer. They were soon followed by the Salzburg Lutherans and a smattering of other Pietist communities. The Moravian and the Salzburg Lutheran communities proved exceptionally prosperous, in spite of the near absence of colonial infrastructure or support.

Within 15 years of its establishment, the idealistic colony was on the verge of failure. In an attempt to revive their experiment, the proprietors repealed their bans on alcohol and slavery in 1749, but they eventually returned the colony to the English Crown in 1752. Even the royal government, however, had difficulty maintaining political and religious jurisdiction over the widespread colony. While the Anglican Church was officially established in the colony upon its original founding, priests and parishes were intermittent at best. Interestingly, among the first priests sent to serve the Georgia parishes were John Wesley, who went on to develop Methodism, and George Whitefield, who was arguably the most significant evangelist of the Great Awakening.

New Netherlands: New York, New Jersey, Pennsylvania, and Delaware

The Mid-Atlantic region was first settled by the Netherlands to the north and Sweden to the south. Through a charter to the Dutch West India Company, the Netherlands claimed the area of present-day New York and Northern New Jersey in 1609. Because the company's main focus was in expanding the fur trade, colonization efforts in New Netherlands were minimal in comparison to the extensive immigration to the English colonies at that time. The founding of New Sweden in 1638 was also primarily motivated by the fur trade. Sweden, however, was interested in developing the settlement. The government sponsored immigration to the Delaware Valley and even established a Swedish Lutheran Church as part of that effort. Sweden's aspirations were short-lived, however. The government abandoned its presence in the New World, stranding the small group of Swedish and Finnish colonist who soon yielded to Dutch rule in 1655. The regime change had little immediate impact on their daily lives, and they were even permitted to conduct Lutheran Church services in Swedish. The settlement's population stayed extremely small, but they remained a significant ethnic enclave through the 17th and 18th centuries.

While sparsely populated and slow to grow, the New Netherlands ultimately constituted the most consistently diverse population in the American colonies. Moreover, even though the Dutch governors ruled with greater political and economic authority over their subjects, they were often lenient with respect to religion. Settlers of the Mid-Atlantic thus escaped the religious austerity of the surrounding English colonies. By the time the Dutch surrendered New Netherlands to the English in 1664, England's royal governors had realized the fiscal benefits of socially liberal rule.

England divided New Netherlands into the colonies of New York, East and West New Jersey, Pennsylvania, and eventually Delaware. New York proved to be a particularly difficult colony for the English to reestablish. In the mid-17th century, its population was relatively small and ethnically diverse. With the exception of a fervent group of Long Island Puritans, who despised the English Crown, the first New Yorkers showed almost total apathy toward both government and religion. But upstate New York became home to the Shakers in 1774. The Shakers were founded in England in 1770, by Quaker Ann Lee. An offshoot of the Religious Society of Friends (Quakers), they were known as the "Shaking Quakers" because they were said to shake as they danced and spoke in tongues during their services. Known as "Mother," Ann Lee's followers came to view her as the female component of Christ's spirit and represented the second appearance of Christ on earth—thus their official name was the United Society of Believers in Christ's Second Appearance. They emigrated to America in 1774, settling in Western New York State in a settlement called Niskeyuna. Eventually they established 18 settlements that stretched from Kentucky to Maine (Portman and Bauer, 2004). Their enduring legacy includes their model of gender equality (institutionalized in their society in the 1780s), their monastic-like communitarian life, and the ecstatic nature of their worship services (similar to the charismatic churches in current times, and in many services during the evangelical fervor of the Great Awakening).

The problems of New York stood in great contrast with East New Jersey, which was chartered for a new wave of English Puritans needing to escape the Great Persecution that followed the Restoration of the English monarchy in 1660. This region eventually became home to many Scotch-Irish Presbyterians who left famine and civil unrest in Northern Ireland during the latter half of the 18th century. Further south, in New Sweden's former colony, William Penn and a small group of fellow Quakers founded West New Jersey in 1674. In less than a year, 800 English Quakers had settled in the Delaware Valley. Their continued persecution in England ensured a steady immigration of Quakers into the region until Penn chartered the Commonwealth of Pennsylvania in 1681. The relative religious tolerance of the Quakers encouraged other persecuted groups, including an evangelical Pietist community of Moravians, to move into Southern New Jersey. By the time the two New Jersey colonies were united in 1702, the colonial charter ensured freedom of religious conscious to all but Roman Catholics.

While the newly formed English colonies tried to account for the preexisting cultural and religious diversity within the New Netherlands settlements, the shift had significant implications for people already residing in each region. Ironically, deeply rooted Old World ethnic enclaves, such as the Swedish Lutherans, found it most difficult to survive in Pennsylvania's atmosphere of extreme religious tolerance. The sudden invasion of new and diverse religions created tension within these traditional communities because they often lacked the resources to stave off pressures brought in by evangelizing groups.

Pennsylvania—the Holy Experiment

William Penn, an English noble and a member of the Society of Friends (Quakers), chartered Pennsylvania in 1681 in order to institute his Holy Experiment of religious tolerance and pluralism. Like many of the English colonies before it, Pennsylvania was founded with the intent to be a salvation for religious refugees. Unlike previous colonies, however, the Commonwealth of Pennsylvania promised nearly complete freedom of religious conscience, welcoming anyone who believed in God.

As the proprietor of Pennsylvania, Penn's secondary goal was undeniably economic, and he initially granted substantial tracts of land to anyone who promised to settle it. His was an attractive offer for many Europeans, and the colony's population exploded. In 1683, 60 ships docked in Philadelphia, and by the following year, Philadelphia had more than 350 homes and as many neighboring farms. The primarily Quaker population grew quickly, easily surpassing the New England colonies' rapid rate of expansion. Toward the mid-18th century, the enthusiasm for Quaker ideals began to fade. Quaker membership became a nominal matter based in birthright, Penn's sons converted to Anglicanism, and the daily concerns of Pennsylvanians generally emphasized economic and secular activities.

The decline in Pennsylvania's Quakerism coincided with an increase in new European immigrants to the colony. Among the largest of these new immigrant groups included Scotch-Irish Presbyterians, who entered the port of Philadelphia at a rate of 12,000 per year by 1740. In addition, an estimated 120,000 German-speaking immigrants landed in the English colonies between 1683 and 1820, which made them the largest non-English-speaking ethnic group in North America, and they ultimately were the single largest national-origin immigrant group, reaching more than 7 million (LeMay, 1987: 21–22). Many of these German-speaking immigrants resided in Pennsylvania, where, by the turn of the 19th century, one-third of the population was of German ancestry. Most German-speaking immigrants were members of the German Lutheran or German Reform churches. Small communities of German Pietist and radical Protestants, who faced persecution from both Roman Catholic and Protestant Reform governments, saw Penn's Holy Experiment as an opportunity to establish a home of their own. While the native stock of English speakers treated them as one people, they were a diverse group splintered by regional strife in their homeland, and along religious lines. They often came in entire groups of hundreds, as Mennonites, Dunkers, Lutherans, Calvinists, and even a few Jews. Geographically, they came from the assorted German principalities of the time: they were Palatines, Salzburgers, Wurttenburgers, and Hanoverians (LeMay, 1987: 23). Collectively, they expanded the American frontier and developed a Pennsylvania German culture that blossomed throughout the 18th and 19th centuries (the Pennsylvania Dutch, an English version of the German Dutch).

The *Anabaptists* or rebaptizers began as a reformation movement in 1525 in Zurich, Switzerland, preaching adult baptism as a public sign of Christian faith and stressing a double separation: church and state, and separation of the church from the evils of the larger society. They encountered severe persecution, as they seemed to threaten the very fabric of 16th-century European society. Thousands were killed as both civil and religious authorities sought to repress the movement (LeMay, 2009: 193).

The Anabaptist sect known as Mennonites was named after Menno Simons, a prominent leader and bishop who united with a Dutch group in 1536. The Amish split off as a separate sect in 1693, in what is today the Alsace region of France. The Anabaptist leader, Jacob Ammann, began a new practice of community life that included social avoidance—shunning—of persons who had been excommunicated from the church, as well as advancing other practices that enforced an even greater separation between the church and the minority society. They migrated to the United States and Canada in the 18th century. The Old Order Mennonites and the Old Order Amish set up small congregations centered in the Northkill Settlement, in groups of 500 or so, in Berks County, Pennsylvania, and in Lancaster County, Pennsylvania, in 1710. These two settlements became the mother colonies of both the Amish and Mennonite communities that were established throughout Pennsylvania and south to Virginia and the Carolinas. The Amish and the Old Order Mennonites maintained their cultural separatism from the broader American society by use of the *Ordnung,* or understandings, that prescribed expectations of Amish life—the do's and don'ts of Amish and Mennonite practices (Nolt, 1992; Kraybill and Nolt, 1995: 12; LeMay, 2009, 193–200).

Pennsylvania German Communities

German-speaking immigrants to Pennsylvania came from many culturally diverse states and principalities that were both in and outside of present-day Germany.[3] These disparate communities became German in heritage due to the extreme linguistic and cultural differences they encountered relative to other immigrants, particularly the dominant English-speaking population.

The increased appearance of German-speaking immigrants during the mid-18th century was caused by both the growing religious tolerance in North America and the resurgence of Pietism in Central Europe. The Pietist movement aimed to complete the Reformation by amending traditional Protestant beliefs to emphasize the importance of spiritual rebirth, evangelism, and the cultivation of inner spirituality. Many Pietists viewed themselves as being part of the German Lutheran Church, but more traditional Lutheran Churches saw these beliefs as being far beyond the scope of their theology.

Upon Pennsylvania's inauguration, William Penn granted 25,000 acres of land to a group of German Lutheran Pietists who subsequently founded Germantown. The settlement quickly attracted many German-speaking communities and soon became the cosmopolitan nexus of German culture in America. Members of the Church of the Brethren, or Dunkers, were among the most influential of the groups to move to Germantown. Dunkers were a small radical community of Pietist Anabaptists from the German Palatinate, who initially emphasized celibacy, shared property, and the practice of ancient Christian rites. The entire community of Dunkers left Germany in 1719 to help build Pennsylvania's German-speaking community. They began in 1708 near the village of Schwarzenau, Germany, along the Eder River. They originally called themselves the New Baptists, part of the Anabaptist (rebaptizers) movement. In America, they were among the groups that called themselves Brethren groups that formed and split into numerous submovements in the 1800s. They were more commonly called "Dunkers" by outsiders because they fully immersed or dunked their baptismal candidates three times in nearby streams, and this distinguished them from the sprinkling Lutherans and Methodists, or the pouring Mennonites, or the single dunking Baptists. Their congregations took the names from the rivers or creeks in which the baptisms took place: Beaver Creek, Yellow Creek, Lost Creek, Marsh Creek, Pike Run, Trout Run, Blue River, Eel River, Little River, Valley River, and so on (Gordon, 1998). They immigrated to America between 1719 and 1733, founding settlements throughout Pennsylvania, but also in New Jersey, Maryland, Virginia, and the Carolinas. The Antietam congregation, site of the Civil War battle, was founded in 1795 (Gordon, 1998). Of particular note, Christopher Sauer printed many religious texts in German, including a copy of Luther's Bible. Several Dunkers eventually followed Conrad Beissel westward to found the ascetic Ephrata Community in Central Pennsylvania. This monastic Order of the Solitary was extremely successful through the mid-18th century and acted as a cultural base for rural Pennsylvania Germans.

While some religious communities stayed in Germantown, others, like the Mennonites, used the settlement as a gateway to the Central Pennsylvania countryside. An Anabaptist group, the Mennonites developed out of the Dutch Reform movement. They migrated throughout Northern Europe to avoid relentless persecution and were among the first German-speaking religious communities to arrive in Germantown in 1683. Mennonites maintained a steady flow of immigrants to Central Pennsylvania through 1760. Entire communities of Mennonites slowly began to migrate into open frontier regions in Virginia and the Carolinas. Closely tied to the Mennonites, the Amish pressed for more stringent observance of Mennonite practices. They, too, were persecuted and began leaving their Swiss homeland in 1727. The Amish initially settled in Central Pennsylvania and then moved their colonies westward.

The Schwenckfelders were another insular Pietist group that found solace in Pennsylvania. They followed the teachings of Kaspar Schwenckfeld von Ossig, who focused on the importance of inner spirituality and building the true, or invisible, church. Schwenckfelders were a largely disestablished group, scattered throughout Germany. Count Nicholaus Von Zinzendorf, the founder of the Moravians, protected a small group of Schwenckfelders from further persecution and, in 1734, sent them to settle in Central Pennsylvania. This first group of immigrants was later joined by others from Scandinavia. They have maintained small, but thriving, communities into the 21st century.

The Moravian Brethren were arguably the most vocal and prominent of the German-speaking Pietist communities to immigrate to North America during the 18th century. Their founder, Count Nicholaus Von Zinzendorf, taught "the psychological identification with the suffering of Christ" (Fea, 2001: 52) and the attainment of sinless perfection. As an extreme form of Pietism, they believed that they could communicate directly with God, so had no need to study the scripture. The Moravian Brethren first settled in Georgia in 1735. Later, under the guidance of the evangelical preacher, George Whitefield, they established a central community in Bethlehem, Pennsylvania, but their intense evangelist and conversion efforts extended their influence throughout the colonies.

Finally, brief mention should be made of the Mormons, who although an American-born denomination, drew tens of thousands of converts from Europe to join their communities in New York, Ohio, Missouri, and Utah. Officially, the Church of Jesus Christ of the Latter-day Saints, but better known as the Mormons after their tablets known as the Book of Mormon, began in 1829 in Palmyra, New York. Their founder, Joseph Smith, was born in Vermont in 1805, but his family moved to New York in 1816. He claimed to have been visited by an angel, Moroni, in 1823. He discovered the tablets in 1827, and the church was officially established in 1830. They experienced intense discrimination in New York, and moved to Ohio, then on to Missouri. Smith was murdered there, in Carthage, in 1844. It was in New York, in 1832, that Brigham Young was converted, and the church moved to Kirtland, Ohio in 1832. They built their first temple there in 1833 but abandoned it after the Panic of 1837 because of financial difficulties and some degree of persecution. In 1831–1833, outright conflict broke out between Mormons and the majority society—who they referred to as Gentiles. They started new communities in the Carthage–Panock–Nauvoo triangle in 1833. Begun with a town of 240 settlers, by 1842 Nauvoo had 7,000 settlers, larger than Chicago at the time. In 1840, Brigham Young and a few others were sent as missionaries to England, and in their first year, there converted 9,000, many of whom immigrated to New Zion when Young returned there in 1841. A state of near civil war developed between the Mormons and the Gentiles. Smith was arrested on June 27, 1844, and Joseph Smith and Hiram Smith were martyred. Brigham Young led the great migration of about 4,000 people, many of whom were immigrant converts to the Church, to Utah in 1846. They established, on July 23, 1847, the frontier settlement of Salt Lake City. Mormons, like the Amish, Mennonite, Dunkers, and Shakers, were subject to schisms and splinter groups (LeMay, 2009: 174–76; Abanes, 2002; Davies, 2000; Launius and Thatcher, 1994).

Conclusion: From 13 Colonies to a United Nation

The array of religions in America's spiritual landscape and American attitudes toward religion underwent a revolutionary transformation during the 17th century. The intense religious drama of the medieval era had faded and the Enlightenment philosophies honoring the vitality of individualism were in full bloom. Yet the effects of this earlier age remained. The Protestant Reformation served as a catalyst for challenging authority and for developing grassroots religious movements. The resulting diversity forced laypeople to assess the validity of a number of spiritual beliefs, allowing people to choose their own religion and even implying that multiple religions could be true. By the mid-18th century, the full articulation of Protestant theology in North America resulted in an emphasis on the conversion experience and a belief in religious freedom.

The American colonies provided a testing ground—a Holy Experiment—that allowed for the complete implementation and expression of religions that, in Europe, could only be practiced under narrow governmental constraints. While each colony—and after Independence, each state—differed in its attitudes toward religion and civil governance, this diversity allowed for the coexistence of competing religious philosophies and presented colonists with many possibilities in cultivating personal spirituality. While not all religions were tolerated in all regions, the founding of Pennsylvania and other later colonies demonstrates that the continued growth of religious diversity ultimately increased religious tolerance. In addition, as the American population grew, the population of homegrown Nonconformists and radical Protestant immigrants also grew, pressuring the colonies to become more tolerant. Freedom to choose one's religion was also sometimes countered by ethnic ties that provided meaning and tradition in this unstructured new world. This created the very American dilemma of whether to affiliate with one's cultural heritage or to practice the modern system and choose one's religion. Of course, to add to this conundrum, the American ethos emphasizes individualism, so personal choice becomes its own form of cultural heritage in America.

The 18th-century concerns of Americans and Europeans were vastly different. Many of the religious denominations in the American colonies had diverged from their counterparts in Europe. Communications between parishioners on each continent were lapsed and people on the opposing continents experienced very different pressures when resolving their concerns. Americans became increasingly self-sufficient, relying less on their connections to Europe. For example, both continents experienced a renewed explosion of religious denominations and cults during the 18th century. Their emergence in Europe created close-knit radical Pietist communities. In North America, however, new denominations of Methodism and Baptism were tied to the widespread movement of evangelism, while small religious communities expanded into the American frontier.

The difference in the American and European responses was caused by the significant dissimilarity in the character and infrastructure of the American colonies in comparison to Europe. Obviously, the American colonies had developed regional identities that formed distinct religious characters. More significant, however, was the expansive wilderness territories that posed a problem for recreating the parish infrastructure of Old World churches. Going to church every week or attending parishioner meetings was often not viable because of the distances between settlements. Even in well-populated areas, churches often did not have a priest or a minister.

This problem, however, ultimately led to New World solutions. As occurred in Pennsylvania and Georgia, the opening of the American frontier allowed entire religious communities to migrate to a safe haven. While only a very few of these religious communities became notable beyond their own settlement, this trend further reinforced the immigrant pull factor of religious freedom in the fledgling nation and the establishment of ideological tolerance and independence in the frontier.

The vast frontier also created the perfect setting for the Great Awakening, which encouraged evangelism and conversion. The Great Awakening was a religious revival movement in America characterized in two distinct periods. Revival religious movements began in England, Scotland, and Germany where ardent preachers aroused religious activism and new religious denominations. The first Great Awakening in America began in 1739 and continued sporadically until about 1850. The second Great Awakening coincided with the emergence of new Protestant denominations such as the Mormon, Baptist, and Shaker. In this American brand of Pietism, a person did not need church or scriptural study to cultivate spirituality. Rather, the spiritual revival brought about by charismatic preachers, such as George Whitefield, led to a person's rebirth in Christ. The emphasis on personal spiritual awakening not only diminished the need for a physical church or congregation, but also weakened many of the denominational divisions that had been so significant during the 17th century. People across the colonies were united through a common spiritual heritage that contrasted sharply with the religions of the Old World. This ultimately enforced a sense of a collective American identity during the Revolutionary era.[4]

As the colonies and the churches within them became more firmly established, churches that were not sponsored by the colonies slowly grew into more formal institutions. As a booming metropolis in a colony that endorsed religious tolerance, Philadelphia played a key role in centralizing many of these Nonconformist churches. By the early 18th century, the city was home to the central assemblies for Quaker, Baptist, and Presbyterian Churches. After the American Revolution, Philadelphia was significant in the development of the Protestant Episcopal Church and American Lutheranism. By creating centralized organizations, independent denominations were better equipped to build new churches and meeting houses for their growing congregations in the frontier.

Simultaneous to the centralization of Nonconformist churches was the disestablishment of state-sponsored churches. Leading up to the American Revolutionary War, Americans became increasingly more accepting of religious pluralism. This is demonstrated most clearly in the conversion experience that was such an important part of the evangelism of the Great Awakening. Yet the people's attitudes toward freedom of religious choice contrasted sharply with the laws of the colonial governments. This was particularly true in Virginia, where the ruling Anglican elites meted out severe punishments on evangelical preachers and the newly converted. Religious freedom and choice soon became a rallying point for uniting the American identity. When the colonies became United States, the Bill of Rights provided for the legal separation of the federal government in religious affairs. In 1786, due to the vigorous efforts of Thomas Jefferson, Virginia became the first state to end state-sponsored churches. Written by Jefferson and secured in its adoption by James Madison, it became the model for other states that sought to include freedom of religion in their state constitutions, and formed the basis of the Religious Clauses in the U.S. Constitution's Bill of Rights. Its principle is worth citing here:

> Be it enacted by the General Assembly, That no man shall be compelled to frequent or support any religious worship, place, or ministry whatsoever, nor shall be enforced, restrained, molested, or burthened in his body or goods, nor shall otherwise suffer on account of his religious opinions or belief; but that all men shall be free to profess, and by argument to maintain, their opinion in matters of religion, and that the same shall in no wise diminish, enlarge, or affect their civil capacities. And though we well know that this assembly elected by the people for the Ordinary purposes of legislation only, have no power to restrain the acts of succeeding assemblies, constituted with powers equal to our own, and that therefore to declare this act to be irrevocable would be of no effect in law; yet we are free to declare, and do declare, that the rights hereby asserted are the natural rights of mankind, and that if any act shall be hereafter passed to repeal the present, or to narrow its operation, such act shall be an infringement of natural right. (Hening, 1823: 86)

By 1833, all of the states followed this model (see Miller, 1986; Levy, 1994; Peterson and Vaughn, 1988). These acts solidified the freedom of religious conscious and the voluntary nature of religion in America.

Notes

1. Transubstantiation is the belief that the substance of bread and wine becomes the actual body and blood of Christ. The form of the bread and wine remains the same, but the substance becomes holy through the sacramental rites. While Calvin and most other Protestant groups suggested that the sacrament was a symbolic gesture, Luther held onto the Roman Catholic Church's literal conception of Christ's actual presence within the Holy Sacrament.

2. While traveling from England to his new home in March of 1630, John Winthrop, the newly appointed governor of the Massachusetts Bay Colony, outlined his ideals for the colony's religious authority and economic prosperity. Winthrop's entire statement reads, "We shall find that the God of Israel is among us. . . . For we must consider that we shall be as a city upon a hill, the eyes of all people are upon us" (Ahlstrom, 1972:147).

3. Germany was not officially unified as a nation until 1871.

4. Following the American Revolution, the remaining Anglicans formed the Protestant Episcopal Church in 1785. Their first bishop was consecrated by Scottish bishops of the Anglican church. They soon combined their parish with the Swedish Lutherans in Philadelphia and South Jersey. While there are many similarities between Anglicanism and the traditional Lutheran liturgy followed by the Swedish church, their greater connection may be that they both held onto the ways of the Old World and remained closed to the charismatic evangelism of the Great Awakening.

References

Abanes, Richard. 2002. *One Nation under God: A History of the Mormon Church.* New York: Four Walls Eight Windows.

Ahlstrom, Sydney E. 1972. *A Religious History of the American People.* New Haven, CT: Yale University Press.

Armstrong, Karen. 2000. *The Battle for God.* New York: Ballantine Books.

Baltzell, E. Digby. 1996. *Puritan Boston and Quaker Philadelphia.* New Brunswick, NJ: Transaction Publishers.

Davies, Douglas. 2000. *The Mormon Culture of Salvation.* New York: Ashgate.

Fea, John. 2001. "Ethnicity and Congregational Life in the Eighteenth-Century Delaware Valley: The Swedish Lutherans of New Jersey." In *Explorations in Early American Culture, Volume 5,* ed. George W. Boudreau and William A. Pencak. University Park, PA: Pennsylvania Historical Association.

Free Library of Philadelphia. 2011. *Fraktur Digital Collection.* Philadelphia, PA: Free Library of Philadelphia. Available at: http://libwww.freelibrary.org/fraktur/.

Gordon, Ronald J. 1998. "The Little Dunker Church: A Silent Witness for Peace," August, 1998.Available at: http://www.cob-net.org/antietam/dunkers.htm.

Hening, W. W., ed. 1823. *Statutes at Large of Virginia.* Vol. 12: 84–86.

Kraybill, Donald, and Steven M. Nolt. 1995. *Amish Enterprises: From Plows to Profits.* Baltimore, MD: The Johns Hopkins University Press.

Launius, Roger D., and Linda Thatcher, eds. 1994. *Differing Visions: Dissenters in Mormon History.* Urbana, IL: University of Illinois Press.

LeMay, Michael. 1987. *From Open Door to Dutch Door: An Analysis of U.S. Immigration Policy since 1820.* New York: Praeger, 1987.

LeMay, Michael. 2009. *The Perennial Struggle.* 3rd ed. Upper Saddle River, NJ: Prentice-Hall.

Levy, Leonard W. 1994. *The Establishment Clause and the First Amendment.* Chapel Hill, NC: University of North Carolina Press.
Miller, William Lee. 1986. *The First Liberty: Religion and the American Republic.* Washington, DC: Georgetown University Press.
Nolt, Steven M. 1992. *A History of the Amish.* Intercourse, PA: Good Books.
Olmstead, Clifton E. 1961. *Religion in America: Past and Present.* Englewood Cliffs, NJ: Prentice Hall.
Peterson, Merrill D., and Robert C. Vaughn, eds. 1988. *The Virginia Statute for Religious Freedom: Its Evolution and Consequences in American History.* Cambridge, MA: Cambridge University Press.
Portman, Rob, and Cheryl Bauer. 2004. *Wisdom's Paradise: The Forgotten Shakers of Union Village.* Wilmington, OH: Orange Frazer Press.
Ulrich, Laurel Thatcher. 1991. *A Midwife's Tale.* New York: Vintage Books.

CHAPTER TEN

The Anti-Immigrant Social Movement: Racial and Religious Undercurrents and Their Political Effects

Michael C. LeMay

Introduction

The social movement that came to be commonly known as the Know Nothing movement, and that soon morphed into the Know Nothing Party, was unquestionably the most significant anti-immigrant movement prior to the Civil War. It had precedents in other political parties, such as the Whig and the Free Soil parties. It developed into a true grassroots social movement, a loose collection of secret social organizations; and it coalesced into a third political party in the 1850s, with meteoric political successes and an equally stunning and rapid political demise. This chapter argues, moreover, that its history suggests several significant parallels to what has become known as the Tea Party movement today. The analysis of the movement provides insights for today's politics and current struggles, and debates over the comprehensive reform of immigration policy.

This chapter describes the development of the Know Nothing movement, the attitudes prevalent among its adherents, its organizing principals as it quickly changed from a social movement to a political one, its party platform, examples of its electoral success, as well as its ultimate political demise. The Know Nothing movement was the first truly effective xenophobic movement in the United States. Like some intricate tapestry, the movement was comprised of numerous strands or threads that intertwined and wove together: a sense of cultural identity, a particular economic ideology, nativism, a political ideology, racism, religion and religious fundamentalism and evangelism, xenophobia, and so on. In its various wings, factions, and organizational parts, it was stridently anti-immigrant, anti-Catholic, anti-foreign, and anti-Jew. A substantial portion of its membership—primarily its southern wing—was undoubtedly proslavery and antiblack as well (Anbinder, 1992; Beals, 1960; Bennet, 1988; LeMay, 1987; Overdyke, 1968).

In some of its tactics, the Know Nothing Party, and in particular its violent Plug Ugly faction, was what would be described in today's parlance a terrorist organization that foreshadowed the post–Civil War development of the Ku Klux Klan (Melton, 2005). As both a social movement and a political movement, it was the very embodiment of nativism. It was arguably the purest political manifestation of the WASP (White Anglo-Saxon Protestant) in American politics and society (Billington, 1938, 1974; LeMay, 1987: 30–31).

The Precedents: From Political to Social Movements

In the decades between the founding and 1830, about 350,000 immigrants came to the United States. Between 1830 and 1850, nearly two million immigrants arrived (LeMay, 2009, Table 1.2: 30). This dramatic increase in the rate of immigration, coupled with the all-too-apparent Democratic Party involvement of Roman Catholic immigrants in places like New York City, where they were heavily concentrated, aroused the first manifestation of nativism. Historian John Higham defines and describes the xenophobic characteristic of nativism that was so evident within the movement:

> "The grand work of the American Party," proclaimed one of the Know Nothing Journals in 1855, "is the principle of nationality . . . we must do something to protect and vindicate it. If we do not, it will be destroyed." Here is the ideological core of nativism in every form. Whether the nativist is a workingman or a Protestant evangelist, a southern conservative or a northern reformer, he stood for a certain kind of nationalism. He believed—whether he was trembling at a Catholic menace to American liberty, fearing an invasion of pauper labor, or simply rioting against the great English actor

> William Macready—that some *influence originating abroad* threatened the very life of the nation from within. Nativism, therefore, should be defined as intense opposition to an internal minority on the ground of its foreign (i.e., "un-American") connections. (Higham, 1955: 4; my italics)

The membership of the Know Nothing movement, as we will see subsequently, was limited to Protestants of British ancestry who were over the age of 21. They were predominately middle class. It began in 1843 in New York under the name of the American Republican Party, then spread and became a national party in 1845 with the name Native American Party. It renamed itself yet again in 1855 as simply the American Party; but it has always been better known by its common name, the Know Nothing Party (Wilentz, 2005; Billington, 1938: 337).

This rapid increase in immigration, particularly of Catholics from Germany and Ireland, was especially viewed with alarm by the Whig Party, integral to the Second Party System that formed during the early to mid-1830s largely in opposition to the policies of Andrew Jackson and his Democratic Party (Anbinder, 1992; Howe, 1973; Silbey, 1991). The Whigs favored modernization and protectionism, and congressional rather than presidential dominance in the national government. The party emerged from remnants of the Federalist Party, the National Republican Party, and the Anti-Masonic Party. It adopted its name to invoke the image of the patriots of 1776, who in the style of the day often donned powdered wigs. Thus, the members of the Whig party indicated that they envisioned themselves, like the founding fathers, as opposing tyranny (Holt, 1992: 27–30).

The Whig Party's notable leadership included Senator Daniel Webster, President William Henry Harrison, and especially Senator Henry Clay of Kentucky. The former Federalist president John Quincy Adams joined the party after he was elected back into the House of Representatives in 1831. In the presidential elections between 1836 and 1860, the party nominated two heroes of the War of 1812: Zachary Taylor and Winfield Scott (in an obvious effort to counter war-hero Andrew Jackson). It nominated but lost the election with Massachusetts senator Daniel Webster in 1836. He was narrowly defeated by Martin Van Buren. Abraham Lincoln began his political life as a Whig Party leader in Illinois. The party held its first national nominating convention in 1839. The party succeeded in having two of its presidential nominees elected president only to die in office—William Harrison and Zachary Taylor. Harrison won the 1840 election, in part by promising to serve only one term, which appealed to popular support among the population who favored a constitutionally limited single term for the presidency. Harrison won, in part too, because of President Van Buren's unpopularity resulting from the Panic of 1837 (what today would be called a depression). John Tyler, his vice-presidential running-mate, and a Virginian and states' rights absolutist, succeeded Harrison upon his death after only 31 days in office. Tyler, however, was expelled from the party after his veto of the Whig economic program in 1841. In the 1844 election, the Whigs nominated then former Senator Henry Clay, who lost. The party won with General Zachary Taylor in the 1848 election, along with his vice-presidential running mate, Millard Fillmore, a New York State comptroller. Fillmore became president upon Taylor's death. He was the last Whig to be president, serving from 1850 to 1853. In the 1856 election, the Whigs nominated Millard Fillmore again, along with a former U.S. ambassador, Andrew Jackson Donelson, a nephew of President Jackson. By this time, Fillmore and Donelson were also on the ticket of the American Party (the official name of the Know Nothing Party). The American Party, founded on July 4, 1845, was specifically anti-immigrant and its party advocated the total rejection of the foreigner (LeMay, 1987: 31). In the 1860 election, the last in which the Whigs offered a ticket, the party nominated another former Senator, John Bell, who was also on the Constitutional Union ticket with former Senator Edward Everett as the vice-presidential candidate. That ticket also lost. The party ceased to exist after the 1860 election, with most of its adherents supporting the Republican Party of Abraham Lincoln thereafter, and with its southern wing joining the Democrats (Alexander, 1961; Silbey, 1991).

The issue of slavery so split the Whig Party that the issue essentially led to its demise, with the antislavery faction becoming Republicans, and the proslavery faction joining the southern wing of the Democratic Party, and subsequently, supporting secession (Alexander, 1961; Overdyke, 1968). In the 1852 election, the Whigs nominated General Winfield Scott, who lost badly to Democrat Franklin Pierce, who carried 27 of the then 31 states and won the popular vote by a wide margin. Scott even lost his home state of Virginia. After the election, Abraham Lincoln left the Illinois Whig Party. Rutherford Hayes also left the Whig Party and joined the Republican Party, from which they were elected to office (Holt, 1992; Howe, 2007).

In large measure, the Whig Party was organized in opposition to Andrew Jackson, whom they viewed as dangerously reactionary. They were formed under the leadership of Federalist John Quincy Adams and Kentucky Senator Henry Clay, reelected to the Senate in 1831. The Whig Party controlled the Senate in the mid-1830s and passed the Compromise of 1833 (on tariff policy), as well as a censure motion denouncing President

Jackson as usurping executive power in the face of the true will of the people as represented by Congress. Clay had opposed Jackson in the 1832 presidential election, but had lost the popular vote by a wide margin, and the electoral-college vote to Jackson 219 to 49.

The Whig Party suffered from factionalism throughout its time on the national political scene. Its strength depended on a network of newspapers, such as the powerful *New York Tribune* edited by Horace Greeley. During the 1840s, the Whig Party was particularly successful in the Northeast, with its strong manufacturing base. The party won nearly half of the governorships. In 1854, Know Nothing candidates won control of the Massachusetts legislature. The Know Nothing movement (and later the party) was strong in the same regional base. It wielded power in Ohio, for example, where several newspapers, in Youngstown and Cleveland, touted Know Nothing movement beliefs. Many white Protestants in Ohio dislike the Catholic Church for opposing taxation to finance public schools. Ohio's American Party formed an alliance, in the early 1850s, with the Fusionist Party, a precursor to the Republican Party, and helped Salmon Chase win the gubernatorial election of 1855. The party appealed particularly to the professional and business classes: to doctors, lawyers, merchants, ministers, bankers, shop owners and factory owners (who today would be referred to as small businessmen), commercially oriented farmers (as opposed to the small farmer, or yeoman in Jeffersonian terminology), and large-scale plantation owners.

Protestant religious revivals, quite common in the 1840s and into the early 1850s, injected a moralistic fervor to the Whig Party, as it did so later to the American Party (Anbinder, 1992; Howe, 1973; Voss-Hubbard, 2002). They opposed the Democrats who were strongest in the West and the South, and whose dominant political coalition reached out to Irish and German Catholic immigrants and who voted heavily for the Democrats. In no small measure, the Whig Party's demise can be attributed to their failure to reach out positively to the ever-growing number of naturalized immigrant citizens.

In 1850, the Kansas–Nebraska Act opened new territories to slavery. Southern Whigs supported the act; Northern Whigs opposed it. The Northern Whigs increasingly joined the newly established Republican Party, reacting strongly to the repeal of the Missouri Compromise. Many former Whigs shifted to the Know Nothing Party (the American Party), attracted by its nativist crusade against the corrupt Irish and German immigrants (Anbinder, 1992; Billington, 1974; Howe, 2007; McGreevey, 2003; Mulkern, 1997; "Know Nothing Party," *Encyclopedia Britannica*).

From Social Movement Back to Political Party Movement

In the early 1840s, the increasing rate of immigration gave rise to nativism as a reaction to the growing influence of immigrants in Eastern cities, where Roman Catholic immigrants (both German and Irish) had concentrated. Nativist societies were formed to combat the undue foreign influences and to uphold the American view. These largely local, and often secret associations, spawned a grassroots social movement that quickly took on political party aspirations. The American Republican Party formed in 1843 in New York State. It soon spread to neighboring states under the moniker of the Native American Party, which went national with its Philadelphia Convention on July 4th in 1845 (*Encyclopedia Britannica*). In its declaration of party principles, the Native American Party stated that the danger of foreign influence threatened the very destruction of national institutions, and threatened to poison American policy with the influence of European policy, one at war with the fundamental principles of the Constitution.

German and Irish Catholic immigrants maintained that they were independent from their clergy when it came to politics and to public policy, but the Protestants, who made up the Know Nothing movement, did not believe them. The membership of the movement feared that the Pope (Pius IX, at that time) would adversely influence American politics, as they asserted he had done with regards to European politics over the failed liberal Revolution of 1848. American Protestants generally viewed the Pope and the Catholic Church (and its bishops in Boston, New York City, Philadelphia, etc.) as antiliberty, antidemocracy, and anti-Republicanism. In short, they believed the Catholic Church itself was the ally of tyranny. Their fears were exacerbated by the seemingly growing influence of Irish Catholic bishops, particularly in Boston and New York, who were selected as bishops by the Pope. The social movement that came to be called the Know Nothing movement began organizationally as the Order of the Star Spangled Banner in 1848–1849 in New York City. The order was created by Charles B. Allen. This secret society formed the nucleus of much of the American Party (McGreevey, 2003: 22–25).

As the grassroots social movement began to politicize, it shed its clandestine beginnings, and the Know Nothing movement began to spread rapidly. The movement was somewhat stalled by the Mexican War in 1848. It revived with the founding of the aforementioned secret patriotic society called the Order of the Star Spangled Banner. It quickly formed local chapters in Massachusetts and Pennsylvania, then spread to Rhode Island, New Hampshire, Connecticut, Delaware, Maryland, Kentucky, and Texas

(*Encyclopedia Britannica*). By the 1854 elections, the movement wielded strong influence in Virginia, Georgia, Alabama, Mississippi, and Louisiana (Smith, 1969: 141; Nevins, 1947: 329). That year the American Party won the New York governorship as well as 40 seats in the New York State legislature. By 1855, they elected a host of local government officials as well as eight state governors. They elected 43 of their members to the U.S. House of Representatives, and 5 to the U.S. Senate. The American Party increased in 1854–1855 from 50,000 to an estimated 1 million members (Anbinder, 1992: 75–102).

> The key to Know Nothing success in 1854 was the collapse of the second party system brought about primarily by the demise of the Whig party. The Whig party, weakened for years by internal dissent and chronic factionalism, was nearly destroyed by the Kansas-Nebraska Act. Growing anti-party sentiment, fueled by anti-slavery as well as temperance and nativism, also contributed to the disintegration of the party system. The collapsing second party gave the Know Nothings a much larger pool of potential converts than was available to previous nativist organizations, allowing the Order to succeed where other nativist groups had failed. (Anbinder, 1992: 95)

Despite their elector success, however, the party's elected members were unable to pass significant bills in Congress that called for the prohibition of foreign-born paupers. They failed to enact literacy test for voters in several states where they attempted to do so.

By then, however, debates over the slavery issue dominated the national scene. When that issue seemed to have been briefly laid to rest by the Compromise of 1850, the nativist social movement reemerged when the number of secret orders grew. The most important and notable among them were the Order of United Americans and the Order of the Star Spangled Banner. At first, these loosely knit secret societies baffled political managers of the established political parties. Attempts to subsume them were stifled by their members meeting all inquiries of the parties with the statement that they, in effect, knew nothing of the movement—which gave rise to their becoming commonly known as the Know Nothings, although there never was an organization with that as its official name (Bailey, 1976: 135; Billington, 1938: 337).

The social movement was at first simply anti-immigrant and advocated highly restrictive immigration policy. It became increasingly political, however, when the loose coalition of social-movement groups began increasingly to insist that its followers elect only native-born Americans to office, and agitating for a 20- to 25-year residency qualification for citizenship (naturalization). In 1850, the party sold lithographs that depicted an idealized, white American, known as Uncle Sam's Youngest Son, Citizen Know Nothing. The Library of Congress notes that the portrait represents the nativist ideal of the Know Nothing Party. By 1850, the social movement spread rapidly, and its members and leaders began to align themselves, as we have seen previously, with the group of Whigs who followed Millard Fillmore into the American Party. The American Party came under the leadership of a New York City merchant and political leader, James W. Barker. They nearly captured New York State in the 1854 election, and they had great success in Massachusetts and in Delaware, where they swept the polls. In the 1856 presidential election, Fillmore carried only the state of Maryland, and by then the American Party (the official name of the political movement) took a stance that was too blatantly anti-Catholic to succeed nationally, and in the election it remained purposively silent on the slavery issue. Millard Fillmore received only 874,534 votes and essentially played the role of spoiler, with the presidency going to Democrat James Buchanan, who defeated Republican candidate John Freemont as well as Fillmore (LeMay, 1987: 32; Anbinder, 1992; Mulkern, 1997). By this time, as noted, all of the party's candidates had to be born in the United States, and they led an effort to change the naturalization laws to require an extensive period of residency—clearly designed to disenfranchise Irish Catholics then coming in great numbers, who thereby would be unable to vote for many years.

In many other states, however, they had considerable success in elections for local office. In California, where the population swelled as a result of the 1848 Gold Rush, the party elected city officials in the boom city of San Francisco, as well as several statewide officials. The San Francisco chapter of the party, begun by Sam Roberts, was formed in opposition to Chinese and Irish immigrants (Anbinder, 1992). Following their success, in 1849, a Know Nothing judge serving on California's Supreme Court ruled that the Chinese were forbidden to testify against white men in court (LeMay, 1987: 53). As the social movement spread to the South, by 1854, aided by the increasing disintegration of the Whig Party, the movement began to make strides as a national social movement that was becoming a national party vying for major-party status. In 1855, they assumed the name American Party, and essentially cast aside much of their characteristic secrecy. In the spring of 1855, Know Nothing candidate Levi Boone was elected mayor of Chicago, where he barred all immigrants from city jobs. The party, however, was less effective statewide, which went with Lincoln's newly formed Republican Party. That year, the Know Nothing Party gained considerable strength in Ohio, even winning over

German American Lutherans, Scotch-Irish Presbyterians, and Dutch Reformed Church adherents, to whom the party's anti-Catholicism appealed (Anbinder, 1992: 34–43). In Alabama, the party congealed with a mix of former Whigs, unhappy Democrats, and other political outsiders who ran on state aid to build more railroads. The coalition, however, failed to carry the state as concern mounted that the American Party could not protect the institution of slavery from the influence of the party's northern and staunchly abolitionist wing (Bennet, 1988: 15). Indeed, Historian Michael Holt (1992) argues:

> Know Nothingism originally grew in the South for the same reasons it spread in the North—nativism, anti-Catholicism, and animosity toward unresponsive politicos—not because of conservative unionism (856).

Nationally, the peak year for the American Party was 1854. It scored impressive victories in Massachusetts, taking control of the state legislature, and polled 40 percent of the vote in Pennsylvania. It polled well in the South, attracting especially former Whig members. It was the last election before the newly formed Republican Party emerged as the second major party of the country.

The peak year for the social movement, nationally, was 1855. Its name gained wide, if brief, popularity. Nativism became the rage, with such items as Know Nothing candy, Know Nothing tea, and Know Nothing toothpicks. Stagecoaches were dubbed the Know Nothing, and a shipmaster from Maine even called his freighter, Know Nothing (Bennet, 1988: 15). Table 10.1 summarizes the party platform of 1854, its peak year of success on the national-level electoral scene.

Precisely at the peak of its popularity as a social movement, however, in June of 1855, at a meeting of the political party's national council held in Philadelphia, the Southerners in the social movement, and in the recently coalesced political party, took control of the political side of the movement and adopted a resolution calling for the maintenance of slavery. The contentious slavery issue emerged front and center in American politics after the enactment of the Kansas–Nebraska Act in 1850. Between 1850 and 1856 national election, the slavery issue loosened ties so that many voters who were not yet ready to cast their votes with either the proslavery Democrats or the antislavery forces that were beginning to form the Republican Party, found a temporary home in the Know Nothing Party. Deep-rooted feelings among many in the native stock by the massive immigration following the potato famine aroused fear and hostility that fed the party's rapid rise, and many of its local and state successes. By 1856, however, as

Table 10.1 The Know Nothing Party Platform Planks, 1854

1. Severe Limitations on all immigration, especially from Catholic countries.
2. Restricting political office to native-born Americans of English or Scottish Lineage and Protestant affiliation.
3. Mandating a period of 21 years before an immigrant could be naturalized.
4. Restricting public school teacher positions to Protestants.
5. Maintaining daily reading of the Bible in public schools.
6. Restricting the sale of liquor.
7. Restricting the use of languages other than English.

Source: Anbinder, Tyler G. 1992. *Nativism and Slavery: The Northern Know-Nothings and the Politics of the 1850s*. New York: Oxford University Press.

the party took a position on the all-important slavery question, the movement was essentially broken over the issue. Even the party leader James Barker of New York left the party and supported Abraham Lincoln in the 1860 election (Billington, 1974; Beals, 1960; Nevins, 1947; Smith, 1969).

The American Party declined in the North as rapidly as it had arisen. It was divided over the slavery issue in the 1856 election. Its Northern faction supported former (Whig) President Millard Fillmore for president, and Andrew Jackson Donelson, a nephew of former President Jackson, for vice president. The ticket was designed to appeal to loyalists from both major parties (Whigs and Democrats). Despite its balanced slate, however, the party only received 23 percent of the popular vote. The Supreme Court's decision in the Dred Scott case (1857) proved to be the party's death knell. The antislavery wing joined the Republicans, virtually en masse, and the proslavery wing remained active only at the state and local levels in the South. By 1860, the party was no longer a serious national political movement, and its few remaining members supported the Constitutional Union Party in that election (Anbinder, 1992: 103).

As a loose-knit social movement, the Know Nothings attracted the working class who feared that their jobs would be taken, and that so vast an influx of foreigners would undermine the institutions and the very order of society. They feared the increasing political threat of the immigrants, who began to bloc vote with growing electoral clout in the beginnings of what would emerge as the urban political machine. These fears, of course, were not entirely unfounded. The new immigrants were flocking to the cities. In the eyes of the native stock adherents to the movement, immigrants caused unbelievable overcrowding. Immigrants provided a massive pool of cheap labor when employers were quick to determine that the new immigrants would do almost any job for very low pay (and thus the business elite continued to advocate a totally open-door policy with respect to immigration). Among movement adherents it was widely felt that large-scale immigration led to overall low-pay rates and absolutely deplorable working conditions. This attracted the support of some growing—although then still largely local—labor unions, and of a variety of urban social reformers (LeMay, 1987: 32–33).

Others were attracted to the movement out of a deep-seated fear Catholicism, the denominational affiliation that was evident among ever larger portions of the immigrants flooding into the country after 1840. By then, immigration from Germany had shifted from the Northern and Eastern German states, which were predominately Lutherans, to Southern and Western portions of Germany, then largely Catholic. Likewise, immigrants from Ireland shifted from the mostly Protestant Scotch-Irish of the northern part of the island to the Catholic southern counties. Those attracted to the Know Nothing movement feared that if the Catholic immigrants gained too much political power, they would bring the nation under the control of and take orders from the Pope in Rome. As early as 1834, groups who called themselves "Nativists" chased a group of students and Ursuline nuns from their school and burned the buildings. By 1835, a group of New Yorkers organized a state political party, the Native American Democratic Party, that ran on a platform of opposing Catholics and immigrants. By 1840, other such groups appeared in Baltimore, Philadelphia, and Providence. These groups often appeared and disappeared over time, but eventually the overarching theme of hostility toward the immigrant foreigner began to unite them in opposition to the costs of trying to support and educate the indigent foreigner, and they began organizing on a national basis.

As noted earlier, nearly 1.2 million Irish immigrants came to the United States between 1847 and 1852 alone (LeMay, 1987: 25). They flooded Eastern seaboard cities, especially the major port cities of Baltimore, Boston, New York, and Philadelphia. This famine-induced emigration activated prejudices. The anti-British attitudes of the Irish contributed to the WASPs' antagonism toward the Irish immigrants. Perhaps equally important, their extreme poverty and the rural backgrounds of the Irish immigrants created problems for their adjusting to their new homes as they increasingly became trapped in the nation's seaboard cities. They arrived with high rates of illiteracy and few job skills than had been the case for previous immigrant waves. This situation forced them into unskilled labor. The Irish became the first to face overt job discrimination when advertisements in Boston, New York, and other cities for some time contained the line "No Irish Need Apply" (O'Grady, 1973; LeMay, 2009: 124). The Irish were forced to take whatever work was open to them. Most such jobs were seasonal, low paying, and periodic. The Irish immigrants worked as stevedores, teamsters, ditchdiggers, and dockers—longshoremen in today's terminology. They built the roads and canals, and soon the railroads heading West from the East. The Irish were soon trapped in a grim existence in what was developing as the slums of the major cities like New York, Boston, Baltimore, Philadelphia, and Pittsburgh. Not surprising, many Irish turned to abusing alcohol, which led to the stereotypical image of the Irish as sots, excessive drinkers.

These trends attracted many to the Know Nothing movement and fed a growing rhetorical radicalism in the movement, and the threat and actual use of violence. Know Nothing movement leaders were often antiunion, and the precarious economic position of the Irish led many among them to become active in labor associations, most of which were operating only at the local level prior to the Civil War, but by 1860 they began to emerge at the national level. In 1861, Irish immigrant Martin Burke helped form the American Miners Association (LeMay, 2009: 124).

The extensive urbanization taking place between 1840 and 1850 required rapid increases in local government work forces, especially police departments. The Irish were quick to join, and some rose rapidly to levels of responsibility. By 1863, John A. Kennedy (no relation to President Kennedy) led New York City's police force. Reacting to the prejudice and discrimination against them, the Irish formed protective associations, like the Irish Catholic Benevolent Union, founded by Dennis Dwyer, which by 1870 was playing a significant role in electoral politics (LeMay, 2009: 126).

Movement adherents rose up "to burn Catholic convents, churches and homes, assault nuns, and murder Irishmen, Germans, and Negroes" (Beals, 1960: 9). A violent hate campaign was unleashed and a number of cities where immigrants were concentrated experienced violence against the immigrant.

Philadelphia experienced a series of riots in 1844, from May 6 to 8, and again from July 6 to 7. Referred to as the prayer riots, they began with clashes between nativist Protestants and Roman Catholics over Bible reading in public schools—specifically over which version of the Bible would be used, the Protestant King James version or the Roman Catholic Douai version. Bishop Francis Kenrich had written a letter requesting that Catholic students in the public schools be allowed to read from the Douai version.

Nativist in the Southwark neighborhood of Philadelphia attacked St. Philip Nen's Catholic Church. In the May 6–8 riot, 14 were killed, 50 injured, and about 200 fled their homes. The military was called in to quell the riot. Tensions broke out again in July when nativists attacked the seminary of the Sisters of Charity. They burned down St. Michael's Catholic Church and rectory. Two of the attacking nativists were killed initially, and before the riot ended on July 7th, an estimated 15 to 20 people were killed, another 50 were injured, and some 5,000 militia were needed to quell the riot.

In New York City, mobs of Irish immigrants and Know Nothing members clashed, leaving two dead, and many wounded (depicted fictionally in the 2002 Martin Scorsese movie, *Gangs of New York*). Nativists objected to the undue influence of New York City's Irish Roman Catholic bishop, John Hughes. Tensions were so high in New York City that, in 1849, the Order of United Americans, the movement group related to the Know Nothing Party, organized a distinctively American regiment, legally formed in October of 1850 as the 71st Infantry Regiment of New York, and called the American Rifles. Its founders were Know Nothing leaders J. M. Parker, Hamilton Fish Jr., and William Kellock. The regiment was comprised of eight companies. In 1852, it was enrolled in the New York State militia, and was used for riot control in 1857. It also served in the Civil War.

In Newark, a mob of an estimated 2,000 Protestants and Catholics squared off, leaving one dead, dozens wounded, and a Catholic Church burned to the ground. In 1855, Know Nothing members and Germans in Louisville clashed in an intense riot during which 20 people died, and hundreds were wounded in the mayhem. In Baltimore, where the Know Nothing Party was especially strong, numerous clashes took place and a riot in 1854 left eight dead (Hofstadter and Wallace, 1971: 313). A spin-off group of the Know Nothing movement, the Plug Uglies, was often responsible (Melton, 2005). The Know Nothing Party was anti-immigrant, and the Germans and Irish were the largest groups of immigrants in the 1850s, so the movement was noticeably anti-German and anti-Irish (LeMay, 2009: 97).

Immigrants became easy scapegoats on which to lay blame for all the problems associated with a rapidly urbanizing and industrializing society. As ghetto-like ethnic enclaves formed in the tenement slums of big cities like New York and Boston, social reformers desiring to preserve the nation's institutions and Protestant evangelicals anxious to save the nation's purity joined to form associations like the secret Order of the Star Spangled Banner. And as the Irish and Germans immigrants began to become politically active, the Know Nothing movement's leadership adopted increasingly overt political action as well (LeMay, 2009: 353). They supported stringent restrictions on immigration, the exclusion of the foreign-born from holding public elective office, and residency requirements of 20 to 25 years. The reformers and evangelicals among them sought to limit the sale of alcohol. They insisted on Bible readings in public schools and tried to ensure that only Protestants could be hired to teach in the public schools.

This intricate weaving in and out of the Know Nothing Party as a social movement and a political party—with its followers and leaders belonging first to the predecessor Whig Party, and after to the Republican Party for northern members and the Democratic Party for leaders from its southern wing—is exemplified by the following brief career highlights of several noted people associated with the Know Nothing Party.

Anna Ella Carroll, a noted American political pamphleteer, for example, was from Maryland's Eastern shore area. She first joined the Whig Party as a publicist and pamphleteer. By the 1850s, Irish immigrants were working at the port in Baltimore, then in its railroad yards. Soon street crime became a problem and the relief rolls rose. Planters from the state's Eastern shore, many of whom were Presbyterians and Episcopalians, helped, in 1853, to form the Maryland Know Nothing Party out of three nativist groups. Carroll joined the American Party in 1854, when the Whigs declined. The party became a strong but divisive force in Maryland politics, being pro-Union and antislavery, but many also anti-Catholic and anti-immigrant. Along with other reformers, Carroll campaigned against the urban machine, its corruption, and crime and what was viewed as the threat of the power of the Catholic Church. In 1856, the American Party split nationally over the slavery issue. Carroll campaigned for Fillmore, the then Whig candidate for president. She wrote articles and pamphlets and toured the Northeast on his behalf. In 1856, she wrote two influential anticlerical and anti-Catholic books and several pamphlets. In 1857, she was the chief publicist for Maryland Governor Thomas Hicks. With the election of Lincoln in 1860, Carroll freed her own slaves and turned her activities to oppose secession. She ended up as a Republican and advisor to President Abraham Lincoln.

Another good example is Anson Burlingame, an American diplomat and ambassador to China. Burlingame was born in New York, but practiced law in Boston. He was first an active leader of the Free Soil Party and served in the state senate for them in 1853–1854. In 1855, he was elected to the U.S. House of Representatives as a Know Nothing Party candidate, but by 1861 he was a Republican and served in the Lincoln administration. President Lincoln first appointed him to serve as ambassador to the Austrian Empire, but resistance from the Hungarians, who rejected him, led Lincoln to appoint him ambassador to China, where he served with distinction.

Henry Winter Davis, a member of the House of Representatives from Annapolis, Maryland, was another politician who was first a Whig, then switched to the American Party, and ended as a Republican Party member who became a radical Reconstructionist and opposed President Lincoln's plans for reconstruction during the Civil War.

John Crittenden, from the state of Kentucky, served in both the House of Representatives and the U.S. Senate. He, too, was first a Whig and then, in the mid-1850s, a Know Nothing Party leader, who went on to serve as U.S. attorney general for Presidents Harrison and Millard Fillmore, and then as the 17th governor of Kentucky.

William Allison, from Ohio, joined the Whig Party in 1834, then the Know Nothing Party. He represented Iowa from the Dubuque area from 1863 to 1871 as a Republican, and served as U.S. senator from Iowa from 1873 to 1908, also as a Republican.

Zebulon Vance, of North Carolina, was a Know Nothing governor of the state. In 1858, he was elected to the House of Representatives as an American Party candidate, served one term, and was elected senator. But during the Civil War, he sided with the Confederacy and became a Democrat.

Consider the career of Horace Greeley. The son of a New England farmer and day laborer in New Hampshire, Greeley began his journalism career as an apprentice to a Vermont newspaper editor. In 1831, he went to New York City where, in 1834, he began the news journal, *Log Cabin*. He supported the Whig Party and helped elect William Harrison as a Whig in 1840. In 1831, he launched his most successful newspaper venture, the *New York Tribune*. He became involved with the Transcendentalist movement. He strongly opposed slavery, and opposed the Kansas–Nebraska Act in 1850, which he denounced. He was briefly a Know Nothing supporter in the early 1850s, then in the 1856 election, switched to the Republican Party. He attended the Republican Party national conventions in Pittsburgh, in 1856, and in Chicago, in 1860, where he supported Abraham Lincoln by the time the balloting began. During the Civil War, however, he broke with Lincoln when his abhorrence of slavery led him to support the radical Reconstruction position and to oppose President Lincoln's plan for reconstruction. Greeley likewise opposed Andrew Johnson's reconstruction efforts (essentially Lincoln's plan), and he advocated the impeachment of President Johnson.

Another Whig to Know Nothing to Republican politician who went on to serve as vice president of the United States was Schuyler Colfax. Born in New York City, Colfax moved to Indiana in 1836. He became a friend of Horace Greeley, and wrote articles on Indiana politics for the *New York Tribune*. He became editor of the South Bend *Free Press* in 1845. In 1848, he joined the Whig party and was a delegate to the national convention of the party that year, and to the Indiana Constitutional Convention as well. In the early 1850s, when the Whig party essentially collapsed, he briefly affiliated with the Know Nothing movement and the American Party. By 1856, his stridently antislavery views led him to join the Republican Party that fused with Northern Whigs. Colfax was elected to the House of Representatives, as a Republican, in 1858 and was elected Speaker of the House in 1862. As Speaker, he announced passage of the 13th Amendment, in 1865. In 1868, he was elected as the 17th vice president of the United States, on the ticket with President Ulysses S. Grant.

Finally, there is the career of Henry Wilson, the 18th vice president of the United States. Wilson was born in New Hampshire, but moved to Massachusetts in 1833. He served in the Massachusetts state legislature from 1841 to 1852. He also was a newspaper editor, of the *Boston Republic,* from 1848 to 1851. He served in the state's Constitutional Convention in 1853, then ran for but lost his race to be the governor of Massachusetts in 1854. In 1855, he was successfully elected to the U.S. Senate as a Free Soiler/American Party candidate. He was reelected to that office, as a Republican, in 1859, 1865, and 1871. He resigned from the senate in 1873 to serve as the vice president to Ulysses S. Grant.

On the West Coast, the movement had some differences, but more similarities than not. Chinese laborers were drawn to California by the gold rush (the Chinese name for the United States was the Land of the Golden Hills). The Chinese immigrants were well organized into work gangs led by a single contractor (one of them who spoke English), and as a result, Chinese laborers agreed to do almost any job, including the most undesirable tasks. They served as ranch hands, farm laborers, and domestic servants. The Central Pacific Railroad, building from the West Coast to the East, employed some 9,000 Chinese immigrants a year (Bailey, 1969; Kenefick, 1985). By 1860, they made up about 10 percent of California's population and roughly 25 percent of its work force (LeMay, 2009: 75; Thompson, 1996). This explosive growth rate initiated a xenophobic fear of the Yellow Peril.

By 1850, growing animosity against the Chinese immigrants was evident. In the mining regions, they were often beaten and robbed, and occasionally murdered. And they could not seek redress in the courts, given the Know Nothing judge's ruling, in 1849, that they could not testify in courts against white men. As a result, crimes against them went unpunished.

Miscegenation laws (forbidding men from the Asian race from marrying white women) were but one manifestation of the legal constraints imposed on the Chinese immigrants. By 1850, the Know Nothing Party grew in power at the state level. California essentially expelled Chinese laborers from the mining work camps with enactment, in 1855, of the Foreign Miners' Tax. It required foreign miners (mostly the Chinese) to pay a four-dollar per month tax. Its rate increased each year the miner did not become a citizen. Since the Chinese were legally excluded from citizenship (then only open to whites), they were forced to pay ever higher rates. That act, coupled with increasing violence against them, forced them out of the mine fields. A combination of state and local ordinances forbade their entry into public schools, denied them the right to testify in court against whites, and barred them from obtaining citizenship.

Continuities and Parallels

Although the Know Nothing Party ended in 1860, its anti-immigrant legacy lived on in other groups and associations after the Civil War, both as social movements and as minor political party movements in the United States. The tapestry that was the Know Nothing social movement and the then minor political party organization may have unwound by 1850, but its legacy left the threads that had intertwined to make up the movement still within the fabric of American social and political life. Many of its ideas and concerns continued on through the decades after the Civil War on up to our current politics. As will be noted subsequently, there remain numerous parallels between the Know Nothing movement and subsequent movements in succeeding decades.

For example, some anti-immigrant third, or minor, parties that carried on the tradition of the Know Nothing's opposition to Open Door Immigration Policy include the Prohibition Party in the 1890s, the Workingmen's Party in California in the 1880s and 1890s, the People's Populist Party in the 1890s, and, to some degree, the Progressive Party of the 1920s. There was another American Party in the 1920s that pushed for the Quota Acts to restrict immigration (Divine, 1957; Bennett, 1963). Likewise, in the 1960s, the George Wallace wing split off from the Democrats and he ran for president on the American Independent Party ticket (Safire, 2008: 375–76; LeMay, 2009: 246). The preamble to his party platform is worth citing:

> As this great nation searched vainly for leadership while beset by riots, minority group rebellions, domestic disorders, student protests, spiraling living costs, soaring interest rates, a frightening increase in the crime rate, war abroad and the loss of personal liberty at home; while our national political

> parties and their leaders play homage to the legions of dissent and disorder and worshipped at the shrine of political expediency, only this Party, the American Independent Party, and its candidates, George C. Wallace and Curtis E. LeMay, possessed the courage and fortitude to openly propose and advocate to the nation those actions which are necessary to return this country to its accustomed and deserved position among the community of nations and to offer hope to our people of some relief from the continued turmoil, frustration and confusion brought about through the fearful and inept leadership of our national political parties. (Available at: pbs.org/amex/Wallace/68platform.html.)

Like the Know Nothing Party, these minor parties were all short-lived, rising and declining quickly. Their narrow anti-immigrant policy platforms were too limited to engender a national following large enough to move the party from a minor to a major party status, so they soon unraveled.

A variety of groups exemplify a continuity to the social movement of Know Nothing nativism. Immediately after the Civil War, in 1870–1890, and again as it revived around 1910–1915, the Ku Klux Klan spread not only as an antiblack organization, but also as an anti-Catholic, anti-Jewish, and anti-immigrant movement—the Know Nothing-like political movement of its day (Safire, 2008: 375–76; Reimers, 1990). Like the Plug Uglies of the Know Nothing Party, the Klan used violence to achieve its ends (LeMay, 1987: 52). The Klan lynched a Jewish manager of a pencil factory, Leo Frank, in 1915. Between 1882 and 1959, Klan members lynched 2,595 blacks in nine Southern states (LeMay, 2009: 234, 361).

Similarly, on the West Coast, the Workingmen's Party not only used electoral politics and legislative action to pursue its anti-Chinese and then anti-Asian immigrant goals, but also used riots and violent terrorism against the Chinese, like the Know Nothing movement did against Catholic immigrants. Violence reached a fever-pitch by the mid-1870s. In 1871, 21 Chinese were killed in a Los Angeles riot. In June 1876, the Truckee Raid occurred in which whites burned two Chinese-occupied cabins and shot and wounded the residents, one of whom died of his wounds. In 1880, Denver was rocked by an anti-Chinese riot. The Order of Caucasians advocated elimination of the Chinese through the use of violence (today, it would be labeled "ethnic cleansing"). They raided and burned various Chinatowns, driving hundreds from their homes. In 1885, in Rock Springs, Wyoming, a mob killed 28 Chinese. In Tacoma, Seattle, and Oregon City, mobs expelled hundreds of Chinese from those cities (LeMay, 2009: 76).

The Klan was resurrected again after World War I, and between then and the early 1920s, it advocated for the highly restrictive (and successful) Quota Laws of 1921, 1924, and 1929 (Bennett, 1963; Divine, 1957).

Klan activity then also included the use of terrorism. The Klan inspired a riot in Omaha in 1909 against Greek immigrants, for example, as part of its national campaign to preserve America's purity. (Burgess, 1913: 162–63).

The American Protective Association, founded in Clinton, Iowa, in 1887, went on to become the largest and most powerful of the Protestant secret anti-Catholic societies that campaigned to heavily restrict immigration to the United States and promoted a program of forced assimilation of immigrants already here—aimed at German-speakers and at restricting the South/Central/Eastern European flow (Higham, 1955: 286–98; LeMay, 1987: 55–58).

Out on the West Coast, a new nativist political party, which also called itself the American Party, was formed. It joined the Chinese Exclusion League and its later and broader coalition, the Asian Exclusion League, which successfully advocated several highly restrictive immigration policies from the 1880s to the 1920s. The American Party and the Workingmen's Party were elements of the coalition that helped lead the xenophobic movement that led to the Chinese Exclusion Acts—in April of 1882, May of 1882, the Foran Act of 1885, its amendment in February 1887, the Chinese Laborer Prohibition Act of 1885 (the Scott Act), and the Exclusion of Chinese Laborers Act of 1888 (LeMay and Barkan, 1999: 50–64).

> The Panic of 1873 inspired fears of the Yellow Fever. In 1867, the Workingmen's Party won control of San Francisco. It called for an end to all Chinese immigration. By the 1870s sentiment was so strong on the West Coast that it was virtual political suicide to take their side. (LeMay, 1987: 53)

Also in the 1890s, some Democrats accused the Grand Old Party of being the new Know Nothings in order to attract German votes in Wisconsin, as did Democrat John Altgeld in Illinois when he said:

> The spirit which enacted the alien and sedition laws, the spirit which Actuated the "Know-nothing" party, the spirit which is forever carping about the foreign-born citizen and trying to abridge his privileges, is too deeply seated in the party. The aristocratic and know-nothing principle has been circulating in its system so long that it will require more than one somersault to shake the poison out of its bones. (Jensen, 1971: 220)

In the early 1920s, as Congressional battles raged over the enactment of restrictive laws that became known as the Quota Acts, any number of groups emerged that continued the anti-immigrant movement first led by the Know Nothings:

> In 1921, in the final debate over the bill, and in the later battles in 1923 and 1924, the primary organizational support in favor of the origins bill and concept included: the American Federation of Labor, the American Legion, the Immigration Restriction League, the National Grange, the Ku Klux Klan, the Junior Order of the United American Mechanics, as well as such patriotic associations as the Sons of America and the Daughters of the American Revolution. (LeMay, 1987: 81)

Finally, one can argue that today's Tea Party movement exhibits a number of continuities with and parallels to the Know Nothing movement. Like the Know Nothing movement, the Tea Party movement, since 2009, has sponsored numerous local and nationally coordinated protests opposing taxes and spending. The term is also used to refer to a caucus in the House of Representatives. The Tea Party movement's platform is explicitly populist. Its commonly used name "Tea Party" is a reference to the Boston Tea Party. As of 2010, it remains a movement rather than a national political party, but it has endorsed Republican candidates. It has no central leadership, being composed of a loose affiliation of national and local groups (the Young Americans for Liberty, the Tea Party Express, the Tea Party Patriots, the Tea Party Caucus, the Nationwide Tea Party Coalition, the Tea Party Nation, etc.). Its noted national figures include former Republican representative and now lobbyist Dick Armey, former Alaska governor and vice-presidential nominee Sarah Palin, Libertarian Party activist and Tea Party movement endorsed senator Rand Paul, Minnesota Congresswoman Michele Bachmann, and former Colorado representative Tom Tancredo, among others. The Tea Party caucus in the House of Representatives consists of 49 Republican representatives. U.S. Senators associated with the movement include newly elected Senators Scott Brown (R-MA), Mike Lee (R-UT), Rand Paul (R-KY), Mark Rubio (R-FL), Thomas Cogburn (R-OK), and Jim DeMint (R-SC).

Parallels between the Tea Party movement and the Know Nothing movement include the following:

1. Like the Know Nothing Party claimed, the Tea Party movement claims to represent the true will of the people.
2. Both movements sought or seek to take back our government from a president viewed as tyrannical (the Whigs/Know Nothings versus Andrew Jackson, and the Tea Party advocates who refer to the president as "the Nazi, socialist, communist, illegitimate President Barack Obama").
3. Both movements exhibited or exhibit considerable factionalization.
4. Both depended on the media to popularize their cause—the Know Nothing movement on newspapers, political magazines, and pamphlets of their day;

the Tea Party on talk radio and TV, on Fox News, on the Internet, and on the blogosphere.

5. Both failed to get Congress to enact some of their key legislative goals—the Know Nothing movement's goals of a literacy test, and a ban on foreign-born paupers, or highly restricted immigration laws, and the 20-year residency before naturalization proposals; and the Tea Party's goals of the balanced budget amendment, repeal of the Health Care Act, and of blocking the increase in the national debt ceiling.
6. Both parties came into being during and waged ongoing culture wars.
7. Both were stridently anti-immigrant, exemplified by the Know Nothings anti-Irish and anti-German attitudes, and by the anti-illegal alien (read Hispanic immigrants), of the likes of former Congressman and Tea Party Activist Tom Tancredo of Colorado.
8. Both began with existing political activists and political organization operatives agitating and stirring their respective movements, which then morphed into grassroots social movements, and then formed a new party or took control of an existing political party (Lepore, 2010; O'Hara, 2010; Rasmussen and Shoen, 2010; Zernike, 2010).
9. Both explicitly expressed concern for the constitution, law, and social order.
10. The Know Nothing Party advocated native-born only elected officials; the birthers within the Tea Party movement uphold, against all reason, the belief that President Obama was born in Kenya and is, therefore, an "illegitimate" president, from whom "we must take our government back."

Conclusion

The Know Nothing movement—both in its manifestation as a social, grassroots movement, and in its organized, third- or minor-political party manifestation—was the first embodiment of the anti-immigrant attitudes of nativism in American political life. It grew out of a natural reaction to the economic and social strife that was associated with the transformation of America to a nation of nations, as immigration surged to unprecedented levels and as the nation struggled to adjust to growing urbanization and industrialization. The American Party never succeeded beyond minor party status precisely because its programs and principles were too narrowly based on stridently anti-immigrant and anti-Catholic platform planks. As immigration swelled and as the immigrants became naturalized and politically active citizens, only those parties that reached out to them survived to form the new two-majority party system that has characterized U.S. politics ever since the Civil War. Those parties, like the Know Nothings, that were ideologically and culturally opposed to wide-scale immigration quickly withered and died.

The attitudes that the movement and the party embodied, however, continued on in American politics throughout the remainder of the 19th century, imbued American political struggles in the early part of the 20th century, and exhibit parallels to today's politics of the first decade of the 21st century. Although the Know Nothing movement was meteoric in its rise and decline, its legacy was far more lasting than was its organizational life. Subsequent volumes in this set will detail that legacy as evident in the period between the Civil War and World War II, and from the end of World War II to the present day.

References

Alexander, Thomas. 1961. "Persistent Whiggery in the Confederate South, 1860–1877." *Journal of Southern History* 27(3): 305–29.

Anbinder, Tyler G. 1992. *Nativism and Slavery: The Northern Know-Nothings and the Politics of the 1850s*. New York: Oxford University Press.

Bailey, Ed H. 1969. *The Century of Progress, a Heritage of Service: The Union Pacific, 1869–1969*. New York: Newcomen Society.

Bailey, Thomas. 1976. *Voices of America*. New York: The Free Press.

Beals, Carleton. 1960. *Brass Knuckle Crusade*. New York: Hasting House.

Bennet, David H. 1988. *The Party of Fear: From Nativist Movements to the New Right in American History*. New York: Random House.

Bennett, Marion. 1963. *American Immigration Policies*. Washington, DC: Public Affairs Press.

Billington, Ray A. 1938. *The Protestant Crusade, 1800–1860*. New York: Macmillan, Co.

Billington, Ray A. 1974. *The Origins of Nativism in the United States, 1800–1844*. New York: Arno Press.

Burgess, Thomas. 1913. *Greeks in America*. Boston, MA: Sherman/French Co.

Divine, Robert A. 1957. *American Immigration Policy, 1924–1952*. New Haven, CT: Yale University Press.

Higham, John. 1955. *Strangers in the Land: Patterns of American Nativism, 1860–1925*. New Brunswick, NJ: Rutgers University Press.

Hofstadter, Richard, and Michael Wallace. 1971. *American Violence*. New York: Knopf.

Holt, Michael. 1992. *Political Parties and American Political Development: From the Age of Jackson to the Age of Lincoln*. New York: Barnes and Noble.

Howe, Daniel W. 1973. *The American Whigs: An Anthology*. New York: John Wiley & Sons.

Howe, Daniel W. 2007. *What Hath God Wrought: The Transformation of America, 1815–1848*. New York: Oxford University Press.

Jensen, Richard J. 1971. *The Winning of the Midwest: Social and Political Conflict, 1888–1896*. Chicago, IL: University of Chicago Press.

Kenefick, John C. 1985. *Union Pacific and the Building of the West.* New York: Newcomen Society.
"Know Nothing Party." *Encyclopedia Britannica.* Available at: http://www.britan nica.com/EBChecked/topics/320530/Know-Nothing party.
LeMay, Michael. 1987. *From Open Door to Dutch Door: An Analysis of U.S. Immigration Policy Since 1820.* New York: Praeger Press.
LeMay, Michael. 2009. *The Struggle for Influence.* 3rd ed. Upper Saddle River, NJ: Prentice-Hall.
LeMay, Michael, and Elliott Barkan. 1999. *U.S. Immigration and Naturalization Laws and Issues.* Westport, CT: Greenwood Press.
Lepore, Jill. 2010. *The Whites of Their Eyes: The Tea Party's Revolution and the Battle over American History.* Princeton, NJ: Princeton University Press.
McGreevey, John T. 2003. *Catholicism and American Freedom: A History.* New York: W. W. Norton.
Melton, Tracy M. 2005. *Hanging Henry Gambrill: The Violent Career of Baltimore's Plug Uglies, 1854–1860.* Baltimore, MD: Maryland Historical Society.
Mulkern, John. 1997. *The Know-Nothing Party in Massachusetts.* Boston, MA: University of Massachusetts Press.
Nevins, Allan. 1947. *Ordeal in the Union: A House Dividing.* New York: Charles Scribner and Sons.
O'Grady, Joseph D. 1973. *How the Irish Became American.* New York: Twayne.
O'Hara, John M. 2010. *A New American Tea Party.* Hoboken, NJ: John Wiley.
Overdyke, William D. 1968. *The Know-Nothing Party in the South.* Gloucester, MA: Peter Smith.
Rasmussen, Scott, and Doug Shoen. 2010. *Mad as Hell: How the Tea Party Movement Is Fundamentally Remaking Our Two-Party System.* New York: Harper.
Reimers, David. 1990. *Natives and Strangers.* 2nd ed. New York: Oxford University Press.
Safire, William. 2008. *Safire's Political Dictionary.* New York: Oxford University Press.
Silbey, Joel H. 1991. *The American Political Nation, 1838–1893.* Stanford, CA: Stanford University Press.
Smith, Theodore. 1969. *Politics and Slavery.* New York: Negro University Press.
Thompson, William. 1996. *Native American Issues.* Santa Barbara, CA: ABC-CLIO.
Voss-Hubbard, Mark. 2002. *Beyond Party: Cultures of Antipartisanship in Northern Politics before the Civil War.* Baltimore, MD: Johns Hopkins University Press.
Wilentz, Sean. 2005. *The Rise of American Democracy: Jefferson to Lincoln.* New York: W. W. Norton.
Zernike, Kate. 2010. *Boiling Mad: Inside Tea Party America.* New York: Times Books.

About the Editor and Contributors

About the Editor

Michael C. LeMay is professor emeritus of political science at California State University, San Bernardino, California—where he served as director of the National Security Studies program, chair of the Department of Political Science, and assistant dean for Student Affairs of the College of Social and Behavioral Sciences. Dr. LeMay took his BS and MS degrees from the University of Wisconsin, and his PhD degree from the University of Minnesota.

His 35 years of teaching includes service at several institutions of higher learning. He taught at Seido Juku, Ashiya, Japan; at the University of Wisconsin, Milwaukee; at Frostburg State University, Western Maryland; and at CSUSB. He served as department chair for 18 years and has won awards as a university administrator, as a teacher, and as a scholar.

He has authored 18 published academic books, including several immigration policy titles: *The Struggle for Influence* (University Press of America, 1985), *From Open Door to Dutch Door* (Praeger Press, 1987), *The Gatekeepers* (Praeger Press, 1989), *Anatomy of a Public Policy* (Praeger, 1994), *American Immigration and Naturalization Laws and Issues: A Documentary History* (with Elliott Barkan) (Greenwood Press, 1999), *U.S. Immigration: A Reference Handbook* (ABC-CLIO, 2004), *Guarding the Gates: Immigration and National Security* (Praeger, 2006), and *Illegal Immigration: A Reference Handbook* (ABC-CLIO, 2007). He is currently writing *Doctors at the Borders: Immigration and the Rise of U.S. Public Health.* He has also sole-authored two textbooks that have immigration as a major focus: *The Perennial Struggle: Race, Ethnicity and Minority Relations in the United States* (3rd ed., Prentice-Hall, 2009) and *Public Administration: Clashing Values in the Administration of Public Policy* (2nd ed., Wadsworth/Thomson Learning, 2006).

Dr. LeMay has published in several scholarly journals: *American Politics Quarterly; Teaching Political Science; National Civic Review; Southeastern Political Review; Journal of Politics, Social Science Quarterly; Journal of American Ethnic History;* and *International Migration Review.* He served as a regular reviewer for *International Migration Review; Social Science Quarterly;* and *Journal of American Ethnic History.*

About the Contributors

Mark N. Hoffman is a PhD candidate at the Department of Political Science, University of Minnesota. He took his BA from Vassar College in Political Science and Philosophy and has an MA from Queen's University, Belfast, in political theory and social criticism. Mark has taught courses at the University of Minnesota and sections at Queen's University, Belfast. His publications include *Policing the West: From France to Arizona* by Counterpunch.org; "Securing the Absent Nation: Colonial Governance in the New World" in *Europe and Its Boundaries: Worlds and Words, within and Beyond,* ed. Andrew Davison and Himadeep Muppidi (Lexington Books, 2009); "Conversations with Governor Tim Pawlenty" in *Minnesota Law and Politics* (Spring, 2007); *Becoming Imperialist: An Urgent Warning to Critics of the Iraq Wars* (with Arjun Chowdhury and Kevin Parsneau), series published by Counterpunch.org; *The Can-Do Troops and the New Anti-Politics*" (May 27, 2007); *Counter Terrorism and International Health Care* (June 5, 2007); and "Perspectives on the Northern Ireland Women's Coalition" in *School for International Training Occupational Papers Series* (Winter, 2002).

Mark has presented several papers at the International Studies Association Annual Conventions: *New World Orders? Immigration Management as Colonial Governance in Europe and Euro America* (February 2010, New Orleans); *Border Politics in the Heartland? Analyzing U.S. "Immigration Crisis" in Minnesota* (February 2009, New York); *Border Politics: Biopolitics and National Security: Rethinking Migration in the "New World" Order* (March 2008, San Francisco); and *Psychoanalyzing Colonial Encounters: The Psychoanalytic Turn in Postcolonial Theory* (March 2006, San Francisco).

Sharon Kornelly received her BA from Knox College in sociology/anthropology, and her MA and PhD degrees from Temple University in cultural anthropology. She has taught at Temple University, Rowan University, Moore College of Art and Design, Drexel University, and Philadelphia University. She received an excellence in teaching award from Rowan University. Her research includes contributions to the following: "Fraktur Digital Collection," Free Library of Philadelphia (http:// libwww.freelibrary.org/

fraktur) and "Louis Shotridge Collection" (University of Pennsylvania Museum of Archaeology and Anthropology, forthcoming).

H. James McLaughlin has been a professor for 20 years, at three universities, and is now professor and chair of a department at Florida Atlantic University. His scholarly interests relate to the history and philosophy of education, to research on rural schooling in Mexico, and to work with teachers on school-based action research. His writing has been published in such journals as *Journal of Education and Urban Society; Teaching and Teacher Education;* and *Journal of Teacher Education.*

Dr. McLaughlin's minor area in his doctoral studies was foundations of education. He has coauthored two books, one about the foundations of a democratic education, and a second about classroom management (with Richard Powell and Thomas Savage, 2000, NJ. Prentice-Hall). In both he wrote the chapters related to the history of education. The chapter in this volume is his first opportunity to link immigration with education, within a historical context. He also teaches a doctoral course on the history and philosophy of school curriculum.

Since 1997, Dr. McLaughlin has examined life in Mexican schools. He has published articles on one-room rural schools there, and has created study abroad and student exchange experiences in Mexico for educators. His next project in this area is a manuscript detailing the experiences of one Mexican family in a rural school area that has been affected by emigration to the United States.

In addition, Dr. McLaughlin has worked over many years with teams of teachers to develop research projects related to their own questions, and has written with them about this kind of action research. He continues to consult with teachers on school-wide research projects.

Carla L. Reyes is an associate attorney with Perkins Coie, LLP, Seattle, Washington. She took her BA in political studies from Whitworth University, her JD, *magna cum laude,* and LLM in International and Comparative Law from Duke University School of Law, and a MPP from Duke University Terry Sanford School of Public Policy. Prior to joining Perkins Coie, LLP, as an associate attorney, Carla served as the Perkins Coie public interest fellow to the Volunteer Advocates for Immigrant Justice from October 2009 to October 2010. During her time at Duke University, Mrs. Reyes volunteered with the Durham Battered Immigrants Rights Project, and served as a summer research fellow with the Migrant Farm Worker Unite of the North Carolina Justice Center.

Her publications include "Gender, Migration and Law: Unexpected Effects on the Most Vulnerable Immigrants" in *25 Wisconsin Journal of Law, Gender and Society* (2010: 301), "War Crimes" in *International Crime and Justice* (Cambridge University Press, 2010), and "Note, The U.S. Discovery-EU Privacy Directive Conflict: Constructing a Three-Tiered Compliance Strategy" in *19 Duke Journal of Comparative and International Law* (2009: 357).

Scot J. Zentner is professor of political science at California State University, San Bernardino, where he has been on the faculty since 1993. He earned his BA from the same university, and his MA and PhD from Michigan State University, all in political science. His areas of teaching and research are American politics, American political thought, and political theory. He has published articles and reviews in journals such as *Polity; Presidential Studies Quarterly*; and *Interpretation: A Journal of Political Philosophy*. He is author of book chapters on the early and modern political party systems in the United States. These include "Culture, Compassion and Today's Progressive Party System" in *Modern America and the Legacy of the Founding* (Lexington, 2007) and "Regimes and Revolutions: Madison and Wilson on Parties in America" in *The Progressive Revolution in Politics and Political Science* (Rowman & Littlefield, 2005). He has contributed a review essay on Abraham Lincoln's rhetoric and statesmanship to the *Journal of the Abraham Lincoln Association* and an article on campaign finance regulation to the *Journal of Law & Politics*. He has received fellowships from the Earhart Foundation and the Social Philosophy and Policy Center of Bowling Green State University. His editorials and commentary have appeared in outlets such as the *Los Angeles Times* and the *San Francisco Chronicle*.

Index